FRAMING THE WORLD

D1484251

UNDER THE SIGN OF NATURE

EXPLORATIONS IN ECOCRITICISM

the World

Framing

![tree with roots shown like a film strip frame]

Explorations in Ecocriticism and Film

EDITED BY PAULA WILLOQUET-MARICONDI

University of

Virginia Press

Charlottesville

and London

University of Virginia Press
© 2010 by the Rector and Visitors
of the University of Virginia
Printed in the United States of America
on acid-free paper

First published 2010
9 8 7 6 5 4 3 2 1

Library of Congress
Cataloging-in-Publication Data
Framing the world : explorations in
ecocriticism and film / edited by Paula
Willoquet-Maricondi.
       p. cm.
   Includes bibliographical references and
index.
   ISBN 978-0-8139-3005-3 (cloth : alk. paper)
   ISBN 978-0-8139-3006-0 (pbk. : alk. paper)
   ISBN 978-0-8139-3066-4 (e-book)
   1. Environmental protection and motion
pictures. 2. Human ecology in motion
pictures. 3. Motion pictures—Social
aspects. 4. Ecocriticism. I. Willoquet-
Maricondi, Paula, 1960–
   PN1995.9.E78F73 2010
   791.43'66—dc22

                               2010002944

In memory of

Lucette Willoquet,

Waldemar Maricondi,

and Denise Hamel

Morality is a matter of getting along with one's fellow creatures as well as possible.

—Joseph Meeker

CONTENTS

PREFACE

Over the last twenty years, the growing number of films and film festivals devoted to environmental concerns points to environmentally engaged cinema as a powerful tool for knowledge dissemination, consciousness-raising, public debate, and, many hope, political action. Particularly within the documentary genre, the number of films addressing environmental issues is growing as new and more affordable production technologies, and modes of film delivery through the Internet and DVD markets, make them easily accessible to a broader and more diverse audience, including in the educational context.

Produced with the explicit intent to bring about greater understanding of the environmental challenges facing us today and to inspire action, films such as *An Inconvenient Truth* (2006) and *Everything's Cool* (2006), discussed in this volume, exemplify the emerging genre of *ecocinema*. As attested by their DVD extra features and accompanying Web sites that provide "take action" tips and "activist toolkits" downloads, ecocinema strives to have a social, political, and material impact, and to be a tool for activism.[1] The overt eco-activist intent of ecocinema offers an alternative to more popularized mainstream "environmentalist" fiction films, such as *Erin Brockovich* (2000), also discussed here, whose principal intent is to put a topical subject in the service of entertainment. While environmentalist films can have an impact on audiences' environmental values, the environmental themes in these films function primarily as backdrops to plot development, not as a call to action.

In addition to calling attention to particular films as productive tools for raising awareness and for educating the public about environmental issues, the essays in this volume encourage us to adopt an ecocritically informed standpoint toward all forms of cinematic productions, not just those that overtly focus on environmental issues. Thus, one of the goals of this volume is to offer different approaches to reading a broad range of films *ecocritically.* While highlighting a number of environmentally explicit films, the present essays call us to become more ecologically minded viewers as we adopt ecocritical perspectives to studying films as cultural products, that is, as made and consumed by the culture, *and* as a means through which the culture re-produces itself, its values, and its worldviews.

Thus, *Framing the World: Explorations in Ecocriticism and Film* urges readers to adopt an ecocritical standpoint toward all types of films: (1) those that are explicitly and intentionally about natural systems and environmental threats; (2) those in which the absence of nature is noticeable or in which the environmental dimension of social injustices is obfuscated; (3) and those that incorporate nature and environmental issues into their narratives but whose modes of representation reveal the ideological limitation or shortcomings of the culture vis-à-vis the environment. The mainstream and independent documentary, fiction, and experimental films and videos examined in this collection function as primers for thinking ecocritically so that we may respond personally and politically to the multifaceted environmental challenges facing us today. In this respect, our hope is that this collection will serve as a tool for activist viewing in the service of greater awareness and real-life engagement with ecological and environmental justice issues.

While the knowledge produced by ecocinema aims to have an impact on audience's environmental values and behavior, and thus to inspire viewers to take personal and political action, information alone does not guarantee action. Although assessing these films' actual impact on audience behavior is fraught with complexities that are outside the scope of this volume, recent research in social psychology and the emerging field of community-based social marketing suggests that awareness and understanding of particular environmental concerns have only a limited ability to foster behavioral change in individuals and communities. According to environmental psychologist Doug McKenzie-Mohr, community-based social marketing works to identify the barriers that prevent knowledge from affecting behavior. He argues that "since the barriers that prevent individuals from engaging in sustainable behavior are activity specific, community-based social marketers begin to develop a strategy only after they have identified a particular activity's barriers. Once these barriers have been identified, they develop a social marketing strategy to remove them."[2] The effectiveness of information in bringing about social change thus depends in part on *how* it is conveyed.

An important and often neglected dimension of studying the environmental potential of cinema from an ecocritical standpoint is attention to the specific ways in which visual texts communicate. How information is delivered visually is vital to its effectiveness in meaningfully reaching audiences. For example, in his review of Leonardo DiCaprio's *The 11th Hour* (2007) (another film whose explicit intent is to awaken our consciousness about the despoliation of the planet and spur us to act on that knowledge), Roger Ebert confesses that while he agreed "with every word," the film did not motivate him to act. Ebert blamed the delivery of the message, not the message itself, for this failure to inspire action. He argues that "too much of the footage of *The 11th Hour* is just standard nature photography, as helicopter-cams swoop over hill and dale and birds look unhappy and ice melts. This is intercut with 50 experts, more or less, who talk and talk and talk." Although we "get it," says Ebert, we are not inspired to do anything because we feel bored by this "tedious documentary."[3] The essays in this volume help foster greater visual literacy in two ways: by showing how the construction of images works to shape perceptions and attitudes about the nonhuman world, and by stimulating discussions about the historical, cultural, and ideological dimensions of our visual representations of nature and of environmental issues.

The contributors to this volume do not offer a quantitative measurement of the impact that representations of nature and of environmental issues have on viewers' perceptions and actions. Nonetheless, several of the essays explore how visual culture has contributed to creating and sustaining particular worldviews. These worldviews, in turn, have a material impact on how we inhabit the planet and might help account for the current ecological crisis.

Even if no one film or other cultural product has, single-handedly, the power to bring about large-scale social change, we believe that more should be done to put the cinematic medium in the service of fostering dialogue about pressing issues, in the classroom and in the wider community. Raising consciousness through the study of films is not sufficient to bring about material change, but awareness and understanding are necessary steps in the process of transforming perceptions and motivating social action. Awareness is particularly critical when it involves more than just knowing the "facts," but when it compels us to investigate the ideologies that inform our knowledge acquisition: what we choose to know; how we acquire that knowledge; the values we assign to what we know; and how we choose to act upon that knowledge. Interrogating the "politics of images," that is, how we "frame" the world and its pressing concerns through words and images, is a crucial part of this process.

The ecocritical readings proposed in *Framing the World* also strive to make a contribution to the "greening" of film studies. Just as the field of cultural studies has drawn our attention to the importance of gender, class, race, and ethnicity, cinematic ecocriticism urges us to incorporate ecological considerations into the study of our experiences as producers and consumers of cinema and, in this way, also to acknowledge our role as co-participants with the nonhuman world in the complex symbiotic process we call evolution, a process that includes cultural evolution.

In this respect *Framing the World* builds on Jhan Hochman's *Green Cultural Studies: Nature in Film, Novel, and Theory* (1998), one of the earliest important studies to undertake an ecocentric analysis of cultural texts beyond literary ones.[4] In this study Hochman urges cultural studies to add nature to its list of concerns since culture is embedded in and dependent on nature. *Framing the World* makes a contribution toward this goal. While some of the films were selected for discussion because of their explicit activist intent to bring about social and political changes, others were selected precisely because of their environmental blind spots.

Ecocriticism and film criticism together offer a much needed perspective on the motives and impacts of a culture's portrayal of nature and of environmental justice concerns. This collection hopes to offer a socio-politico-cultural tool in the service of both nature and culture by engaging in the kinds of critiques proper to the greening of all disciplines. As Richard Kerridge succinctly put it, "Direct representations of environmental damage or political struggle are of obvious interest to ecocritics, but so is the whole array of cultural and daily life, for what it reveals about implicit attitudes that have environmental consequences" (530).[5] The essays in this volume bring to light some of the most significant implicit and explicit attitudes about natural systems and human/nature relations.

By engaging with films representing a diversity of cinematic traditions and modes of production, this volume goes beyond the scope of previous studies of the representation of nature and environmental issues that have focused almost exclusively on Hollywood cinema. Moreover, the diversity of ecocritical approaches to reading films adopted here contributes to furthering visual and environmental literacy, and thus to educating for the creation of a socially and environmentally just and sustainable future.

NOTES

1. For a few examples of such calls to action on films' Web sites, including teaching resources, see the following: http://everythingscool.org/article.php?list= type&type=7; http://www.climate crisis.net/takeaction/; http://11thhouraction .com/signup?gclid=CNus5auH_JQCFRKLxwodWASTcQ; http://www.ban.org/; http://www.thirstthemovie.org/resources.html; http://waterfrontmovie.com/ getinvolved.
2. See http://www.cbsm.com/.
3. See Roger Ebert's review, 27 August 2007, http://rogerebert.suntimes.com/

apps/pbcs.dll/article?AID=/20070823/REVIEWS/708230302 (retrieved 20 June 2008).

4. See Jhan Hochman, *Green Cultural Studies: Nature in Film, Novel, and Theory* (Moscow: Univ. of Idaho Press, 1998).

5. See Richard Kerridge, "Environmentalism and Ecocriticism," *The Theory and Practice of Literary Criticism: An Oxford Guide,* ed. Patricia Waugh (Oxford: Oxford Univ. Press, 2006), 530–43.

ACKNOWLEDGMENTS

I am deeply grateful for the generosity, guidance, and encouragement I received over the last three years from all my communities, human and nonhuman. They have been a constant reminder that we are, indeed, absolutely interconnected and interdependent.

This collection of essays owes its existence, foremost, to the community of colleagues whose work is represented here. To all my contributors, thank you for your enthusiasm, dedication, patience, and adaptability.

I wish to thank Marist College for its generous support of this project through conference travel grants, a yearlong sabbatical leave, and the course reductions that helped me complete the work.

The professional organizations and conferences that supported the work of all the authors represented here also merit acknowledgment. In particular, I would like to thank the Association for the Study of Literature and the Environment for providing the principal forum for the exchange of ideas about film and ecology.

I am equally grateful to the *Mid-Atlantic Almanack, Green Letters,* and SUNY Press for granting permission to reprint portions of previously published essays in my "Shifting Paradigms" and "Beyond the Frame" and in Robin L. Murray and Joseph K. Heumann's "Fast, Furious, and Out of Control."

I am indebted to Boyd Zenner, acquisitions editor at the University of Virginia Press, for her encouragement, especially during those difficult times when life got in the way; to the series editors for their steadfast commitment to this book; and to the readers for their insightful and constructive suggestions for revisions.

For their long-standing and unwavering friendship, I thank Monique LaRocque, Richard Cripe, and Erinn McCluney. My deepest thanks to Suse Volk, Sue Fick, and Patti Knoblauch for illuminating the path; to my feline companions, Pepie and Guinnie, for sharing desk space with me during the long hours; and to Victor Kragh for his compassionate love, integrity, and clear "seeing," including in the proofreading of the manuscript.

FRAMING THE WORLD

INTRODUCTION
FROM LITERARY TO CINEMATIC
ECOCRITICISM

. . . .

PAULA WILLOQUET-MARICONDI

Human culture is connected to the physical world,
affecting it and affected by it.
—Cheryll Glotfelty, *The Ecocriticism Reader*

Nature, unfortunately for the organization of academia,
is vexingly interdisciplinary.
—Glen Love, *The Ecocriticism Reader*

Framing the World: Explorations in Ecocriticism and Film owes its greatest debt and inspiration to the field of literary ecological criticism, or ecocriticism; to the seminal texts that helped shape this field since the mid-1990s; to the journal *ISLE: Interdisciplinary Studies in Literature and Environment*; and to the Association for the Study of Literature and the Environment (ASLE), the organization that has supported the growth and strengthening of this field of study.

Since its official inception in the early 1990s and its recognition as a significant academic field of study, ecocriticism has expanded beyond the area of literary analysis to embrace the study of other forms of cultural production, including theoretical discourse, music, photography, virtual environments, and film and video. Karla Armbruster and Kathleen Wallace's collection of essays, *Beyond Nature Writing: Expanding the Boundaries of Ecocriticism*, reflects the perspective of many practitioners of ecocriticism that "one of ecocriticism's most important tasks at this time is expanding its boundaries . . . to address a wider spectrum of texts" (2). Thus, Scott Slovic's observation in 2000 that ecocriticism is "being re-defined daily by the actual practice of thousands of literary scholars around the world" holds true today more than ever and in relation to a wider range of fields and texts (161).

Because of its broad scope of inquiry, ecocriticism remains "methodologically and theoretically eclectic" (Rosendale xv), and does not have a "widely-known set of assumptions, doctrines, or procedures" within the academy as a whole (Barry 248). Serpil Oppermann notes that ecocriticism has no "field defining theoretical model" in place beyond its aim to promote ecological awareness, to bring ecological consciousness to the study of literary texts and other cultural productions, and to understand the place and function of humans in relation to the nonhuman world (105). Ursula Heise agrees that ecocriticism is not an easy field to define partly because of the diverse political and disciplinary influences that have shaped the field. She argues that "somewhat like cultural studies, ecocriticism coheres more by virtue of a common political project than on the basis of shared theoretical and methodological assumptions, and the details of how this project should translate into the study of culture are continually subject to challenge and revision" (506). This "common political project" is complex, multifaceted, at times contradictory, and as a result difficult to delineate. As Heise suggests, however, what is "common" to an otherwise diverse movement are the challenges and critiques of the conceptual dichotomies and simplistic understandings of human progress that have shaped modernity at least since the seventeenth century. Thus, to the extent that ecocritics do share a "common political project," the politics of this project can only be understood in the broadest terms. No common specific political agenda can be said to unify the various manifestations of ecocriticism, ranging from deep ecology to social ecology, animal rights, and environmental justice. This plurality is reflected in the essays collected here, which offer perspectives ranging from those fostering more ecocentric-oriented worldviews to those addressing specific environmental injustices affecting communities worldwide. In the case of films by or about Aboriginal peoples' struggles for self-determination, these seemingly different political agendas often coalesce.

Since the history and scope of ecocriticism has been amply documented by others, the following brief summary will serve to contextualize the essays in the present volume, as well as highlight the continuities and innovations this collection brings to the study of the intersections of nature and culture.

As broadly defined by Cheryll Glotfelty and Harold Fromm in one of the earliest foundational texts for ecocritics, literary ecocriticism, and its manifestations in other fields, takes an earth-centered, environmentally conscious approach to the study of texts and to the investigation of the relationship between these texts and the physical environment. It offers an environmental perspective on culture in the same way that feminist and Marxist criticism have given us, respectively, gender and class consciousness (xviii). Ecocriticism helps us identify works that have an environmental orientation—that is, that fit the three criteria outlined by Lawrence Buell in *The Environmental Imagination*: (1) works in which the nonhuman world is not mere backdrop for human action but helps us situate human history within natural history; (2) works that do not single out human interest as the only significant interest; (3) and works whose ethical orientation includes human responsibility and accountability toward the environment and the nonhuman sphere (7–8). At the same time, and as some of the essays in this collection will make clear, ecocriticism enables us to identify other types of texts that are not "self-evidently about nature" (Barry 259) but that nonetheless offer us needed perspectives on the relations between the human and the nonhuman.

Ecological literary studies became a recognizable and consolidated critical school in the early 1990s, although its origins date back to the 1960s and '70s. The term "ecocriticism" has a history of its own, having first been used in 1978 by William Rueckert to refer in a more restrictive way to the application of ecological concepts to literature (Glotfelty xx). Literary ecocriticism today includes the study of nature writing as a genre; it examines the role of the physical setting in literary productions, the values expressed in relation to the environment, and the correlation between what a culture says about the environment and how it treats it; it conceives of *place* as a critical category; it looks for correspondences among gender, class, ethnicity, and nature; it asks how culturally produced texts affect our relationship with the natural world; it traces changes through time in a culture's concept of environment; and it examines representations of the environmental crisis in literature. In short, ecocriticism acknowledges that the world is composed of the social sphere and the ecosphere, that the two are interrelated, and that the former cannot be considered outside the context of the latter.

The practice of something analogous to literary ecocriticism has even older roots. Before the term was ever used, the study of textual engagement with the nonhuman world from an ecological standpoint had already commanded the attention of students of philosophy, ethics, and critical theory. One of the first efforts to address the ecological crisis from within critical theory, and at a time when ecological consciousness was only beginning to surface in popular discourse, is Joel Whitebook's 1979 essay "The Problem of Nature in Habermas." In this essay Whitebook argues that the domination of nature is a constitutive feature of what we call the modern era, roughly spanning from the seventeenth century to now, notwithstanding our current claims as postmoderns. Whitebook begins his investigation by asking whether a strictly anthropocentric perspective could meet the challenges of an ecological crisis of such unprecedented dimension. He writes, "Even if it could be shown *theoretically* that it is not necessary to move from the standpoint of anthropocentrism to formulate solutions to the environmental crisis, a question would still remain at the level of social psychology. For it is difficult to imagine how the conflict between society and nature is going to be resolved without a major transformation in our social consciousness of the natural world—for example, a renewed reverence for life" (307). The dilemma elucidated by Whitebook in this passage is one that has been at the core of current debates in ecology, environmental ethics, and ecocriticism, and one that will inform a number of the essays in this volume: the debate between an anthropocentric and a biocentric outlook.

C. A. Bowers, writing about the connections between education, culture, and the environmental crisis, notes that the only adequate test of the viability of a culture is whether its beliefs and practices are environmentally sustainable over multiple generations. In *Education, Cultural Myths, and the Ecological Crisis,* Bowers takes up the task of revealing the anthropocentrism of our textbooks: for example, he points out how our very use of language in expressions such as "the earth you live *on*" as well as our dating system, which emphasizes a linear sense of history, reinforce the myth of human progress and supremacy. In *Educating for Eco-justice and Community,* he proposes strategies to reform education so it will meet the environmental challenges facing us and help us develop greater moral responsibility for the long-term effects of our actions on the ecosystem. What Bowers calls an "eco-justice pedagogy" must

> combine a responsibility for contributing to social justice (in the domains of both culture and natural ecology) while at the same time helping to conserve traditions essential to communities that retain the mutuality and moral reciprocity of the commons. . . . The task of conserving what contributes to the recovery of the ecological and cultural commons, in turn, requires an understanding of local interest, needs, and traditions. This understanding needs to be framed within the larger context of worldwide ecological trends such as global warming and the toxic contamination of the environment. (25)

Similarly, Lawrence Buell rightly notes that the responsibility for addressing the most pressing problem of the twenty-first century, environmental sustainability, can no longer be relegated to only a few specialized disciplines such as ecology or public policy, but must fall on "*all* the human sciences" ("Ecocritical Insurgency" 699).

Several of the essays in this volume engage in a questioning of the anthropocentrism built into our filmic representations of nature. This exploration is grounded on the belief that education can offer avenues for a change in paradigm; as Bowers puts it, academic freedom "may still serve an essential purpose if it can be situated within a moral framework that recognizes the interdependence of natural systems and that human cultures must evolve newer or recover non-exploitative forms of relationships" (*Cultural Myths* 202). Bowers shares the position of other advocates of an ecocentric ethic that solutions to inequities among humans and to environmental injustices have to be framed in relation to values and practices that discourage the overuse of nonrenewable resources, halt environmental pollution and degradation, and preserve the diversity of cultures, organisms, and ecosystems (156).[1] It is the case, as Michael McDowell has noted, that any textual attempt, literary or filmic, "to listen to voices in the landscape . . . is necessarily anthropocentric. It's our language, after all, that we're using, and we inevitably put our values into the representation" (372). What follows from this observation is not that we should accept our anthropocentrism unquestioningly; but rather, that to study our representations of nature, whether linguistic or imagistic, to scrutinize how we give nature a voice in human artifacts, is to probe into our values and culturally constructed beliefs about the nonhuman world.

A shift in paradigm from an unquestioned anthropocentric perspective to an ecocentric one would require, for instance, taking climate change as well as other environmental problems caused by human action into account when considering development projects in both richer and poorer countries, or when assessing personal and broader cultural lifestyle choices in developed countries and their "export" to developing countries. With such a shift in perspective, what we regard as the signs of "progress," "growth," and "development" in richer countries can no longer automatically serve as models, or paradigms, for development in poorer countries. Our very understanding of what constitutes "development" and "progress" needs to undergo scrutiny and debate.

To assure the viability and sustainability of the planet, and thus the future of human societies, would we not need, as Bill McKibben reminds us in *Deep Economy: The Wealth of Communities and the Durable Future*, some "new measure that would more accurately reflect progress (or regress) by subtracting for pollution or disease" (28)? Findings regarding the causes and consequences of global climate change, for example, strongly indicate the need to reconsider what we mean by "development" and to shift globally to living practices that are ecospherically sustainable and environmentally just. As McKibben further states, "One consequence of nearly three hundred years of rapid economic growth has been stress on the natural world: we've dug it up, eroded it away, cut it down" (18). The degree of environmental damage we have enacted brought a panel of 1,300 scientists to a consensus view that "human actions are depleting Earth's natural capital, putting such strain on the environment that the ability of the planet's ecosystems to sustain future generations can no longer be taken for granted" (quoted in McKibben 18).

This line of questioning is further exemplified in the following remarks by Sir John Houghton at the opening of a 2007 online conference devoted to exploring the ethical, political, and sociocultural aspects of climate change:

> The wealth of the world's rich countries has come largely as a result of cheap energy from fossil fuels, without realization of the damage being caused—*damage that is tending to fall disproportionately on poorer countries.* There is therefore an inescapable moral imperative for wealthy countries: first, to take action to reduce drastically their emissions of carbon dioxide and, secondly, to use their wealth and skills to assist those in poorer countries to develop in sustainable ways. (my emphasis)[2]

The disproportionate impact of environmental despoliation on poorer countries, indigenous peoples, and racial, ethnic, and gender minorities in both richer and poorer countries has been at the heart of the grass-roots movement known as environmental justice (EJ), or ecojustice, and is the focus of several of the essays in this volume.[3]

These issues, many feel, have been either overlooked or not sufficiently addressed by traditional environmentalism and academic ecocriticism. T. V. Reed contends that "ecocriticism is in danger of recapitulating the sad history of environmentalism generally, wherein unwillingness to grapple with questions of racial, class, and national privilege has severely undermined the powerful critique of ecological devastation" (145). Richard Kerridge, in summarizing the variety of ecocritical endeavors that seek to "find ways of removing the cultural blockages that thwart effective actions against environmental crisis" (532), stresses the important function to be played by ecocritics responsive to environmental justice issues. Environmental justice ecocritics, he writes, "will bring questions of class, race, gender, and colonialism into the ecocritical evaluation of texts and ideas, challenging versions of environmentalism that seem exclusively preoccupied with preservation and wild nature and ignore the aspirations of the poor" (531). Thus, in responding to environmental justice concerns, ecocriticism can make a contribution to bringing about a needed cultural change that is more likely to promote a biocentric worldview—that is, one that enlarges our "conception of global community to include non-human life forms and the physical environment" (Branch et al. xiii).

Michael P. Cohen has shown that ecocriticism should not limit itself to praising environmental narratives but should also question "the nature of environmental narrative" (23). Similarly, cinematic representations of nature and of environmental issues must be examined critically for the assumptions and ideologies they foster and reinforce, through their modes of production and also their deployment of the vocabulary and techniques particular to the visual medium.

While some ecocritics have advocated a return to the mimetic tradition of realism in environmental writing, others have raised the question of "how accurately literature can represent the natural environment," or "how exactly language refers to reality" (Oppermann 111). Any representation of the physical world and of our engagement with it, whether through words or images, is a "product" with value added. In other words, if representations are never transparent windows onto the world, then the study of representations needs to take into account what the act of representing, with its methods, values, and rules, adds to the represented.

For many film viewers, cinema is a deceptively transparent medium, creating the illusion of an immediate, direct, and objective access to reality. This, in part, is due to what Robert Romanyshyn calls a "cultural habit of mind" (349), initiated by the invention of linear perspective, to see images as having an indexical relation to reality, a relation created by the mechanical (now digital) apparatus that appears simply to "capture" events, freezing them in time, without shaping them. What we know is thus always partly a function of what brings us this knowledge—whether that be our physical senses, our measuring and recording tools, or our values and beliefs. Cinema is masterfully adept at projecting "an effect of reality" (Oppermann 112). Representations of nature, whether linguistic or imagistic, "create a model of reality that fashions our discourses and shapes our cultural attitudes to the natural environment. The roots of the ecological crisis, for example, are traced back to such a model known as the dualistic paradigm, or model of reality, in the social sciences" (Oppermann 112).

Thus, it is not that representations directly shape nature but that they shape our perceptions of nature, perceptions that in turn inform and pattern our actions in relation to nature; our actions, in turn, shape nature by preserving ecosystems or by despoiling them. Derek Bousé's study of the representation of wildlife in nature films extrapolates from these ideas by showing how an inherent conflict of interests arises between the subject matter—nature—and the conventions of cinema used to represent nature by molding it "to fit the medium" (4). The use of formal devices such as camera angles, close-ups, and slow motion, argues Bousé, "may do less to acquaint us with nature than to alienate us from it, and . . . repeated exposure to nature and wildlife through a shroud of cinematic conventions may help make us less, not more, sensitive to it" (8). Furthermore, audiences' expectations about nature are increasingly shaped by their own consumption of media images of nature more than by their personal experiences of natural settings or environmental threats; thus, audiences are more likely to accept these images at face value, having nothing else but other images against which to weigh them. Bousé rightly asks to what extent audience members remain cognizant that the creative medium is not a transparent window onto the world when this medium is so "adept at *realism*" even when it "cannot convey reality in its fullness" (7). A representation's degree of "reality," he notes, is often assessed on the basis of content and not of technique, as if content could be separated from how it is conveyed. This leads him to the conclusion that the depiction of animals in wildlife films lies somewhere between representation and simulation (13).

Literary ecocriticism has examined what a writer's use of language and metaphor reveals about his/her perception and experience of nature. Cinematic ecocriticism, what others call "green film criticism" or "eco-cinecriticism" (Ivakhiv 1), must engage with how visual representations position nature and natural features, how these are framed by the lens of the camera or shaped by the editing process. While the camera does foster a greater illusion of objectivity and realism—objective representations being the product of a particular dominant ideology and way of seeing—nothing is more ideologically predetermined than the so-called invisible style of classical cinema that strives to hide the constructed nature of images.

Bousé's study is an important one for ecocritics interested in examining the function of images in molding our perceptions of and attitudes toward nature, as is Gregg Mitman's *Reel Nature: America's Romance with Wildlife on Film*. While neither work proposes itself as an instance of ecocriticism, the insights they offer us about the politics of representation, both of the camera and of the institution of filmmaking, are crucial to the elaboration of a cinematic ecocriticism. Nature in films is socially constructed by a number of factors: the capabilities of the cinematic technology, the filmmakers' objectives, the economics of the entertainment industry, the prevailing concepts of nature, and the perceived tastes of viewers. Recalling Aldo Leopold's observation that "wilderness is the raw material out of which man has hammered the artifact called civilization" (quoted in Mitman 4), Mitman shows how the reverse has become the norm:

> Longing for the authentic, nostalgic for an innocent past, we are drawn to the spectacle of wildlife untainted by human intervention and will. Yet, we cannot observe this world of nature without such interventions. The camera lens must impose itself, select its subject, and frame its vision. The history of nature films reverses Leopold's claim. Cultural values, technology, and nature itself have supplied the raw materials from which wilderness as artifact has been forged. (4)

This study builds on several other works concerned, in their different ways, with what David Ingram calls "the interplay of environmental ideologies at work in Hollywood movies" (x). In *Green Screen: Environmentalism and Hollywood Cinema*, Ingram offers a broad analysis of "environmentalist" films, defined as those in which environmental issues are central to the narrative but where the environment is merely a backdrop to human drama. Being the first of its kind, Ingram's study "covers as large a field as possible in order to indicate directions for further research" (ix). Focusing on fictional Hollywood narratives, Ingram explores the way Hollywood applies the well-tested conventions of melodrama to representing environmental issues. Among the topics covered are the symbolic function of wilderness and its construction as a pristine Edenic space; the aesthetics of landscape cinematography; the anthropomorphic representation of wild animals and the "starification" of certain species such as dolphins, wolves, and bears; the effects of gendering the representation of nonhuman nature; and the representation of technologies of progress, such as the automobile and nuclear energy, and their ecological implications. Ingram approaches the films he selects for discussion as "mediators of social issues." The present volume furthers the study of some of the topics explored by Ingram in relation to genres not covered, such as animation, documentary, experimental, art cinema, and Native cinema.

Ingram's definition of environmentalist films is also crucial to the investigation of the emerging genre of ecocinema undertaken in part 1. The term *ecocinema* has gained currency to describe films that overtly engage with environmental concerns either by exploring specific environmental justice issues or, more broadly, by making "nature," from landscapes to wildlife, a primary focus. As a category of media, ecocinema cuts across genres and modes of production, encompassing full-length and short fiction, documentary, and experimental films/videos that actively seek to inform viewers about, as well as engage their participation in, addressing issues of ecological import. Thus, these films strive to play an active role in fostering environmental awareness, conservation, and political action. Ecocinema also encompasses those films that in a broader, more philosophical way compel us to reflect upon what it means to inhabit this planet: that is, to be a member of the planetary ecosystem or "ecosphere" (see Rowe) and, most important, to understand the value of this community in a systemic and nonhierarchical way.

Other books that have contributed to the study of Hollywood films and ecology include Robin Murray and Joseph Heumann's *Ecology and Popular Film: Cinema on the Edge,* Deborah Carmichael's *The Landscape of Hollywood Westerns: Ecocriticism in an American Film Genre,* and Pat Brereton's *Hollywood Utopia: Ecology in Contemporary American Cinema.* Murray and Heumann analyze a variety of environmental themes, including environmental politics, ecoterrorism, ecodisasters, and the presence of tragic and comic eco-heroes. They look at how environmental issues are sometimes obscured by a film's focus on spectacle and conflicting messages, but also at how films that seem to "promote environmental degradation" help call attention to this degradation by putting it on display (205). Addressing a broader base of readers, they also raise the important issue of the environmental impact of the film industry and the steps taken by production companies and trade journals to address that impact; they cite, for example, *An Inconvenient Truth* and *Syriana* as examples of carbon-neutral productions that lowered their carbon footprint by partnering with companies that offset carbon emissions through renewable energy credits (204).

Carmichael's edited collection examines the importance of the natural setting as a central motif in both documentary and fiction films set in the American West. Noting that studies of the western genre have tended to give only a "supporting-role status" (1) to the land—the very land that helped define the genre—Carmichael reminds us that the central conflicts of this genre are predicated on the way humans respond to the natural environment. Thus, she argues, "Cinematic representations of the American West offer students a unique opportunity to explore both current and historical perspectives on the role of nature in nation building and national identity. . . . The western march of civilization can often be read as future ecological disaster within a confident present tense of a particular historical era" (15).

Stories of settlement, both in literature and film, show the natural world as simultaneously offering possibilities for profit and posing dangers, thus inspiring the drive toward conquest and control of what appeared to the early settlers to be limitless natural resources. Not only were the vastness of the continent, and the ever-expanding frontier with its apparent inexhaustibility of both space and resources, crucial formative influences on the American psyche, but "the conquest of western land remains embedded in our national myth" (3). This historical analysis of how landscapes have been portrayed in western films, and how they have functioned in the formation of cultural identity, helps provide a context for the essays in part 3 dealing with the presence, absence, and transformation of land.

Brereton's study is more controversial in arguing for the presence of "utopian ecological themes" in mainstream Hollywood films, a body of work not generally regarded as offering many progressive conceptions of nature. As Brereton notes, "Relatively little academic effort is given over to understanding and appreciating rather than dismissing the utopian spatial aesthetic that permeates Hollywood films" (12). Brereton looks at the impact of consciously foregrounded and excessive representations of nature and landscapes. These excesses, he argues, are means through which the films "dramatize and encourage raw nature to speak directly to audiences" and "promote an ecological meta-narrative, connecting humans with their environment" (13).

While Brereton may be overly optimistic in attributing to these representational excesses the power to mobilize audiences around environmental issues, his exploration of Steven Spielberg as an "eco-*auteur*" provides a useful context for the essays in part 4, dealing with art-cinema directors whose body of work exhibits an identifiable eco-consciousness. For Brereton, Spielberg is the Hollywood director with "the most successful embodiment of nature and ecology on film," helping "consolidate a uniquely Hollywood range of representations of nature," even if these representations have not always promoted "ecological praxis" (67). The limits of Brereton's reading of Spielberg as an agent of ecological awareness is well captured in Adrian Ivakhiv's remark that "Spielberg's films celebrate not so much the power of nature as the power of cinema." Spectacular effects, even those "ostensibly celebrating the power of nature, [are] hardly guaranteed to generate social mobilization" (Ivakhiv 11).

While the persistence of "ecological questions" (Brereton 72) in the work of a director does not automatically qualify him or her as an eco-auteur, an auteur studies approach informed by ecocriticism is one of a number of productive next steps in the "emergence of a more full-fledged and mature ecological cinema criticism" (Ivakhiv 24). The potential to locate eco-auteurs and ecocinema is more fully realized in independent and experimental productions, and in the auteurist art-cinema tradition exemplified by directors such as Werner Herzog, Peter Greenaway, and Kiyoshi Kurosawa, discussed in this volume.

Experimental cinema, in particular, offers the greatest potential for a truly consciousness-altering cinematic experience, as shown by Scott MacDonald's exploration of the genre's power to retrain perception by challenging our viewing habits and expectations. While not offering an ecocritical approach, strictly speaking, MacDonald's *The Garden in the Machine: A Field Guide to Independent Films about Place* and his subsequent article "Toward an Eco-cinema" bring to our attention an important body of not widely known experimental and avant-garde films about place: urban, rural, and wild. Beyond that, MacDonald draws from a rich body of research ranging from art history to environmental philosophy to engage with issues pertinent to ecocriticism and to environmental studies: how films explore the idea of an "original American nature" (xxii); depictions of the American West; representations of the development of the modern city and the stresses of urban existence; and critiques of romantic conceptions of both city and country.

A final book that provides a valuable context for the present study is Sean Cubitt's *EcoMedia*. Cubitt's contribution to ecocriticism is to stress the need to study how environmental concerns, such as biosecurity, overexploitation of resources, global climate change, ecoterrorism, and genetic modification, are mediated by popular film and television programs. "In the absence of citizen's media," he writes, "we have no better place to look than the popular media for representations of popular knowledge and long-term concerns so little addressed in dominant political and economic discourse" (1). Cubitt argues that the utopian content of popular media can be a source of much insight about the weaknesses of our ecological thinking and environmental politics. He finds that films are rich in contradictions, making them not only emotionally but also ethically and intellectually satisfying. More than simply "symptoms of their age," says Cubitt, popular media are effective in voicing the contradictions of their age precisely by appealing "directly to the senses, the emotions and the tastes of the hour"; by sacrificing "linear reason for rhetoric or affect"; and by "abandoning the given world in favour of the image of something other than what, otherwise, we might feel we had no choice but to inhabit" (2).

Cubitt focuses much attention on the dual function of technology, arguing on the one hand that technologies can permit communication between human and natural worlds and thus should not be seen as mere instruments of domination over nature or other humans. On the other hand, he points to the paradox of using sophisticated technologies to define a "pristine nature," citing as examples the highly complex and sophisticated lighting techniques and digital grading processes used by David Attenborough in his eight-part natural history of the ocean, *The Blue Planet*. What enables audiences to see the darkness of the ocean at eight hundred meters deep, or the bioluminescence of certain species, also reveals how "scientific realism is often a matter of readjusting the unobservable so that it can be observed" (54), a comment that echoes Bousé's contention cited above that, in film, nature is often molded "to fit the medium."

This paradox is further explored in several of the essays in this volume specifically addressing issues of representation, of how and why we "frame the world." Cubitt speaks of the need to invent "a mode of looking that encourages the world's unmotivated upsurges to well up into us, clasp itself to us, merge with the salt water in our veins" (59). This "mode of looking" Cubitt calls for is perhaps more likely to be found in experimental rather than mainstream cinema, and in ecocinema rather than environmentalist films. Cubitt remains more optimistic about the role of technology in bridging the gap between human and nonhuman nature than some of the contributors to this volume; his perspective thus serves as an important balance to the orientation adopted here. Arguing that scientific rationalism is not the cause of but the response to our estrangement from nature, Cubitt proposes that "human, natural and technological are three moments of a single process, for if we cannot know, we cannot care, and if we cannot recognize nature as at once ecologically bound to our own survival as a species and an utterly distinct and to a great extent unknown category of existence, there can be no way of mediating the needs of these two torn halves of an integral world" (58).

All other differences aside, Cubitt's comments echo Aldo Leopold's often-quoted dictum that "we can be ethical only in relation to something we can see, feel, understand, love, or otherwise have faith in" (251). This is a sentiment with which all contributors to the present volume would agree. The means by which we "see, feel, understand" is where divergences of opinions arise.

While the essays in the present volume are mostly concerned with the politics of representation at the level of content and form—that is, with cinema's "perceptual ecologies" (Ivakhiv 24)—the application of ecocriticism to film studies must also expand to include the study of the environmental impact of the production, distribution, and exhibition of films, what Ivakhiv calls the "political economy of the industry" (21), or cinema's "material ecologies" (24). Harri Kilpi notes that

> an environmental audit of the film industry would highlight how cinema also produces as a matter of fact concrete, real-world effects on the environment. It does so by being an industry engaged in the uses of raw materials and locations. Therefore, instead of focusing on people, a critical look at the film industry from the perspective of nature would focus on the usage of raw materials and on environmental strains caused by film production. In effect, this kind of research would trace the ecological footprint of a given production and help contribute to the environmental audit of the industry.[4]

Addressing the ecological footprint of all of our choices and actions, including how our entertainment is produced and consumed, is another crucial next step for an ecocritical study of culture that is world-relevant and has a real material impact on our prospects for a sustainable future.

Framing the World is divided into four sections engaging with different but interrelated sets of issues. Part 1, "Ecocinema as and for Activism," focuses more specifically than subsequent sections on the consciousness-raising and activist potential of cinema. In "The Rhetoric of Ascent in *An Inconvenient Truth* and *Everything's Cool*," Mark Minster offers a rhetorical analysis of two popular ecodocumentaries on climate change that provides a partial response to the question of how successfully ecocinema can spur audiences to action. Minster identifies in both films a "rhetoric of assent" that makes these films surprisingly optimistic in inciting audiences to take personal and political action. These two films are among the best examples of how ecocinema might approach educating, raising consciousness, and inspiring activism through a rhetoric of optimism and humor that does not sacrifice the seriousness of the message.

In "Shifting Paradigms: From Environmentalist Films to Ecocinema," I discuss two different avenues for ecocinema that set films within this genre apart from environmentalist films. The Canadian environmental justice documentary *Power: One River Two Nations* brings a minority viewpoint to public attention, overtly informing and engaging viewers in relation to specific environmental injustices affecting the Cree community in Northern Quebec. The Slovenian independent experimental video *Riverglass: A Ballet in Four Seasons* compels us to reflect philosophically on what it means to be a part of the ecosphere. Understanding the differences in the values expressed in ecocinema such as these, as opposed to environmentalist films, helps us gain an appreciation of the causes and effects of privileging a narrow anthropocentric worldview over a more expansive ecocentric perspective on human/nature relations.

The next essay, "Ecocinema, Ecojustice, and Indigenous Worldviews: Native and First Nations Media as Cultural Recovery," focuses on the activist potential of indigenous ecocinema to foster an ecocentric world-view. Jennifer Machiorlatti argues that "indigenous cinema is, at its roots, an activist endeavor that looks to the past in order to make visible the enduring effects of colonization, to reclaim annihilated ways of be-ing, and to envision an affirmative future for contemporary Native peo-ples" (65). The author approaches Native and First Nations film narra-tives as expressions of a specifically indigenous worldview, one more closely aligned with an ecocentric rather than an anthropocentric ethos. Drawing from an "aesthetics of interdependence" (63), Machiorlatti dis-cusses Shelly Niro and Anna Gronau's *It Starts with a Whisper* and George Burdeau's *Backbone of the World: The Blackfeet,* highlighting three central themes: (1) the disconnection of humans from each other and from the Earth's kingdoms; (2) the cultural recovery function of Native film and video; and (3) the relationship of individual media texts to an ecocentric worldview of interdependence.

Part 2, "Bodies That Matter: Environmental Justice in Fiction and Doc-umentary Films," focuses specifically on films dramatizing environ-mental justice issues. Linking ecological wholeness with social and eco-nomic justice, the emerging field of environmental justice, or ecojustice, "does not mean merely another aspect of justice," argues William Gib-son. Rather, "the term eco-justice retains the ancient claim upon human moral agents to build and nurture responsible, equitable, compassion-ate relationships among humans in the social order. And it incorporates the realization that has come like a revelation to our own time, that human societies cannot flourish unless natural systems flourish too" (Gibson 7).

The essays in this section raise questions that are central to environ-mental justice struggles: How do injured bodies come to matter within the larger sociopolitical community? How is access to legal and medical remediation negotiated by victimized bodies? How do particular por-trayals of the land reveal the links between the environment and gender, race, and class dynamics?

Cory Shaman's "Testimonial Structures in Environmental Justice Films" looks at the challenges and obstacles to developing successful environmental justice testimonial strategies through an analysis of Stephen Soderbergh's *Erin Brockovich* and Slawomir Grünberg's independent documentary *Fenceline: A Company Town Divided.* These films, argues Shaman, seek to "'reframe' bodies and places by representing how frequently unrecognized dimensions of threatened bodies and environments become intelligible in activist formation and advocacy contexts." These landmark films have helped bring public attention to environmental injustices and have offered support to activist campaigns by making visible the environmental justice advocacy work that originated in the 1980s and 1990s.

In "Disposable Bodies: Biocolonialism in *The Constant Gardener* and *Dirty Pretty Things,*" Rachel Stein offers an analysis of the pressing issue of third world persons' biomaterial as "natural resources" for first world consumption and profit. Stein looks at the biotechnological colonization of third world bodies through the administering of risky drug trials by transnational pharmaceutical corporations and through the illicit transnational trade in human organs. Her analysis points out the potential of fictional cinema to illuminate for mainstream audiences actual contemporary instances of commodification of third world bodies for first world consumption.

The next essay, "Engaging the Land/Positioning the Spectator: Environmental Justice Documentaries and Robert Redford's *The Horse Whisperer* and *A River Runs Through It,*" provides a transition into the next section focusing on the representation of place. Beth Berila analyzes the implications of particular portrayals of the land by focusing on how two different genres and modes of production position spectators in relation to the environment and to environmental justice issues. The author juxtaposes two acclaimed Robert Redford films that revere the western landscape with two independent environmental justice documentaries that interrogate a community's responsibility for addressing environmental degradation. Linking to the environmental justice issues brought up in the previous two essays, the two documentaries discussed here, *Toxic Racism* (1994) and *Drumbeat for Mother Earth* (1999), show the brunt of environmental abuse falling on poor communities of color. These films offer an explicit analysis of the racial, gender, and class dynamics that shape our relations to nature. Berila's discussion of the Redford films begins to engage with the politics of image construction explored in subsequent essays in part 3 by arguing that these films foster a dominating and colonizing relationship to the land portrayed as spectacle.

Part 3, "Positioning Ecosystems in Fiction, Documentary, and Animation," brings together four essays addressing the different ways in which cinema reflects and shapes our relationship to particular places, and to the human and nonhuman beings that inhabit them. While environmental issues continue to be central to the narratives of most of the films discussed in this section, the focus here shifts to an examination of how films construct, represent, and mediate our experiences of and relationships to particular places and ecosystems.

Harri Kilpi's essay, "The Landscape's Lie: Class, Economy, and Ecology in *Hotel Rwanda*," develops the issues of the spectator's positioning and accountability to place as these themes relate to the portrayal of the 1994 genocide in Rwanda. Specifically, Kilpi discusses *Hotel Rwanda*'s lack of representation of nature, ecology, and land-related economic issues as they relate to the genocide. The essay situates the film's discourse on Rwanda and the genocide within multiple contexts, including ecological, historical, economic, and fictional. Kilpi argues that *Hotel Rwanda* deploys conventional rhetorical devices in its depiction of war and atrocities, but that it leaves out the proper representation of the ecological causal frameworks of the conflict. The erasure of the ecological context from the film not only militates against our gaining a more complex understanding of the conflict but also has the ideological effect of absolving the West's indirect responsibility for the magnitude of the genocide.

In "Fast, Furious, and Out of Control: The Erasure of Natural Landscapes in Car Culture Films," Robin Murray and Joseph Heumann look at another form of erasure and displacement, focusing on the urban context. The essay engages with the often neglected issue of urban nature, particularly its erasure from the awareness of urban dwellers. Murray and Heumann push the limits of an ecocritical reading of films by applying their analysis to a group of films that de-emphasize nature, rendering it invisible even when present. They analyze several recent remakes of the 1955 John Ireland film *The Fast and the Furious* to show how these car culture films celebrate not only speed and control but also "the transformation of the natural landscape into a man-made landscape that is, in turn, itself transformed without questioning the environmental expense" (155).

In "The Screaming Silence: Constructions of Nature in Werner Herzog's *Grizzly Man*," Elizabeth Henry focuses on the German filmmaker's interpretative portrayal of bear activist Timothy Treadwell. Through an analysis of Treadwell's footage of himself, the land, and the animals he interacts with in Alaska, as well as the use Herzog makes of this footage and of Herzog's own footage, Henry explores the ways in which both "filmmakers" exploit the myth of the American frontier in the service of "anthropocentric modes of relating to the nonhuman world." Henry argues that in their interactions with and representations of nature, Treadwell and Herzog "insist on their separation from nature" (172). At the same time, Henry's essay calls attention to moments in the film when an ecocentric view seeps through the footage that both Treadwell and Herzog have captured. For Henry, these moments hint at "what a truly environmentalist and ecocentric approach to our experience of the natural world might consist of" (171).

In the final essay in this section, "*Bambi* and *Finding Nemo:* A Sense of Wonder in the Wonderful World of Disney?" Lynne Dickson Bruckner captures the complexities of assessing environmental attitudes and messages in children's animated films. Environmentally themed children's animation confronts us with the tension between our environmental and our consumer drives. These popular and financially successful films have helped promote environmental awareness and sensitivity both through their narratives and through additional DVD features; at the same time, they also encourage the commodification of creatures and ecosystems through the marketing of nature-themed consumer products. These contradictions make it that much more crucial that we approach animated nature films and the "green packaging" Disney provides as starting points for ecological discussions. Left alone, these films only superficially foster greater ecological literacy in viewers. Bruckner's essay significantly challenges recent studies that unproblematically rescue Disney films' proclivity for sentimentalizing nature from academic criticism.[5]

Part 4, "Art Cinema Eco-auteurs," turns to the work of two distinctly different international art-cinema directors, Peter Greenaway and Kiyoshi Kurosawa, to suggest an avenue for the future of both film studies and cinematic ecocriticism: the study of the eco-auteur. The essays in this section build on the notion of the film director as the equivalent of the literary author introduced by French film critics writing in the late 1950s for *Cahiers du cinéma.*[6] While the essays do not provide a comprehensive and exhaustive ecocritical analysis of the directors' bodies of work, through the analysis of specific films they reveal the filmmakers' underlying environmental consciousness and overt expression of environmental themes and subjects. Although Greenaway and Kurosawa are not self-proclaimed eco-auteurs, the essays in this section provide models for approaching particular directors whose films consistently manifest an ecological sensibility. They also point to the need for film critics and ecocritics to explore more systematically the tradition of art cinema, as has been done with Hollywood, for what it contributes to the development of cinematic ecocriticism.

In "The Rules of the World: Japanese Ecocinema and Kiyoshi Kurosawa," Tim Palmer turns his attention to the neglected phenomenon of Japanese ecocinema by exploring the environmental perspectives conveyed both during the classical era of Japanese cinema and today as Japan experiences a film renaissance. Palmer centers his discussion of contemporary Japanese eco-horror on the work of Kiyoshi Kurosawa, particularly his 1999 film *Charisma*, which the author sees as providing a poignant portrait of contemporary Japanese environmental malaise. This essay situates the study of a particular eco-auteur within a broader national cinema tradition. While classical Japanese cinema was characterized by its treatment of Japan as a lush garden paradise, contemporary Japanese cinema has taken on a more experimental and hybridized form to present a dystopian view of Japan "as a badlands in crisis, a megalopolis poised on the brink of environmental disaster" (210). Japanese cinema today is set in an urban milieu characterized by catastrophe in the form of curses, virulent plagues, and natural and supernatural contaminants, as well as violent social and environmental breakdown.

In the final essay, "Beyond the Frame: The Spirit of Place in Peter Greenaway's *The Draughtsman's Contract*," I examine Peter Greenaway's treatment of nature *as character* in his first commercial feature, *The Draughtsman's Contract*. Addressing the power of the image to reflect and shape our perceptions of reality, and thus to inform our actions in the world, the essay argues that the film itself interrogates the *idea* and the *politics* of visual representations of nature. It does so through a philosophical investigation of one of the most fundamental tools of representation: the frame. To the power of the picture frame to contain and fix reality, Greenaway juxtaposes the archetypal figure of the Green Man, or Genius Loci. While the nature of his existence remains somewhat ambiguous in the film, I read this figure's function allegorically and symbolically, as a trickster who helps us perceive, experience, and reconnect to the world around us from a more ecocentric sensibility.

Building on a rich and expanding body of ecocritical analyses, then, *Framing the World: Explorations in Ecocriticism and Film* engages with a wide range of questions that have informed the study of culture from a "green" standpoint, while focusing on those aspects that are particular to the study of the visual medium. What kinds of images of nature do films create? What stereotypes, distortions, omissions, or emphases are to be found in cinematic representations of nature? What insights about our relationship to the nonhuman world do the absence and veiling of natural settings in films provide us? What role does the physical environment play in relation to human and nonhuman characters and to plot development? Which filmmakers make nature the focus of their work? How do changes in the representation of nature reflect changes in cultural conceptions of nature? How do gender, class, race, and ethnicity affect the way nature is portrayed? How are environmental threats and responses to these threats represented? What strategies are deployed to educate and inspire action in viewers? Finally, are the values expressed in particular films supportive of an ecological consciousness of interconnectedness, interdependence, and survival?

NOTES

1. For a thorough investigation of the complicit role of education and educational institutions in the ecological crisis, and for suggestions on how to reorient education and the curriculum in the service of the "biophilia revolution," see also David Orr, *Earth in Mind: On Education, Environment, and the Human Prospect* (Washington, DC: Island Press, 1994). Orr encourages us to rethink education by starting with the premise that "all education is environmental education. By what is included or excluded, students are taught that they are part of or apart from the natural world" (12). See also the Greening of the Campus movement (http://www.bsu.edu/greening/) and the many campus sustainability initiatives under way. For resources on campus sustainability, see the Association for the Advancement of Sustainability in Higher Education (http://www.aashe.org/).

2. Sir John Houghton is a former professor of atmospheric physics at the University of Oxford (1976–83), chief executive of the Meteorological Office (1983–1991), and co-chairman of the Scientific Assessment Committee for the Intergovernmental Panel on Climate Change (IPCC 1988–2002). The quotation is from his opening remarks on April 14, 2007, to the online conference EcoRes Forum, "From Anthropocentrism to Ecocentrism: Making the Shift," 14–30 April 2007, http://www.eco-res.org/shift_econf.html. The conference's Web site contains a number of resources on the ethical, political, and economic dimensions of the climate crisis (http://www.eco-res.org/shift_resources.html).

3. See for example, Richard Hofrichter, ed., *Toxic Struggles: The Theory and Practice of Environmental Justice* (Salt Lake City: Univ. of Utah Press, 2002); Joni Adamson, Mei Mei Evans, and Rachel Stein, eds., *The Environmental Justice Reader: Politics, Poetics and Pedagogy* (Tucson: Univ. of Arizona Press, 2002); William E. Gibson, ed., *Eco-justice: The Unfinished Journey* (New York: SUNY Press, 2004); Winona LaDuke and Rachel Stein, eds., *New Perspectives on Environmental Justice: Gender, Sexuality, and Activism* (Piscataway, NJ: Rutgers Univ. Press, 2004).

4. See Harri Kilpi, "Green Frames: Exploring Cinema Ecocritically," *WiderScreen,* January 2007, http://www.widerscreen.fi/2007/1/green_frames-exploring_cin ema_ecocritically.htm.
5. See, for instance, David Whitley, *The Idea of Nature in Disney Animation* (Aldershot: Ashgate Publishing Limited, 2008), and my review of the book in *Animation: An Interdisciplinary Journal* 4.2 (2009): 203–11.
6. The foundational essay for the *auteur* theory is François Truffaut's "A Certain Tendency of the French Cinema," originally published in French in 1959 and in English in 1967. See *Cahiers du cinéma* 1 (1967): 30. See also Andrew Sarris, "Notes on the Auteur Theory in 1962," *Film Theory and Criticism: Introductory Readings* (6th ed.), ed. Leo Braudy and Marshall Cohen (Oxford: Oxford Univ. Press, 2004), 561–64.

WORKS CITED

Armbruster, Karla, and Kathleen R. Wallace, eds. *Beyond Nature Writing: Expanding the Boundaries of Ecocriticism.* Charlottesville: Univ. of Virginia Press, 2001.

Barry, Peter. *Beginning Theory: An Introduction to Literary and Cultural Theory.* Manchester: Manchester Univ. Press, 2002.

Bousé, Derek. *Wildlife Films.* Philadelphia: Univ. of Pennsylvania Press, 2000.

Bowers, C. A. *Education, Cultural Myths, and the Ecological Crisis: Toward Deep Changes.* Albany: SUNY Press, 1993.

——. *Educating for Eco-justice and Community.* Athens: Univ. of Georgia Press, 2001.

Branch, Michael, Rochelle Johnson, Daniel Patterson, and Scott Slovic, eds. *Reading the Earth: New Directions in the Study of Literature and the Environment.* Moscow: Univ. of Idaho Press, 1998.

Brereton, Pat. *Hollywood Utopia: Ecology in Contemporary American Cinema.* Bristol: Intellect Books, 2005.

Buell, Lawrence. "The Ecocritical Insurgency." *New Literary History* 30 (Summer 1999): 699–712.

——. *The Environmental Imagination: Thoreau, Nature Writing, and the Formation of American Culture.* Cambridge, MA: Harvard Univ. Press, 1995.

——. *The Future of Environmental Criticism: Environmental Crisis and Literary Imagination.* Malden, MA: Blackwell Publishing, 2005.

Carmichael, Deborah A., ed. *The Landscape of Hollywood Westerns: Ecocriticism in an American Film Genre.* Salt Lake City: Univ. of Utah Press, 2006.

Cohen, Michael P. "Blues in the Green: Ecocriticism under Critique." *Environmental History* 9.1 (January 2004): 9–36.

Cubitt, Sean. *EcoMedia.* Amsterdam, New York: Rodopi, 2005.

Gibson, William E., ed. *Eco-justice: The Unfinished Journey.* New York: SUNY Press, 2004.

Glotfelty, Cheryll, and Harold Fromm, eds. *The Ecocriticism Reader: Landmarks in Literary Ecology.* Athens: Univ. of Georgia Press, 1996.

Heise, Ursula K. "The Hitchhiker's Guide to Ecocriticism." *PMLA* 121.2 (2006): 503–16.

Ingram, David. *Green Screen: Environmentalism and Hollywood Cinema.* Exeter: Univ. of Exeter Press, 2000.

Ivakhiv, Adrian. "Green Film Criticism and Its Future." *Interdisciplinary Studies in Literature and Environment* 15.2 (Summer 2008): 1–28.

Kerridge, Richard. "Environmentalism and Ecocriticism." In *The Theory and Practice of Literary Criticism: An Oxford Guide.* Ed. Patricia Waugh. Oxford: Oxford Univ. Press, 2006. 530–43.

Leopold, Aldo. *A Sand County Almanac.* 1949. New York: Ballantine Books, 1970.

MacDonald, Scott. "Toward an Eco-cinema." *Interdisciplinary Studies in Literature and Environment* 11.2 (Summer 2004): 107–32.

——. *The Garden in the Machine: A Field Guide to Independent Films about Place.* Berkeley: Univ. of California Press, 2001.

McDowell, Michael J. "The Bakhtinian Road to Ecological Insight." *The Ecocriticism Reader: Landmarks in Literary Ecology.* Ed. Cheryll Glotfelty and Harold Fromm. Athens: Univ. of Georgia Press, 1996. 371–91.

McKibben, Bill. *Deep Economy: The Wealth of Communities and the Durable Future.* New York: Times Books, 2007.

Mitman, Gregg. *Reel Nature: America's Romance with Wildlife on Film.* Cambridge, MA: Harvard Univ. Press, 1999.

Murray, Robin L., and Joseph K. Heumann. *Ecology and Popular Film: Cinema and the Edge.* Albany: SUNY Press, 2009.

Oppermann, Serpil. "Theorizing Ecocriticism: Toward a Postmodern Ecocritical Practice." *Interdisciplinary Studies in Literature and Environment* 13.2 (Summer 2006): 103–28.

Reed, T. V. "Toward an Environmental Justice Ecocriticism." *The Environmental Justice Reader: Politics, Poetics, and Pedagogy.* Ed. Joni Adamson, Mei Mei Evans, and Rachel Stein. Tucson: Univ. of Arizona Press, 2002. 145–62.

Romanyshyn, Robert. "The Despotic Eye and its Shadow: Media Image in the Age of Literacy." *Modernity and the Hegemony of Vision.* Ed. David Michael Levin. Berkeley and Los Angeles: Univ. of California Press, 1993. 339–60.

Rosendale, Steven, ed. *The Greening of Literary Scholarship: Literature, Theory, and the Environment.* Iowa City: Univ. of Iowa Press, 2002.

Rowe, Stan. "What on Earth Is Environment?" Originally published in *Trumpeter* 6.4 (1989): 123–26. Revised version at http://www.ecospherics.net/pages/RoWhatEarth.html. Retrieved 14 April 2007.

Slovic, Scott. "Ecocriticism: Containing Multitudes, Practicing Doctrine." *The Green Studies Reader: From Romanticism to Ecocriticism.* Ed. Laurence Coupe. London: Routledge, 2000. 160–62.

Whitebook, Joel. "The Problem of Nature in Habermas." *Minding Nature: The Philosophers of Ecology.* Ed. David Macauley. New York: Guilford Press, 1996. 283–317.

PART I
ECOCINEMA
AS AND FOR
ACTIVISM

THE RHETORIC OF ASCENT
IN AN INCONVENIENT TRUTH
AND EVERYTHING'S COOL

MARK MINSTER

Given that the explicit purpose of both *An Inconvenient Truth* and *Everything's Cool* is to convince viewers to help fight global warming, the title of my essay might equally well be "the rhetoric of *assent*." Both documentaries call for an end to nearly two decades of dilatory, unproductive debates about whether the planet's climate really is changing, or whether anthropogenic emissions of greenhouse gases have caused "some" or "most" of the troposphere's warming. The science is as clear as it can possibly be, both films insist, and the time for discussion is over. The time for action is *now*. Toward this end, eliciting assent and inciting action, both films marshal a host of rhetorical devices.

Throughout Al Gore's *An Inconvenient Truth* (produced by Laurie David and eBay billionaire Jeff Skoll and directed by Davis Guggenheim) we see audiences laughing and nodding in agreement with him, one of the film's many shrewd decisions for building consensus. "Rhetoric of *assent*" reflects the film's remarkable success in doing what so few works of environmentally oriented film and literature have *ever* been able to do: taking an issue generally perceived as an activist concern and making millions of Americans ready to act, at least with their votes.[1] Even as recently as late 2006, global warming was hardly a viable ballot issue for politicians in the United States. It has become so since the film's release, as suggested by the platforms of all of the major Democratic presidential candidates and at least one of the Republican candidates in the 2008 election.[2] *Time* and *Newsweek* ran cover stories on Gore and climate in 2007, and even Rupert Murdoch's Fox News—which has given more airtime over the last decade to the Competitive Enterprise Institute than to climatologists, broadcasting documentaries of doubt and dubious merit—even Fox News announced, in late spring of 2007, that the company now vows to reduce emissions and bring climate messaging into its programs.[3] And even though, as global warming skeptics are fond of pointing out, "correlation is not causation," my sense is that Gore's film has had more to do with this transformation in values than did the appearance, in February 2007, of the most recent report of the Intergovernmental Panel on Climate Change (IPCC).

Even if the film has not single-handedly raised America's consciousness or changed the country's mind, it is a rhetorician's dream. *An Inconvenient Truth* is a model of the art of persuasion, from Gore's winning sense of humor ("I'm Al Gore. I used to be the next President of the United States") to his role as skeptical semiotician, decoding cigarette ads and newspaper clippings, defusing his opponents' counterclaims; from the film's anticipation and bridging of its multiple audiences (the unconvinced as well as the committed) to its blurring of genres and deployment of Aristotelian modes of reasoning.

In *Everything's Cool*, Daniel B. Gold and Judith Helfand, the same directors who made the ecodocumentary *Blue Vinyl*, take exemplary persuasion yet one step further. If *An Inconvenient Truth* wants to persuade viewers that global warming is real and dangerous, and that we have the capacity and moral responsibility to stop it, *Everything's Cool* weaves together profiles of a number of activists—"global warming messengers," the film's Web site calls them—who are actively attempting to do just that. It moves from the lecture halls of *An Inconvenient Truth* into the sets and dressing rooms of the Weather Channel, the home offices of an investigative journalist and a governmental whistle-blower, and the garage of a Big Lebowski–like ski bum who experiments with biodiesel. The film literally takes to the streets, following a fifteen-foot truck (wryly called "The Do You Care? Mobile") that was driven across the country in 2004, and walking along with Bill McKibben's activist march in Vermont in 2007.

Whatever their differences, both films realize that audiences are persuaded to action not primarily by facts or prophecies of doom—nor, as Michael Shellenberger says in *Everything's Cool,* by abstract calculations about a rise in the price of maple syrup, nor by pictures of polar bears drowning. Rather, we are persuaded by likeable characters we can trust and maybe even emulate. We are persuaded by humor and believable emotion, by shared values and deeply embedded cultural narratives. Even though the films are documentaries, not works of fiction—indeed, perhaps *because* they are not fictional—they are successful at making us care about large, global issues by making us care about the people involved, and by convincing us that if we are not ourselves activists and "messengers," we might still strive to be like them.

It is worth spending some time with this question: how does successful ecocinema spur us to action? *An Inconvenient Truth,* in particular, has been accused of being yet another environmental jeremiad, prophesying apocalypse.[4] Perhaps the filmmakers come closest to this fear-inducing mode when they present images of numerous airborne diseases, showing an animated graphic (which looks strikingly like an old Atari game) with several enormous mosquitoes rising up a comparatively small mountain as the temperature rises. Gore slightly oversimplifies the scientific evidence to imply that many, many ominous-looking diseases will result *directly* from global warming, whereas most epidemiologists say that the transmission dynamics of infectious diseases are affected by numerous other factors as well, including a widespread increase in global travel and the cost and availability of mosquito control strategies.[5] Here—and in the film's emphasis on Hurricane Katrina, particularly in the image used as the film's cover in which a single smokestack emits a spiral cloud that looks decidedly like a hurricane—the film does seem to emphasize the worst-case scenarios of what current science knows for certain about global warming.[6] This is about as close to Jeremiah as Gore comes, however, in a film that is far more positive than doomsaying, and one that is, I hope to show, rhetorically uplifting as well.

Both films, in fact, are surprisingly optimistic, arguing that it is imperative for their audiences to take personal and political action, without coming close to taking Jeremiah's dark pleasure in predicting the collapse of humankind. The films do depict global warming as an urgent problem, but not as the all-too-certain I-told-you-so end of the world. As Michael Shellenberger quips in *Everything's Cool,* "Martin Luther King didn't give the 'I Have a Nightmare' speech, he gave the 'I Have a Dream' speech."

Contrast the tones of *An Inconvenient Truth* and *Everything's Cool* with the very title of Jonathan Schell's *Fate of the Earth,* or with the best-known fictional film about global warming, *The Day After Tomorrow,* which glosses over and even revels in the deaths of many millions of humans (and presumably other species as well). It is a last-man-standing film in which the audience is invited not to sympathize with the dead and dying and endangered, but to identify with the few Crusoes and Ishmaels who alone survive to tell the tale. When Dr. Jack Hall (Dennis Quaid) abruptly draws a line across the United States, telling the president to sacrifice the northern half of the United States (eliding, of course, the existence of Canada) to the calamitous storms that encircle the globe, we are meant to see how dire the situation is, but more important, we are supposed to sympathize with Hall, who is finally being taken seriously. Hall later picks his way over the frozen bodies of those who were duly warned and should have believed.

In *The Day After Tomorrow,* those who remain unconvinced about global warming are cast as villains or deserving victims, whereas in *An Inconvenient Truth* and *Everything's Cool* they are merely the audience, while the true villains are those who deliberately obfuscate science for the sake of greed and the status quo.[7] *Everything's Cool,* admittedly, does permit us to laugh at Americans at fairs and truck stops who do not believe that global warming is as real a threat as terrorism or atheism. According to one woman interviewed in New Orleans wearing Mardi Gras beads, "Before Noah, we had global warming."

If the films fit the pattern of an early American literary genre, it is not so much the jeremiad—which implies invective, judgment, and blame[8]— as the conversion narrative, the account related by one who was lost but now is found and has had his or her life transformed, in a pattern that mirrors other believers' transformations, inducing *assent.*[9] Each convert's life story fits the same narrative pattern as the one that other believers tell about themselves, which fits with the larger narrative of salvation history. We identify with the minister who is also a convert, convicted by his or her harrowing experiences of having descended into the miry clay, only to be raised up, ascending, in the waters to new life. This is "ascent" as it is spelled in my title. Gore is one such convert-turned-minister, pairing the story of his own awakening to the realities of climate change with accounts of how the Gore family learned to give up tobacco farming, and how Gore has dedicated himself to telling others about the problems and solutions associated with greenhouse gases.

Everything's Cool presents several more exemplars, mostly people who started as writers but have become traveling lecturers, more active activists. Ross Gelbspan was a journalist who had to be persuaded that global warming is real before devoting most of the 1990s to writing books and articles on the interests that conspire to make the climate crisis seem unreal, and then joining the lecture circuit—"I didn't get into this because I loved the trees," he tells us. Rick Piltz was a government researcher who became a government watchdog when his work was undermined by presidential appointees funded by the oil lobby, so he took his writing from Capitol Hill to the *New York Times.* And Bill McKibben, whom the filmmakers present reverentially as the "Poet Laureate of global warming," the man "who wrote the book on the subject," *The End of Nature,* now lectures and leads demonstrations and campus action groups.

Both films end with a kind of altar call, presenting solutions not just as easy things anyone can do, but as difficult ways to change our lives. In Gore's film Melissa Etheridge enjoins us to "Wake Up," as a short montage of suggested solutions flashes across the screen, interspersed with the closing credits. "If you can, buy a hybrid." "When you can, walk or ride a bicycle." "Where you can, use light rail + mass transit." While the sentences change, the words "you can" remain on-screen, the new words in the next sentence rising into place from the bottom of the screen. In *Everything's Cool*, the credits roll while the Flaming Lips play "The Yeah Yeah Yeah Song (With All Your Power)" to show that real action begins when films are over. Through the song, the film asks us how we would use our power to affect the world: "If you could blow up the world with the flick of a switch / If you could make everybody poor just so you could be rich / Would you do it?"

For Aristotle, the rhetorician's art consists of three main kinds of appeals, or modes of persuasion: logos, ethos, and pathos (*Rhetoric* 1.2.2).[10] *Logos* indicates an attempt to persuade with evidence, reasoning, using what Aristotle called "proof, or apparent proof" (1.2.5). *Ethos* is the attempt to persuade by the character and authority of the speaker. "We believe good [people] more readily than others," Aristotle writes, going on to say that "character may almost be called the most effective means of persuasion" (1.2.3). *Pathos* is an appeal to emotion but also, and perhaps more important, it is an appeal to shared values, shared narratives. "Our judgments when we are pleased and friendly are not the same as when we are pained and hostile," he writes (1.2.3). Therefore, skilled rhetoricians will make sure not to pain or unnerve their audiences unduly.

While both of these films might seem to be about presenting evidence, appeals to logos are the least of what they do. *Everything's Cool* takes the scientific evidence for global warming as a fait accompli. The very first shot of the film shows seven rows of packing boxes with labels such as "Sea Ice," "Exxon," "N_2O," "Greenland," as a voice-over says that "several thousand tons of scientific studies on climate change all led to the same conclusion." The boxes pile up until they all topple over. Filmmakers Daniel Gold and Judith Helfand set out to show not that global warming is a serious problem facing the world today—this they present as a given—but that, despite the vast quantity and relative clarity of the evidence, there is a sharp divide between what "scientists tell us" and Americans' general inability, or unwillingness, to accept this evidence and act on it.

Repeatedly, the film uses the visual metaphor of a widening rift, or chasm, between the left and right halves of the screen. On one side stands what we know from science. On the other stand the corporate lobbyists with their campaign of disinformation. All scientific evidence in the film is presented off-screen, as backstory. NASA scientist James Hanson is shown only briefly, testifying before Congress. Ross Gelbspan mentions how he was persuaded only by collaboration with the scientist Paul Epstein, and by the discovery that global warming skeptics were funded by the coal industry. Rick Piltz was responsible for assimilating reams of data at the Climate Change Science Program, data represented on-screen as stacks of files and government documents. Instead of walking the audience through charts and graphs, the film portrays evidence as piles of papers on desks, which we trust the experts have read. Even Heidi Cullen, the climate expert for the Weather Channel, is not in the film to persuade us with logos, abstract reasoning, scientific experiments, or laboratory results. She tells us just enough to establish her credentials. She functions, rather, to represent how challenging it is to present evidence to a general American television audience without having that evidence distorted by either the medium of television or the organizational politics of the Weather Channel. If she provides evidence, it is evidence for the rift between how much we know about climate change and how little we have done about it.

In *An Inconvenient Truth*, by contrast, the systematic, authoritative presentation of evidence appears to be the film's reason for being, though its logical argument is leavened with stories of Gore's growth as a person, and with cartoons of polar bears looking forlorn and Matt Groening's animation of thuggish greenhouse gasses bossing around rays of sunlight. Graphs that function as axes of evidence frequently appear, and they multiply. And yet these graphs operate less for the sake of logos than for the sake of ethos—they tell us at least as much about Gore's credibility as they do about the chemical composition of the earth's atmosphere. The content of these graphs, in other words, is scientific. But what the graphs *mean* in the context of the film, the film's ultimate argument, is that Gore himself has mastered much of the science that has already been done, long before we arrived, and can authoritatively mediate that science for us. His encounters with the evidence are more persuasive than the evidence itself.

When Gore discusses Dr. Charles Keeling, for example—whom he describes as "faithful and precise," and "hard-nosed" about the data—he presents numerous images of the famous Keeling curve that has recorded atmospheric concentrations of carbon dioxide above Mauna Loa since 1958. Its saw-toothed pattern reflects seasonal changes, but its overall upward rise is unmistakable, from 320 parts per million fifty years ago to nearly 400 parts per million now. The image appears at least thirty times: behind Gore as part of his slideshow, on his laptop in windows small and large, in an old-looking textbook figure, as raw tabular data. During Gore's discussion of Keeling's research, one grainy black-and-white pan-and-scan shows pages of strikingly similar graphs tacked to a wall. The color and texture of the shot, and much of the sequence, lend the graph historical authority, while the replication of the Keeling curve functions as "proof" of its veracity—the visual pattern of the graphs is what we notice.

Back in the film's present tense, Gore's presentation software slowly recreates the graph, automatically drawing the jagged upward line of CO_2 concentrations and simultaneously running a counter of the last fifty years. Gore compares the graph's saw-toothed pattern, created by seasonal variations, to the breathing of the planet, as an image of the earth pulses with blue light. As the computer draws the Keeling curve, the planet pulses, and the counter ticks along the years, Gore narrates his own involvement in the fight against global warming during the very years that flash across the screen. "It just keeps going up," he says of the Keeling curve, "it is relentless." Interestingly, this "it" has no clear antecedent: "it" could almost as easily refer to Gore's own growth as an activist, the relentlessness of his efforts attempting to catch up with the increase in atmospheric CO_2 concentrations, an effort propelled, it almost seems, by the breathing of the earth.

A few minutes later, this blurring of logos and ethos becomes even clearer as Gore reveals a theater-sized image of a version of the IPCC's controversial "hockey-stick" graph, which uses a single red line to trace variations in temperature in the Northern Hemisphere over the last millennium.[11] This graph, too, just keeps going up, and is multiplied as well, with a single line that records CO_2 concentrations, first over the last 1,000 years, and then over the last 650,000 years, and then a temperature graph for the last 650,000 years. Though they are evidentiary, these curves are not abstract data, but a literal backdrop for Gore to walk along and participate in.

This is argument by character far more than by reason. Gore is involved in the evidence he presents, both narratively—he tells his own story while the earth breathes in and out—and corporeally—he walks along the x-axis and ascends the y-axis with an electric elevator he calls a "contraption."[12] As CO_2 levels continue to rise, Gore rises alongside them. There is more than a little bit of P. T. Barnum here, certainly. We may be persuaded by data, but we are convinced less by the data themselves than by the replication of the shape of the curves—multiple graphs, all going up—and even more by Gore's personal involvement in those curves. He himself goes up.

If ethos is more fundamental to both films than logos is, it is also more problematic. *Everything's Cool* depicts many of its characters as completely heroic. Gelbspan sits *in pater familias*. Piltz's teen daughter realizes that while her father used to seem normal, "Now he's all, like, big." Michael Shellenberger and Ted Nordhaus, the "Bad Boys of Environmentalism," are shown in a limo on their cell phones, and McKibben is positively glorified, introduced by a nun as "one of the great prophets of our age." Gore's autobiographical narratives make the science of global warming digestible, and yet the visual style in which he is often shot renders some of this autobiography unpalatable. He looks wistfully out the windows of planes and cars and taxis, works single-handedly on his slideshow on his laptop, and uses the word "friend" to describe scientists and politicians all over the world. He is frequently depicted as a man of the people, with his folksy humor, his black-and-white snapshots taken of his family farm when he was a child, his wearing a suit without a tie, all portraying him as one of us. The decision to include nearly a full minute of Gore walking through airport security at Los Angeles International Airport invokes heightened security conditions after 9/11 and foregrounds a hassle we can all identify with. "It is extremely frustrating, to me . . . ," Gore says in a voice-over (though he is talking about something else) as he prepares to walk through the metal detector. The long scene functions as a transition for Gore's visit to China, but it also characterizes Gore as a weary traveler, an everyman, even as it backgrounds the CO_2 tonnage emitted on his flights around the world (for which he has repeatedly been taken to task).

Contrast the Gore of the people with the apotheosized Gore, whom we encounter especially near the very end of the film. The last time we see him, he is walking out of a green room before giving his slideshow, up a tunnel backstage to the cheering of adoring fans, into a spotlight, which fades to a still frame of haze that turns out to be an image of Katrina. Throughout the walk, Gore's voice-over speaks: "There's nothing that unusual about what I'm doing with this. What is unusual is that I had the privilege to be shown it, as a young man. It's almost as if a window was opened, through which the future was very clearly visible. 'See that,' he says, 'see that? That's the future in which you are going to live your life.' "

Who this "he" is, is not exactly clear. What is clear is Gore's prophetic sense of having been chosen, alongside the identifiable ascent of the rock star taking the stage. We are left only with his silhouette as he trades his commonplace identity for onstage stardom.

In between the prophetic and the popular, the film establishes for Gore a pair of more interesting and likeable roles, in a way that seems to give almost unmediated access to his "true" personality: Gore the semiotician and Gore the comedian. These two roles overlap repeatedly, when his witty skepticism satisfies our personal need for comedy relief and our larger cultural desire for critique. He systematically defuses his opposition, wryly pointing out the rhetorical strategy used by global warming skeptics—"Reposition Global Warming as Theory rather than Fact"—and then quickly juxtaposing this spin with the rhetoric used by the tobacco industry, which he can count on his audience to both distrust and dislike. His slide of a vintage cigarette ad that claims "More Doctors Smoke Camels" elicits ironic laughter from his audience, and then applause. A few minutes later, he displays some information about the career of Philip Cooney, who worked for the American Petroleum Institute before being appointed as chief of staff to the White House's Council on Environmental Quality. Gore reveals a copy of a memo that Cooney edited (despite having no scientific expertise), then returns to Cooney's bio sheet to show that the day after Cooney resigned from his political appointment, he took a job for ExxonMobil. This sequence culminates with a screenshot of a quote from Upton Sinclair: "It is difficult to get a man to understand something when his salary depends upon his not understanding it." Gore has only to read the statement for the audience to laugh and applaud.

Moments later he shows a visual prepared by the White House labeled "Balance" that depicts a scale balancing six gold bars on the left with, on the right, a picture of the globe. As he looks at the gold bars, he delves into stand-up comedy, shaking his head and saying, "Mmm, mmm, mmm. Don't they look good? I'd just like to have some of those gold bars. Mmm, mmm." "And on the other side of the scales," he continues, "the ENTIRE PLANET!" The laughter continues for nearly fifteen seconds as Gore pretends to consider this option, reducing his opposition's argument to the absurd, deflating their symbols, emptying them of significance. In a sentence that needs no conclusion, he says, "This is a false choice . . . If we don't have a planet . . ."

Since the overall goals of both films are so similar, it makes sense that Everything's Cool establishes its ethos similarly, presenting its global warming messengers as both prophets and ordinary people, since both movies need us to believe that, when it comes to issues like climate change, everyone has prophetic authority. Both films also blend the comedic with the semiotic, revealing those who attempt to "reposition global warming as a theory" as ridiculous. And yet there are two major differences in how the films establish ethos. First, the sheer number and variety of characters allows the characters' roles to be distributed more effectively than in *An Inconvenient Truth,* which focuses solely on Gore. Gore plays his various roles well, but because he is one man, he simply cannot portray the range of emotions and values that ten people can. He is not as much a man of the people as Bish Newhouser, the Utah snow groomer with the beat-up old diesel whose experiments with biodiesel melt the plastic in his kitchen blender. He does not live somewhere affected directly by global warming, as do the children from Shishmaref, Alaska, a village that had to move because the melting permafrost destroyed their homes' foundations.[13] The children speculate about techniques for moving a whole village ("A barge?" one boy says), and what they might take with them ("some clothes," "my dog," "Gameboy"). He does not have an offbeat voice or tone like the narrator of *Everything's Cool,* Daniel Gold. He can convey experience, clout, and conviction, but not the exuberance of Shellenberger and Nordhaus, nor the passionate first steps of activist Vermonters marching to raise awareness. The multiplicity of characters means *Everything's Cool* is less likely to succeed or fail based upon our identification with one character. Bill McKibben may be especially knowledgeable and articulate, but he does come across as relatively humorless when compared with Bish Newhouser, who more than makes up for what he lacks in reasoned exposition with his ability to hot-wire a 1975 Mercedes.

A second difference between the two films' appeals to ethos is that, while *An Inconvenient Truth* wants us to trust and like Gore so that we will identify with his moral anger and relentless determination, *Everything's Cool* spends much more time with its characters' frustrations, so that we come to sympathize with those activists who have been trying to narrow the gap between what we know about global warming (much) and what we have been able to do about it (little). In other words, Gore's film leaves us convinced that global warming is a problem we need to act on, but Gold and Helfand's film leaves us convinced that *doing nothing* about global warming is the real problem we need to act on, that the main obstacles to taking action are psychological: depression, frustration, and fear. The title, *Everything's Cool,* stands not as a statement of disbelief from the filmmakers, but as an incredulous, ironic quotation of what skeptics have convinced most Americans about global warming.[14] Across the animated chasm that recurs throughout the film, we see animated stick figures trying to reach across the gap to shut it: trying to do "something that frankly seemed impossible," Gold narrates, "a seismic shift in the public's perception of one of the most serious problems ever to confront humanity."

Global warming is the problem, of course, but what seems impossible and perpetually frustrating is changing the public's mind. "I've tried every way I could think of, over the years, to get people to pay attention," McKibben says. "To think and work about global warming can be a pretty depressing business." Rick Piltz talks with his daughter about his having resigned from his job compiling climate research, "just completely letting that go." And yet he goes on to show the filmmakers the research reports made by the National Climate Assessment, recounting how the second Bush administration "deep-sixed the National Assessment, they just sent it into a black hole, suppressed any use of it, or even any reference to it . . . a black hole, just sent it into a black hole."

Our interest in Heidi Cullen is closely tied to our sense of her as an outsider, "the new kid on the block," as she calls herself, struggling to bridge the gap between science and popular media. She listens as a Weather Channel managing editor points out the flaws with her delivery and even with her content. She voices frustration when an acting coach tells her that audiences pay far more attention to how newscasters look than to what they actually say: "Which I just, I don't, I don't believe." More frustrating for her is the way global warming skeptics "molest the truth," preying upon science's every attempt to speak judiciously as if speaking responsibly meant having serious doubts. "The part that I find so challenging," Cullen says, "is trying to convince someone that you don't have an agenda, that you're just trying to say . . . that you're not trying to cry wolf . . . that this isn't just *crap* that we've created, it's the mother of all problems."

Gelbspan is the best example of our identifying with the activists' frustration. "I think people really still don't get it in a really profound way," he says, cleaning out his office at home, sorting through videotapes of his appearances on national television programs, "and it's just really sad seeing what's happening and how the world is not responding, especially in the U.S. It's very sad to go through all of this and see how much work went into all this stuff and how it's made no dent. Or very little dent." Later in the film he reflects, candidly and poignantly, on his efforts to raise public awareness of climate change:

> I feel like I'm one of a number of people who've sort of thrown their bodies across the tracks, probably to no avail. A lot of us probably feel like Paul Revere without a horse, you know? . . . I certainly have no

misgivings about anything that's happened in the sense that, personally, it's been a great ego trip. . . . But at the larger level it feels like, it feels like the title of a Yeats poem, you know, "To a Friend Whose Work Has Come to Nothing." Not personally, but in terms of the larger aims of it, it does. And that's a very defeated kind of feeling . . . My daughters Thea and Joby, I'm really proud of what they're doing, but knowing what's happening with the planet, a part of me wants to say to them, "Why bother?" And I don't *ever* want to say that to them.

Rhetoric is, for Kenneth Burke, "a symbolic means of inducing cooperation in beings that by nature respond to symbols" (*Rhetoric of Motives* 43). As humans, we are symbol-makers; according to Burke, one of our key symbols is negation, which divides us from the natural world that has no negatives. There is no absence, no negation, not even in parasitic wasps or species loss, until we invent it. This symbol of the negative, of proscription, the "no" or "not," gives birth to ethics (the "thou shalt not"). Our separation from the eternal affirmations of nature, not to mention our essential division from one another, begets in us a cycle of the desire for return, through which desire we seek to transcend our lost unity, and so we seek in language, in communication, what he calls "consubstantiality," to be substantive with other substances.

The key point here, for our purposes, is that for Burke persuasion is less the goal of rhetoric than identification is. It is not so much that films about environmental issues are trying to change audiences' minds, but that they are tapping into latent desires their audiences already have to join the whole, the common. And Burke's notion of consubstantiality suggests that persuasion is not primarily antagonistic, nor even agonistic, but cooperative and community-building: "Rhetoric seeks . . . a sense of oneness amid diversity of conflicting interests and values" (Crusius 28). Films like *An Inconvenient Truth* and *Everything's Cool* attempt to persuade us by deploying a range of symbols; but more, they seek to build consensus, having us identify with their characters and speakers. Thus, Gore's nodding, cheering, and laughing audience members within the film are remarkably effective at nurturing our desires for consubstantiality, at least as effective as any graphs could be. McKibben's books, as far as the movie is concerned, do less for us than the image of him speaking before a crowd of marchers at the end of their journey, scratching his head and admitting that this was his most hopeful day in twenty years. Gelbspan's books are far less effective than the image of him on the couch with his wife and daughter, talking about his newfound optimism in 2006, his sense that people are finally getting the message. "Now Paul Revere has a horse."

Yet it is also Burke's culminating preoccupation with hierarchy that interests me, and in particular the phrase "the rhetoric of ascent," which Arthur Quinn uses to characterize the end of *The Rhetoric of Motives*. We are motivated to identify with others for multiple reasons, chief among them the desire for collective rising, a desire for ascent. We long for a sentimental reunion with a lost unity—with nature and with each other; but we also long for some kind of transcendence and are particularly susceptible to the rhetoric of transcendence, which elsewhere Burke calls "the machinery of transcendence" (see "I, Eye, Ay"). Ascent, then, is one of our key human symbols, or clusters of symbols: mountaintops, climbs, ladders (or elevator platforms), chains of being.

Burke's terms help explain why these two instances of ecocinema are so successful. Both documentaries emphasize collective ascent, overcoming, a communal attempt to transcend the ecological crises facing the planet. In *An Inconvenient Truth*, this ascent is literal as well as figurative. The Keeling curve and the hockey-stick graph both rise literally, representing the rising temperatures and concentrations of greenhouse gases, the threat of global warming. And yet Gore ascends alongside them, literally on the elevator platform, and figuratively from a young politician and member of a tobacco-farming family, past the merely political setbacks of his failed presidential campaigns, to a position beyond politics. But the film portrays ascent ethically, in the manner of the conversion narrative and the tent revival meeting.

Herein lies the film's appeal to pathos. The film may be more about ethos than logos, more character than reason, but it is pathos, the appeal to shared values, that ultimately makes the film so effective. "Are we, as Americans, capable of doing great things even though they are difficult?" Gore asks near the conclusion of his slideshow. "Are we capable of *rising above ourselves* and above history?" The affirmative answer to these rhetorical questions is accompanied by a picture-book narrative of political history: the Declaration of Independence, the Emancipation Proclamation, the Nineteenth Amendment, Iwo Jima (a classic visual instance of the rhetoric of ascent), Brown v. Board of Education, the Apollo Program, the fall of the Berlin Wall. While Gore acknowledges that global warming is different from problems the world has confronted in the past, the nearly automatic procession of images here positions what Gore wants to see happen—a dramatic change in direction for the United States—as a *continuation* of American democracy, not as a drastic swerve from it. It is remarkably positive as a portrayal of what needs to happen: revolution, emancipation, suffrage, civil rights, the end of the Cold War, all presented bloodlessly, all presented not as consumer or corporate restraint, not as population control or emissions reductions, but as a rise.

While the visual logic of *Everything's Cool* operates on a horizontal access, the film is nevertheless an attempt to lift up its audience. The leitmotif of the film is not an upward curve on a graph, but a chasm widening from the top of the screen to the bottom, which positions the science of global warming on the left and the skeptics and energy industry lobbyists on the right. Instead of encouraging us to rise up to meet the challenge, Gold and Helfand enjoin us to help close the gap, which nevertheless implies a narrative of ascent and transcendence, overcoming a threatening divide. The filmmakers' pervasive sense of humor is one example of its upbeat nature; the similar trajectory of each of the global warming messengers, all of whom have overcome some sort of obstacle, is another. The film's Web site insists that the goal of the film is to portray to its audience the serious challenges posed by global warming, "and still leave them optimistic and willing to do something."

Neither film says anything about the accelerating growth of the human population, nor anything critical of consumerism, or the dynamics of global capitalism, or patterns of individual consumption. It would be irresponsible not to acknowledge that. Neither seriously treats the probability that stopping global warming altogether may already be too late. But how could they, how could any film? Presenting strategies for mitigating the effects of global warming is the role of politics and science. The role of ecocinema, by contrast, is to lift us up to a point where we can see the challenges facing the planet, to raise our emotions, our identification with one another, our values, so that we can do as much as possibly can be done.

NOTES

1. *Uncle Tom's Cabin* is often taken as "probably the most influential book ever written by an American" (Tompkins 122), as is Rachel Carson's *Silent Spring* the most influential environmentalist work. For a point-by-point comparison of Gore and Carson, see Stephen Bocking, "The Silent Spring of Al Gore," *Alternatives Journal* 33.1 (2007): 34–35.

2. In April 2007 the League of Conservation Voters Education Fund prepared a one-page chart, together with more detailed analysis, that would allow voters to compare candidates' positions on climate change. Similarly, the Web site of the Council on Foreign Relations maintains an "Issue Tracker," compiled from press releases and public statements. According to these sources,

as of August 2007, Democratic candidates Biden, Clinton, Dodd, Edwards, Gravel, Kucinich, Obama, and Richardson had all declared support for some kind of cap on carbon emissions. Among the Republican candidates, McCain co-sponsored a bill in favor of capping carbon emissions, while Romney and Brownback encouraged voluntary reductions in carbon emissions. Hunter, Paul, and Tancredo did not make official statements about global warming, Giuliani equivocated, and neither Huckabee nor Cox believed climate change poses a serious threat.

Since the writing of this essay, major changes have obviously taken place. As President, Barack Obama has delivered a number of speeches on the subject of global warming, most recently (November 2009) alongside China's President Hu Jintao. The U.S. House of Representatives even passed a climate-change bill in June 2009. But while discussions continue, the Senate will likely not take up the issue until the spring of 2010. See "U.S. Climate Debate" at http://www.eenews.net/special_reports/us_climate_debate/ (accessed 19 November 2009).

3. Global warming made *Newsweek*'s cover on April 16, 2007, and *Time*'s cover story, "The Last Temptation of Al Gore," appeared on May 28. Rupert Murdoch's announcement about the greening of New Corporation came on May 9 (Little). Examples of Fox News's skeptical coverage of global warming abound, with talk show hosts Bill O'Reilly and Sean Hannity leading the list. In addition, Steven Milloy—who works as an "adjunct scholar" at the Competitive Enterprise Institute—maintains a "Junk Science" column at FoxNews.com that may be taken as representative. His August 2007 column is entitled "Junk Science: New Science Challenges Climate Alarmists." In 2007 alone, Competitive Enterprise Institute spokesperson Chris Horner has appeared on Fox News at least a dozen times. Documentaries that have aired on Fox News include 2005's "The Heat Is On," a relatively balanced presentation, and 2007's "Global Warming: The Debate Continues."

4. One of the most quoted journalistic responses to the film is Warren Bass's report in the *Washington Post*, "Al Gore's Inconvenient Jeremiad" (28 May 2006): BW08. Countless other reviews use the term, which may simply reflect the reviewer's obligatory visit to the thesaurus, but often enough seems meant as a dig. For an excellent review of the merits and failures of *An Inconvenient Truth*, see Jayson Harsin, "Eco-apocalypse and the Powerpoint Film," *Bright Lights Film Journal* 53 (August 2006), http://www.brightlightsfilm.com/53/gore.htm (retrieved 13 August 2007).

5. See, for instance, *Emerging Infectious Diseases* 4.3 (July/August 1998), a special issue focusing on "Global Climate Change and Infectious Diseases." Gore's simplification may have been a necessary result of adapting the austerities of scientific journals for a popular film audience, but the enormity of the mosquitoes hardly seems necessary. Nevertheless, the World Health Organization *does* cite malaria as one of the chief factors in their estimation that climate change is indirectly responsible for 160,000 deaths annually (Henson 147).

6. While there are plenty of examples of unanimity or near-unanimity in climate science—*everyone,* for example, now accepts the data that show the earth is warming—the topic of hurricanes is not one about which scientists agree. In fact, according to Robert Henson, "tropical cyclones" constitute "one of the liveliest arenas of climate science debate" (122). *Everything's Cool* tackles this Katrina question more explicitly in an exchange between Heidi Cullen and a Weather Channel anchorwoman who wants a definitive answer to her questions "Are we entering a new era of super-hurricanes?" and "Is this related to global warming?" Cullen responds responsibly, that such questions are difficult for a scientist to answer definitively, linking any one event with global warming as a whole, but that there *does* seem to be a correlation.

7. As I wrote this, Leonardo DiCaprio's film *The 11th Hour* was being released in a few theaters across the country. The title alone sounds far more apocalyptic than either of the films I am discussing here. A handful of reviews imply this as well: Manohla Dargis, for example, writes in the *New York Times* that "the images in 'The 11th Hour' are pointedly horrifying, not reassuring, pacific or aestheticized"; and *Entertainment Weekly* claims that "in contrast, *An Inconvenient Truth* feels positively hushed" (Schwarzbaum). More recently, films such as *The Day the Earth Stood Still* (2008) and *The Age of Stupid* (2009) have failed to make much of an impact.

8. According to Donna Campbell's "Forms of Puritan Rhetoric," "The term *jeremiad* refers to a sermon or another work that accounts for the misfortunes of an era as a just penalty for great social and moral evils, but holds out hope for changes that will bring a happier future. It derives from the Old Testament prophet Jeremiah who in the seventh century BC attributed the calamities of Israel to its abandonment of the covenant with Jehovah and its return to pagan idolatry, denounced with 'lurid and gloomy eloquence' its religious and moral iniquities, and called on the people to repent and reform in order that Jehovah might restore them to his favor and renew the ancient covenant."

9. The genre flourished in New England during the middle decades of the seventeenth century. For analyses of Puritan conversion morphology, see Daniel B. Shea, *Spiritual Autobiography in Early America* (Princeton, NJ: Princeton Univ. Press, 1968), and Patricia Caldwell, *The Puritan Conversion Narrative: The Beginnings of Expression* (Cambridge: Cambridge Univ. Press, 1985).

10. Jimmie Killingsworth argues that the common translation of *pisteis*, "appeals," is not as accurate as either "modes" or "means of persuasion" (250).

11. The graph is the work of a team of scientists led by Michael Mann. The controversy stems largely from the wide variability in data before 1600, which other versions of the graph portray as a temperature range, not simply as a single line.

12. The laissez-faire economist Stephen Hayward, who works with the American Enterprise Institute, has made a skeptical film in response to *An Inconve-*

nient Truth in which he climbs a stepladder to analyze a graph, and comments that he is lowering his carbon footprint by not using an electric device.

13. Shishmaref is also profiled in the best single book about global warming to date, Elizabeth Kolbert's *Field Notes from a Catastrophe: Man, Nature, and Climate Change* (New York: Bloomsbury USA, 2006).

14. *Everything's Cool* also uses the strategy employed by journalists from *60 Minutes* to the *Daily Show*, giving the opposition enough rope to hang themselves. "It's weather," a blasé Chris Horner from the Competitive Enterprise Institute says. "When we see cooling, it's global warming. When we see warming, it's global warming. When we see drought, it's global warming. When we see rain, it's global warming." "Wealthier is healthier," he repeats. Myron Ebell, when asked what he will be doing on "the day after tomorrow," laughs at the reference to the film and says, intending it to sound ironic, "Just beating up on my enemies, that's all I do."

WORKS CITED

Aristotle. *Rhetoric*. Trans. W. Rhys Roberts. Internet Classics Archive. http:// classics.mit.edu/Aristotle/rhetoric.html.

Burke, Kenneth. "I, Eye, Ay: Concerning Emerson's Early Essay on 'Nature,' and the Machinery of Transcendence." *Language as Symbolic Action*. Berkeley and Los Angeles: Univ. of California Press, 1966. 186–200.

——. *A Rhetoric of Motives*. Berkeley and Los Angeles: Univ. of California Press, 1950.

Campbell, Donna M. "Forms of Puritan Rhetoric: The Jeremiad and the Conversion Narrative." *Literary Movements* 21 May 2007. http://www.wsu .edu/~campbelld/amlit/jeremiad.htm. Retrieved 13 August 2007.

Crusius, Timothy W. "A Case for Kenneth Burke's Dialectic and Rhetoric." *Philosophy and Rhetoric* 19 (1986): 27–28.

Dargis, Manohla. "Helpful Hints for Saving the Planet." Review of *The 11th Hour*. *New York Times* 17 August 2007. http://movies.nytimes.com/2007/08/17/ .movies/17hour.html?8mu&emc=mua1. Retrieved 17 August 2007.

The Day After Tomorrow. Dir. Roland Emmerich. Twentieth Century-Fox, 2004.

Everything's Cool. Dir. Daniel B. Gold and Judith Helfand. Toxic Comedy Pictures, 2007.

Henson, Robert. *The Rough Guide to Climate Change*. London: Rough Guides, 2006.

An Inconvenient Truth. Dir. Davis Guggenheim. Lawrence Bender Productions, 2006.

Killingsworth, M. Jimmie. "Rhetorical Appeals: A Revision." *Rhetoric Review* 24.3 (2005): 249–63.

League of Conservation Voters Education Fund. "Current Positions of Presidential Candidates on Climate Policies (April 20, 2007)." *The Heat Is On* 2008. http://www.heatison.org/index.php/content/news_item/lcvef _releases_guide_on_where_08_candidates_stand_on_global_warming/. Retrieved 13 August 2007.

Little, Amanda Griscom. "Thinking Outside the Fox." *Grist: Environmental News and Commentary* 9 May 2007. http://www.grist.org/news/maindish/2007/05/09/murdoch/index.html?source=daily. Retrieved 13 August 2007.

Quinn, Arthur. "Teaching Burke: Kenneth Burke and the Rhetoric of Ascent." *Rhetoric Society Quarterly* 25 (1995): 231–36.

Schwarzbaum, Lisa. Review of *The 11th Hour. Entertainment Weekly* 15 August 2007. http://www.ew.com/ew/article/0,,20051856,00.html. Retrieved 17 August 2007.

Tompkins, Jane. "Sentimental Power: *Uncle Tom's Cabin* and the Politics of Literary History." *Sensational Designs: The Cultural Work of American Fiction, 1790–1860.* New York: Oxford Univ. Press, 1985. 122–46.

SHIFTING PARADIGMS
FROM ENVIRONMENTALIST
FILMS TO ECOCINEMA

. . . .

PAULA WILLOQUET-MARICONDI

An idea, a relationship, can go extinct, just like an animal
or a plant.—Bill McKibben, *The End of Nature*

The proliferation of international and domestic film festivals dedicated to environmentally oriented films attests to the crucial function of the emerging genre of ecocinema to "challenge and broaden audiences' perception and understanding of the complex world that surrounds us."[1] The annual Environmental Film Festival in Washington, DC, one of the largest, showcases a wide selection of fiction, documentary, and experimental films, with themes ranging from the vital connections between healthy food, fresh water, and the environment, to the patenting of genetically modified seeds, fresh water shortages and privatization, climate change, world hunger, and the impacts of globalization on indigenous peoples and environments.

While environmental film festivals educate viewers about a range of environmental issues, they also help bridge the gap between activist filmmakers, the general public, and educators. The Eckert College Environmental Films Festival, for example, integrates film screenings with discussion sessions lead by academic scholars. The Wild and Scenic Environmental Film Festival not only makes its films available for rental to the local community but also packages the best films of the festival for nationwide tours. The tours aim to "expose people to forward-thinking ideas and global awareness" through films that not only "highlight the concerns but [also] provide solutions."[2]

As the variety of subjects and approaches featured in the films showcased in these festivals grows, so does the understanding of what constitutes an "environment." For example, the Finger Lakes Environmental Film Festival markets itself more comprehensively than other festivals, as a "multimedia interarts extravaganza" that engages in larger global conversations about diverse issues such as "labor, war, health, disease, music, intellectual property, fine art, software, remix culture, economics, archives, AIDS, women's rights and human rights."[3] This shifting and expanding conception of "environment" to include virtual and human-made environments—such as software and archives—can pose a challenge to narrowing the definition of ecocinema as a genre whose identifying characteristic is its focus on matters of environmental health and justice. Another challenge in defining this genre is the ease with which the prefix "eco" tends to get attached to words and concepts so as to "greenwash" them, casting over them an appealing aura of environmentalism and potentially making the notion of an "eco" cinema sometimes suspect. Should all films touching on issues relating to the environment be given this label? Should all "environments," including virtual ones, be given the same value and consideration as living ecosystems in regards to preservation and survival?

As Lewis Ulman has noted, virtual and material landscapes often inform and affect one another. As these two "worlds" become increasingly bound, we are compelled to define parameters for ethical and healthy relations between them. "If our virtual models of whatever sort are leading us into unhealthy relationships with our environment," writes Ulman, "then we need to change those models, not fantasize about abandoning virtuality" (355). By virtue of being *re-presentations* of the "real" world, films are a type of virtual environment that at the same time model for us ways of perceiving and engaging with material and organic environments. From this standpoint, as a specific type of environmentally oriented cinema, ecocinema can offer us alternative models for how to represent and engage with the natural world; these models have the potential to foster a healthier and more sustainable relationship to that world.

Thus, films whose overt intent is to educate and provoke personal and political action in response to environmental challenges must be distinguished from those films David Ingram calls "environmentalist." The prefix "eco" in ecocinema serves the specific function of reminding us of the Greek *oikos*, meaning "house" or "home." As the geo-ecologist and environmental ethicist Stan Rowe points out, the prefix "eco"

> has the double advantage of reminding humanity where it is domiciled, while expressing no prejudice in favour of organisms, hence no denigration of earth, water and air as less than organisms, as merely their environment. It implies equal importance among all components, while also implying that everything existing within the Ecosphere, including the human race, is a product of it, a subdivision of it, a part of it, and therefore less important than it. The Whole Home

is the prime reality; all else within is fragmentary, disarticulated, lost, and meaningless until conceived and experienced in the context of the Ecosphere.

An important distinction I wish to establish between "environmentalist" films and ecocinema is the latter's consciousness-raising and activist intentions, as well as responsibility to heighten awareness about contemporary issues and practices affecting planetary health. Ecocinema overtly strives to inspire personal and political action on the part of viewers, stimulating our thinking so as to bring about concrete changes in the choices we make, daily and in the long run, as individuals and as societies, locally and globally. The capacity to choose consciously, with an awareness of the planetary consequences of our choices, is uniquely human. Ecocinema helps us examine our choices and question whether they are expressive of "ecological wisdom" or "ecological insanity," as Joseph Meeker puts it (163). "Human behavior," says Meeker, "has generally been guided by presumed metaphysical principles which have neglected to recognize that man is a species of animal whose welfare depends upon successful integration with the plants, animals, and land that make up his environment" (163). Ecocinema can assist us in redressing this shortsightedness.

Films falling within the genre of ecocinema can work on our perceptions of nature and of environmental issues through a variety of approaches. A lyrical and contemplative style can foster an appreciation for ecosystems and all of nature's constituents—air, water, earth, and organisms. Alternatively, ecocinema can deploy an overt activist approach to inspire our care, inform, educate, and motivate us to act on the knowledge they provide. These divergent approaches are exemplified, respectively, by the two films analyzed here: the independent experimental video *Riverglass: A Ballet in Four Seasons* (1997) and the environmental justice documentary *Power: One River Two Nations* (1996).[4] An understanding of the differences in the values reflected in these films helps distinguish ecocinema from environmentalist films; this distinction, in turn, helps us explore the contrasting values reflected by an anthropocentric and an ecocentric worldview.

SHIFTING PARADIGMS:
FROM ANTHROPOCENTRISM TO ECOCENTRISM

The ecocentric values to be found in ecocinema constitute a paradigm shift, that is, a shift in the way we regard the place and function of humans on the planet and the way we value ecosystems. For many environmental thinkers, this paradigm shift moves us from a narrow anthropocentric worldview to an earth-centered, or ecocentric, view in which the ecosphere, rather than merely the human sphere, is taken as the "center of *value* for humanity" (my emphasis; see Rowe).[5] My preference for the term "ecocentric," rather than the more common "biocentric," is based on Rowe's definition of the ecosphere as the "prime reality" comprising the four spheres—the atmosphere, the hydrosphere, the lithosphere, and the biosphere. As Rowe notes, "Humanity came into being within regional ecosystems—forest, savannah, grass-land, seashore —as symbiotic parts of them, co-evolved with them, inseparable from them, along with a host of companion organisms of equal merit and importance. Living things arose within the ecosystems that the Ecosphere comprises. Thus the truth: Life is a phenomenon of the Ecosphere."

In many respects, Darwinian evolutionary theory already was an expression of such a shift in understanding the place of humans on the planet. Darwinian and post-Darwinian science initiated the decentralization of humanity, both in relation to a hypothetical evolutionary "path" and in relation to all other life forms. It deteleologized evolution and helped undermine the idea of a progressive and cumulative development by noting that evolution occurs over both periods of stability and periods of dramatic transitions.

Neo-Darwinian theories of evolution also enlarged Darwin's concept of adaptation to mean coadaptation between organisms and their environment. The nineteenth-century model of evolution as competitive was replaced with a cooperative model that emphasizes coadaptation and symbiosis. Recognizing symbiosis as an evolutionary force, notes Fritjof Capra, "has profound philosophical implications. All larger organisms, including ourselves, are living testimonies to the fact that destructive practices do not work in the long run. In the end the aggressors always destroy themselves, making way for others who know how to cooperate and get along" (243).

In addition to its scientific roots in Darwinian theory and the science of ecology, ecocentrism's intellectual roots can be traced to various modern Western as well as traditional East Asian philosophies. Lawrence Buell, for example, provides a broad overview of the influence of certain continental philosophies, holistic environmental ethics, and Eastern philosophies/religions on the ecocentric ethos, singling out the writings of Aldo Leopold (land ethic), Arne Naess (deep ecology), Martin Heidegger (ontology), Maurice Merleau-Ponty and Gaston Bachelard (phenomenology), Spinoza (ethical monism), as well as the influences of Gandhi and of Buddhism and Taoism.[6]

To speak of ecocentrism as an alternative to anthropocentrism seems paradoxical: the word itself reintroduces the spatial image of a "center," and the user of the term is, after all, human. How do humans speak on behalf of the ecosphere without being anthropocentric or anthropomorphic in this very act of speaking? This, argues Warwick Fox in *Toward a Transpersonal Ecology*, is the "anthropocentric fallacy," for even if all valuations are generated by humans, they need not be human-centered (21). The word "center" should not be taken to express a simple prioritizing.

Rather, ecocentrism denotes a shift in values that takes into consideration the well-being of the whole ecosphere, which *includes* humanity. There is no paradox, then, since humanity is part of the biotic community, one of the components of the ecosphere. But also, as Buell notes, "It is entirely possible without hypocrisy to maintain biocentric values in principle while recognizing that in practice these must be constrained by anthropocentric considerations, whether as a matter of strategy or as a matter of intractable human self-interestedness" (134). To be ecocentric, albeit in an "anthropogenic" or "anthropologic" way, makes sense and is perhaps inevitable. To be anthropocentrically biased in humanity's favor is in the long run, as Paul W. Taylor suggests, "irrational" (78).

Another way to approach the anthropocentric/ecocentric paradox, one taken by Joseph Meeker, is to acknowledge that human and nonhuman nature share certain qualities and interests, and that our survival interests are not in opposition to those of nonhuman nature, but are interconnected and interdependent with it. Rather than leading to an anthropomorphizing of nonhuman nature for the sake of promoting a narrow anthropocentric agenda, such recognition can help us put the "nature" back into the "human," and place human nature in a more harmonious relationship with the rest of nature, not at its center.

ECOCINEMA AND THE LIMITS OF ENVIRONMENTALIST FILMS

In his study of environmentalism and Hollywood, David Ingram defines environmentalist films as those in which environmental issues are central to the narrative but where the environment is merely another "topical issue" at Hollywood's disposal. Environmentalist films, argues Ingram, are "ideological agglomerations that draw on and perpetuate a range of contradictory discourses concerning the relationship between human beings and the environment" (viii).

While the degree to which these films might offer a "pro-environment," "pro-conservation," or "pro-sustainability" perspective varies greatly, their fundamental message is one that affirms rather than challenges the culture's fundamental anthropocentric ethos. As Ingram notes, "Hollywood environmentalist movies often use their concerns with non-human nature, whether wilderness or wild animals, as a basis for speculation on human relationships, thereby making those concerns conform to Hollywood's commercial interest in anthropocentric, human interest stories" (10). Given Hollywood's commercial imperative, it is not surprising that ecocinema is more likely to reflect an independent and experimental approach to production, play at film festivals, art houses, and on public television, and often be distributed through the Internet or grassroots organizations.

Since the publication of Ingram's book, a number of environmentalist fiction films have been released that could well be included in that study and that fall short of fulfilling the goals of ecocinema outlined here. For example, Steven Soderbergh's *Erin Brockovich* (2000) was hailed by the press and audiences alike as offering a model of environmental activism. The film is structured around an environmental justice issue, and its female protagonist, played by Julia Roberts and based on the real-life Brockovich, does serve as a model of activism for audiences. However, by the end of the film, the contamination of soil, water, and human life that should have remained the focus of the narrative is upstaged by the individual courage and heroism of the main character and also by the material rewards that come with such heroism: the expensive downtown high-rise office, the shiny red gas-guzzling SUV, the $2 million in the bank, and, of course, the media fame.

It is not my intention to minimize the real-life Brockovich's dedication to raising awareness about water contamination and corporate malpractice; after all, we do need examples of people taking action in the face of corporate disregard for human and environmental health. But by the end of the movie, not only are the working-class affected families, bodies, and environments forgotten by the film but so is any serious discussion of a way of life that demands ever-increasing dependence on nonrenewal and polluting sources of energy, not to mention obscene profit margins. By focusing on Chromium 6—rather than the more widespread mercury contamination of rivers and streams, for example—the film exploits our fears only to reassure us that we have nothing to fear, as long as heroic individuals like Brockovich can be counted on.

In fact, our dependence on nonrenewable sources of energy, such as chlorine chemical plants and coal-fired power plants, is a significant contributor to the contamination of streams, wetlands, reservoirs, and lakes with mercury, and to global climate change. Scientific studies continue to show widespread mercury contamination in fish, and the U.S.

Environmental Protection Agency has issued fish consumption advisories because of mercury contamination for all but seven states. There are no Hollywood films about this.

One of the appeals of Hollywood films is that, striving to reach a broad audience and maximize box office receipts, they often and easily lend themselves to multiple and even conflicting readings. This is why, for example, Pat Brereton can argue that the "utopian ecological themes" that abound in Hollywood films "help to promote an ecological meta-narrative, connecting humans with their environment" (12, 13). They also permit us to emphasize those aspects that resonate with our own concerns and sensibilities, our own ideological predispositions. The visual excesses in the representation of Erin Brockovich's body—she's beautiful, she's sexy, and she never wears the same outfit twice—are pleasing, and paradoxically serve to draw our attention to the body's vulnerability to toxic contamination. While the film links human and environmental damage, it does so by focusing our attention and investment on Brockovich's beautiful and healthy body, rather than on the "toxic bodies" of the affected community members.

Like *Erin Brockovich,* the 2004 global warming disaster movie *The Day after Tomorrow* might be approached as a "purely escapist" experience, or as a reflection of the utopian ideals that for Brereton are potentially useful to the ecological cause (23). From an ecocritical standpoint, however, the film's reliance on dramatic exaggerations, instant consequences, and dazzling special effects; its absolute apocalyptic premise and minimal attention to science; and its emphasis on the individualistic heroic actions of the male protagonist upstage any real concern and engagement with the reality of global warming. In his analysis of the film, Ingram notes that

> environmental problems such as global warming, ozone pollution, industrial pollution . . . are usually slow to develop, not amenable to fast solutions and are often caused by factors both invisible and complex. None of these facts fit easily into the commercial formulae of Hollywood or mainstream narratives like *The Day after Tomorrow,* which favour human interest stories in which individual protagonists undergo a moral transformation or they resolve their problems through heroic actions in the final act.[7]

Moreover, Hollywood films such as this one have made environmental calamities "perversely attractive" but ultimately inconsequential, adds Ingram. Presenting environmental apocalypse in such melodramatic and spectacular ways, and placing the narrative focus on the heroic actions of one individual and on survivors rather than on the victims, serves to protect spectators from the causes and implications of the drama enacted on screen, which we can enjoy unproblematically. While we wait for scenarios like those in *The Day after Tomorrow* to unfold and for heroic individuals to come forth and save the day, shall we ignore the less spectacular, by Hollywood standards, but much more real and devastating impacts of human action on the ecosphere?

As a strategy for creating audience identification, the focus on a heroic individual is certainly effective and commonly used, even by documentaries. The global warming documentaries *An Inconvenient Truth* and *Everything's Cool* offer us compelling characters whom we are invited to trust, admire, identify with, and emulate. In *An Inconvenient Truth,* Al Gore deploys the Hollywood strategy of the "heroic" individual, casting himself in the role of seer and savior. While this is an aspect of the film that was met with mixed reactions, there is no denying that, generally, humans respond positively to other humans with whom we can identify and depend on for guidance, inspiration, and encouragement. But what happens when the "messenger" is a bear, a frog, an owl, an insect, an ecosystem, or dramatically altered weather patterns? How can film bring about concern for and identification with the nonhuman without anthropomorphizing it, essentially inviting us to cross species lines in order to connect and empathize?

In his study of ecologically oriented avant-garde and experimental cinema, Scott MacDonald defines ecocinema as a type of cinema able to provide "an evocation of the experience of being immersed in the natural world," or, alternatively, as creating "the illusion of preserving 'Nature'" (108). One of the functions that MacDonald attributes to avant-garde films in general, and one that certainly is reflected in ecocinema, is that of "a retraining of perception, as a way of offering an alternative to conventional media-spectatorship" (109). By prompting us to engage differently with representation, in part by acknowledging representation as such and by not confusing the technologically mediated "evocation of experience" with direct multisensorial experience, experimental and avant-garde ecocinema can help create the conditions for alternative modes of engaging with both cinema *and* with the natural world.

There are many approaches to retraining perception, and the films I single out here do so in different ways. The experimental video *Riverglass: A Ballet in Four Seasons* invites us to adopt a different relationship vis-à-vis the natural environment, of which we are a part and on which we depend for survival, by prompting us to adopt a different relationship to film spectatorship itself. *Riverglass* helps us practice a particular form of ecocriticism; it invites us to question the implications of our traditional, culturally determined representations of natural features and elements. The environmental justice documentary *Power: One River Two Nations,* on the other hand, focuses on grassroots models of activist citizenship while also offering us alternative perspectives on human/ nature relations.

LYRICAL ECOCINEMA: RIVERGLASS: A BALLET IN FOUR SEASONS

As we become more conscious of the ways nature tends to be represented, of how we process these representations, and of what we come to expect from representations of nature, we gain more sensitivity to the ideological origins and impacts of these representations on our lived relationships to people and places. How these relationships are understood and lived in turn directly informs our positions and responses to specific issues, from global warming and environmental contamination to the control of essential communal natural resources such as water.

In an essay entitled "Toward an Environmental Justice Ecocriticism," T. V. Reed argues that our aesthetic appreciation of nature, and of representations of nature in literature, photography, film, advertising, and the like, has paradoxically worked to veil the causes and effects of environmental degradation. I would like to explore further this problematic issue of the aesthetic appreciation of nature in representation, an issue linked to the function of technology in representing nature, by discussing the potential of a film such as *Riverglass: A Ballet in Four Seasons* to stimulate a shift in consciousness and in expectations about the natural world and our relationship to it.

Andrej Zdravic's *Riverglass* is a 41-minute-long lyrical video that visually immerses viewers into the crystal-clear emerald waters of the river Soča in Slovenia. The Soča has been described as the jewel of the Slovenian rivers; the Slovenian poet Simon Gregorčič called it the "lucid daughter of the mountains, graceful in all her natural beauty" in his poem "To the Soča."[8] *Riverglass* is not an activist, polemical, or political film. It does not deal with "issues" in the traditional sense. It is not about injustices. It has no human characters—except briefly at the end when we see in an extreme long shot what appears to be a small human figure waking across a shallow part of the river. It has no dialogue. It has no story. Or rather, it has no human-based story. The "story" it tells is of a different "nature."

However, the demands that the film's length and approach make of viewers are polemical and political: they are the product of a political action because they are transformative of our perceptions and awareness of nature; they reframe our experience of ourselves as consumers of representations of nature and as members of the biotic community that includes us and the river. By challenging our habits of perception, our ways of seeing—including our relationship to real and filmic time as well as our expectations about the representation of nature—*Riverglass* opens up a space in which we might meditate on our relationship to the natural world and how that world has come to function in representation, and in reality.

MacDonald has pointed out that film viewers are conditioned to experience beautiful landscapes as "*not* something deserving of sustained attention or commitment" (113). *Riverglass* challenges this conditioning by giving us nothing else on which to focus our attention for 41 minutes but the flow of the river, from within the river, through the span of the four seasons. In these 41 minutes, either the river comes to matter or it does not; and *Riverglass* compels us to make that choice, and to acknowledge it as a choice.

At the same time, *Riverglass* does not allow us to forget that we are watching a recorded, manufactured image of the river—although it does not idealize the technology that produced the images as films generally do, overtly or covertly. A glass box that houses the camera is revealed whenever the water level of the river changes, as the seasons change, as the snow melts, as the summer storms disturb the often quiet flow of the river. We see the water sliding down the transparent walls of the box. At times, we see both the inside of the river and the river's surroundings in a split-screen effect created by the glass box and the water, not by special effects or editing, giving us an opportunity to reestablish our bearings temporally and spatially.

Riverglass transforms our conditioned relationship to time by demanding that we be patient and appreciative of something to which we rarely lend our attention. It asks us to see the river in its own terms, not in ours; to experience the river for itself, not for what resources it can provide us. It challenges our conditioned relationship to space as well by making us uncomfortably aware of the dark screening room, the chairs we sit on, the sometimes restless audience. But we are also captivated by the space represented in the film—the river, in all its clarity and calm, its energy and vitality.

Riverglass creates the conditions for an exploration of a different kind of relation to the nonhuman world, what wildlife ecologist and writer Aldo Leopold defined as a relationship founded on a land ethic that enlarges the boundaries of the community to include the land, in the broadest sense. This land ethic, says Leopold, "changes the role of *Homo sapiens* from conqueror of the land-community to plain member and citizen of it" (240).

Riverglass does this subtly and indirectly: by slowing down time; by demanding that we notice the "insignificant" details of the life of the river; by suggesting to us, through its self-reflexive elements, that there is no dichotomy between the river as "object" and the human as "subject"; by proposing that our experience of the river in the film is an expression of "being-in-nature." The making of *Riverglass* did not require that nature adapt to our needs. *Riverglass* gives us breathtaking views of nothing but details, not only skipping the sweeping landscape vistas found in most nature films but also not assigning a role or function to the landscape.

Riverglass is as close to a cinematic rendition of nature writing as I have seen. It is a metaphorical expression of the symbiotic relationship between people and nature, a relationship that need not be exploitative or invasive of nature in a damaging way, but that suggests instead the possibility of a healthy exchange and coexistence. *Riverglass* is a visual evocation of the deep ecological insight expressed by Canadian geneticist David Suzuki, following his initial encounter with First Nations people:

> When I first encountered First Nations people, I was struck by the way they referred to the earth as their "mother." They would tell me things like: we are made of the four sacred elements—earth, air, fire, and water. And as I reflected on that, I realized we framed the environmental problem the wrong way. There's no environment "out there" and we have to interact with it. We are the environment, because we are the Earth. And we're made by the four sacred elements— earth, air, fire, and water. And that's not meant in a metaphorical or poetic way of speaking. They mean that in the most scientifically profound way. And for me, that began a whole shift in the way that I looked at the issues that confront us and the way we live on this planet.[9]

Shifting the way we look at what we call the "environment," the way we see our own position in relation to the rest of the biotic community, is fundamental to bringing about a shift in the way we live. That is essentially what *Riverglass* compels us to do: readjust our perception.

Perhaps the central predicament that the study of representations enables us to address, as we address specific manifestations of social and environmental degradation and injustice, is that of perception—or misperception. We have erected a social structure, a civilization, based on a perceptual error regarding the place of humans within the biotic community. Since the visual arts deal in matters of perceptions and representations, they might help us regain a proper perspective. *River-glass* exemplifies how ecocinema can help us shift and readjust our perceptions, and therefore our actions, in directions that are more environmentally sound—that is, that are sustaining and affirming of all life. This is one of the activist functions open to ecocinema.

ACTIVIST ECOCINEMA: *POWER: ONE RIVER TWO NATIONS*

The perceptual habits and ideologies that define nature in aesthetic and utilitarian terms (nature as beautiful and nature as mere resource and raw material) are the same ones that have historically defined indigenous peoples and lands as invisible and underdeveloped. The opening images of Magnus Isacsson's 1996 documentary, *Power: One River Two Nations*, enact a critique of this ideology by giving us a bird's-eye view of the Northern Quebec territory that reminds us of how film has traditionally supported the rhetoric of "Native invisibility," casting the land and its people as remnants of a forgotten, wild, and desolate frontier, needing to be rescued from underdevelopment. This portrayal is immediately challenged by the caption asserting that "most of the world's great rivers have been dammed and destroyed by hydroelectric projects," by the choice of traditional music, and by the montage sequence juxtaposing Canadian premier Robert Bourassa's statements in support of the hydroelectric project and shots of a group of Cree on a speed boat, flying their native flag. As one critic has noted, "Native film must establish a different visual rhetoric of sovereignty. The presentation of a map of Cree and Inuit land alone will not establish it as a human habitat."[10]

Funded by the National Film Board of Canada, Telefilm, and TV Ontario, and made by nonindigenous filmmakers, this film chronicles the events that led to the Cree's defeat of Hydro-Québec's plan to establish a new hydroelectric plant on the Great Whale River; however, more important, in the process of documenting these events, the film asks us to rethink our understanding of land: not as scenic landscape or economic resource, but as *place* and as intimately linked to culture, identity, and survival.

This film is also an example of the role of activist media in the service of indigenous struggles for self-determination. The camera becomes a witness and an agent for change in the transnational political struggle that culminates in New York governor Mario Cuomo's decision, in 1992, to cancel the $17 billion contract to buy electricity from Hydro-Québec. The film specifically addresses a nonindigenous audience; to that end, it effectively uses symbolic events such as the Earth Day celebration, and known political figures such as Robert F. Kennedy Jr. and New York state assemblyman Bill Hoyt, both of whom demanded that a certifiable environmental impact statement be done on the project. One of the film's challenges is to make its Western audience sympathetic to the plight of a people who, for many in the industrialized world, simply do not exist. One New York state representative is reported to have said that before this issue came to his attention, he had never even heard of the Cree. As Assemblyman Hoyt explains in the film in a 1990 statement issued on the steps of the New York state legislature in Albany, "To many New Yorkers and Americans, it's way out there. And what's there? Tundra, muskeg, a couple of Black Spruce trees?"

To the extent that indigenous populations do exist in the minds of Western audiences, they are often perceived as either unfortunate or misguided in their resistance to the inevitability of development, usually defined in economic and technological terms. In this case, Hydro-Québec is the instrument for emancipation and progress, and the Cree are an obstacle to progress. As a representative of Québec Manufacturers' Association put it in the film, "Fifteen thousand people are holding hostage the rest of the province and its economic development." An alternative way to understand "development" would be to assess the environmental impact of technological innovations. For example, writing about the impact of the James Bay I project on the La Grande reservoir system, Winona LaDuke points out that the resulting mercury contamination from large amounts of vegetation decay is six times safe levels. "About two-thirds of the people downstream from the reservoirs have mercury contamination in their bodies—some at thirty times the acceptable level" (103).

The other challenge that *Power* faces, and perhaps the film's greatest challenge, is to evoke a different kind of understanding of human relationship to land: land as not merely territory or resource, but as a cultural, political, historical space and the sacred repository of culture, identity, and (bio)diversity. This approach to understanding our relation to the nonhuman world echoes Aldo Leopold's call for a land ethic. Whether the film succeeds in evoking this relationship has been a matter of debate. One commentator notes that the film's visual rhetoric is closer to that of mainstream environmentalist films, where "landscapes are depicted as pristine wilderness, and a few shots of the extraordinary harshness of the winter seem to echo the prejudices of the south that Northern Quebec does indeed remain the uninhabitable, untamable frontier."[11]

But this critique of the film's appeal to images of "pristine wilderness" fails to take into account other elements in the film, elements that infuse these images with a different meaning. For instance, the film consistently shows the interdependence of people and land, visually and verbally, as in a segment where a Cree woman explains through a voice-over that "the land is our connection to re-strengthening our spirit as a people. The more land is destroyed, the more our spirit is destroyed." The woman's voice is accompanied by the sounds of drums and Native chanting, and by visual elements that evoke this interconnection; the film joins her words to a montage of aerial views of the land, in all its expansiveness and diversity. At one point in the segment the woman's voice is overlaid with the sound of running water as the camera cuts to a close-up of a body of water.

This segment is bracketed by two moments that illustrate the complexity both of the situation the Cree face today and of the relations within the larger Cree community. The film thus avoids lapsing into a simplistic and romanticized portrayal of the Cree as "noble savages," showing instead the inner conflicts and disagreements over self-determination that they face as a "unified nation" struggling to survive, coexist with, and respond to the pressures of another nation striving to meet its growing energy needs.[12]

The scene immediately preceding the one referenced above shows Grand Chief Matthew Coon Come signing a controversial agreement consenting to additional flooding in the James Bay area, where Hydro-Québec had built the first project in 1975. In return, the Cree would receive $50 million in compensation. In reaching this compromise—thus preserving the land by the Great Whale River that would have been affected by the construction of James Bay II—the Grand Chief further sacrifices a river he says is "already dead" in order to safeguard the Cree Nation's mission to continue working to preserve their land. A paradox, no doubt, but one that the Cree have been faced with since England took possession of their territory in 1670. The scene that follows the segment suggesting the intimate connection between people and land shows the community in the town of Chisasibi chanting and performing dance rituals while demonstrators display signs linking genocide to ecocide, denouncing mercury contamination of water, land, and animals, and proclaiming that the "Earth does not belong to man. Man belongs to the Earth."[13]

While the film does not overtly challenge the developed world's unquestioned dependence on increasing amounts of energy, it creates a space in which we might begin to examine our Western conception of progress and the values that inform our relations to the nonhuman world. Since we can no longer deny the impact of water, soil, and air contamination, as well as of climate change, on the ability of ecosystems to sustain life, why is it such a challenge for the developed world to acknowledge that for us, too, "the land is our connection to re-strengthening our spirit as a people"?

The constructions of dams and of hydroelectric projects, such as the James Bay project, are but two examples of the overexploitation of river systems affecting communities all over the world, in developed and developing countries. In 2002 Maude Barlow and Tony Clarke published *Blue Gold: The Battle against Corporate Theft of the World's Water*, a devastating account of the looming global water shortages that would make it "the most threatening ecological, economic, and political crisis of the twenty-first century" (from the book's jacket).[14] Calling for a new water ethic, and noting the acute plight of indigenous peoples who "have been disproportionately hurt by the construction of megadams and water diversion projects" (215), Barlow and Clarke echo the ethical world-view of the Cree Nation: that their fate as a people is bound to the fate of the land, the ecosystem on which they (and we) depend materially and spiritually. "Water is also a foundation of spiritual life for Indigenous peoples—a further reason that their proprietary interest in waters on their traditional lands must be respected, say Barlow and Clarke" (215–16).[15]

Power is exemplary of the overt activist potential of ecocinema to document (and also to intervene in) communal action for the preservation of self-determination and local control over communal rights. It urges a reconsideration of what constitutes a community, of what it means to belong to the human and biotic community. This film confronts us with a clash between cultures, worldviews, and perceptions of nature. It invites us to understand culture as more than a matter of racial and ethnic differences, but as a matter of differences in values that either promote or hinder the ability of human communities and environments to secure a sustainable future.

We cannot isolate ecosystems from their relation to society and culture, and vice versa. We also cannot ignore the disproportionate impact of environmental degradation on Native people, people of color, and poor people. As Reed notes, "Any serious environmentalist must now realize that for decades the worst forms of environmental degradation have been enabled by governmental and corporate policies of dumping problems on communities of color, poor whites, and Third World" (146).

If we are to enter a sustainable environmental era, we must acknowledge the ways in which human relationships with the land are mediated by cultural norms and practices, including the practice of cinema, and are bound to power dynamics in relation to gender, race, ethnicity, and class. Films such as *Riverglass* and *Power* prompt us to respond to the values, beliefs, and patterns at work in the films as well as in the culture at large, particularly when those patterns are counter to an ecologically sound and sustainable way of being-in-the-world.

NOTES

Part of this essay was first published in "Ecocinema as Environmental Activism," *Mid-Atlantic Almanack* 16 (2007): 125–45, and is used here with permission.

1. From the Washington, DC, Environmental Film Festival, quoted in "Wild Film News" (http://www.wildfilmnews.org/calendar.php).
   "Wild Film News" provides a calendar of environmental film festivals around the world.
2. See http://www.wildandscenicfilmfestival.org/.
3. See http://www.ithaca.edu/fleff/.
4. *Power: One River Two Nations* may be acquired through Forum 5 Inc., 5505 St. Laurent Blvd., Suite 3008, Montreal, QC H2T 1S6 Canada. *Riverglass: A Ballet in Four Seasons* is available through Canyon Cinema at http://www.canyoncin ema.com/.
   Portions of this material were presented at the conference "Arts and Ecology: Toward an Eco-cinema," Bristol, UK, 28–29 September 2005.
5. For succinct and clear definitions of the terms anthropocentrism, biocentrism, and ecocentrism, see the "Glossary of Selected Terms" in Buell 134–35, 137–38. Anthropocentrism posits the interests of humans as having priority over those of nonhumans; biocentrism acknowledges that all organisms, humans included, are part of a larger web of life or biotic community "whose interests must constrain or direct or govern the human interest" (134); ecocentrism posits the interest of the ecosphere as primary over those of individual species and "points to the interlinkage of the organismal and the inanimate" (137).
6. For an overview of the convergences between Deep Ecology and other eco-centric modes of thought, see Bill Devall and George Sessions, *Deep Ecology: Living as if Nature Mattered* (Salt Lake City: Peregrine Smith Books, 1985).
7. From a talk by David Ingram at the conference "Arts and Ecology: Toward an Eco-cinema," Bristol, UK, 28–29 September 2005.
8. Quoted in http://www.vlada.si/en/about_slovenia/geography/waters_in_slovenia/rivers_the_mellifuous_eyes_of_slovenia/print.html (retrieved 20 November 2009).
9. From *It's Not Just Empty Space*, a 30-minute video directed by Tony Papa as part of the second season of *Natural Heroes*, the national television series of inde-

pendently produced films on the environment; see http://www.greentreks
.org/naturalheroes/season2/notjustemptyspace.asp.

10. I thank Michelle Stewart for bringing this film to my attention and for sharing
    her unpublished essay "*Power* and the Representation of Sovereignty," which
    I have taken the liberty to quote.

11. Ibid.

12. While archeological evidence estimates that the Cree's presence in the re-
    gion extends back 3,500 years, some historians believe they were the first
    people to occupy the northern region as far back as 8,000 or 9,000 years ago.
    Until the mid-twentieth century, they were a nomadic hunting and gathering
    culture occupying a land area of approximately 133,158 square miles. Esti-
    mated to have a population of about 5,000 from the time Europeans first
    started keeping records, today the 12,000 Cree occupy nine communities.
    The Cree have survived modern times through a series of adaptations, start-
    ing in 1670 when King Charles of England transferred the lands to his cousin
    Prince Rupert. The lands were transferred to the Government of Canada in
    1868 and to Québec in 1898. For an overview of the Cree's past and present in
    the region, see "The Crees of Yesterday and Today," http://www.gcc.ca/pdf/
    TRD000000002.pdf.

13. The relationship between the Cree and Hydro-Québec is quite different today
    than it was at the time the film was made, although internal disagreements
    continue to exist. Under the leadership of their current Grand Chief, Ted
    Moses, the Cree have entered into agreements with Hydro-Québec on two
    new hydro projects, the EM-1 and EM-1A/Rupert, as part of a larger develop-
    ment deal signed in 2002. Divisions in the community continue, as nearly
    one-third voted against the 2002 agreement with Québec, and advocacy
    groups such as Rupert Reverence continue to oppose the damming of the
    Rupert River. I would like to thank Kreg Ettenger from the Department of
    Geography and Anthropology at the University of Southern Maine for helping
    me understand the intricacies of the situation. Professor Ettenger is working
    on a project to document the Cree cultural heritage of the area that will be
    flooded.

14. Since the publication of this book, a number of books and films on water
    scarcity and privatization have been released. One of the most comprehen-
    sive examinations of the global water crisis I have seen so far is *FLOW: For the
    Love of Water*, directed by Irena Salina (http://www.flowthefilm.com/index
    .php). See also *Blue Gold: World Water Wars* (2008), directed by Sam Boso (http://
    www.bluegold-worldwaterwars.com/) and based on the book *Blue Gold* (2002)
    by Maude Barlow and Tony Clarke. For an excellent resource on water issues,
    including an up-to-date listing of water-related documentaries and books,
    see http://waterfortheages.org/.

15. These are the sentiments expressed in Articles 25 and 26 of the United Na-
    tions Declaration on the Rights of Indigenous Peoples, adopted by the Human
    Rights Council on June 29, 2006, by a vote of 30 in favor, 2 against, and 12

abstentions, with Canada voting against it. The United States is not a member of the Human Rights Council. Article 25 states: "Indigenous peoples have the right to maintain and strengthen their distinctive spiritual and material relationship with the lands, territories, waters and coastal seas and other resources which they have traditionally owned or otherwise occupied or used, and to uphold their responsibilities to future generations in this regard." Article 26 states: "Indigenous peoples have the right to own, develop, control and use the lands and territories, including the total environment of the lands, air, waters, coastal seas, sea-ice, flora and fauna and other resources which they have traditionally owned or otherwise occupied or used. This includes the right to the full recognition of their laws, traditions and customs, land-tenure systems and institutions for the development and management of resources, and the right to effective measures by States to prevent any interference with, alienation of or encroachment upon these rights." See "Resolution and Declaration," http://www2.ohchr.org/english/issues/indigenous/declaration.htm.

WORKS CITED

Barlow, Maude, and Tony Clarke. *Blue Gold: The Corporate Theft of the World's Water.* New York: New Press, 2002.

Brereton, Pat. *Hollywood Utopia: Ecology in Contemporary American Cinema.* Bristol: Intellect Books, 2005.

Buell, Lawrence. *The Future of Environmental Criticism: Environmental Crisis and Literary Imagination.* Malden, MA: Blackwell Publishing, 2005.

Capra, Fritjof. *The Web of Life: A New Scientific Understanding of Living Systems.* New York: Anchor Books, 1996.

The Day after Tomorrow. Dir. Rolan Emmerich. Twentieth Century-Fox, 2004.

Erin Brockovich. Dir. Steven Soderbergh. Universal Studios, 2000.

Fox, Warwick. *Toward a Transpersonal Ecology: Developing New Foundations for Environmentalism.* Boston: Shambhala Publications, 1990.

Ingram, David. *Green Screen: Environmentalism and Hollywood Cinema.* Exeter: Univ. of Exeter Press, 2000.

LaDuke, Winona. "A Society Based on Conquest Cannot Be Sustained: Native Peoples and the Environmental Crisis." *Toxic Struggles: The Theory and Practice of Environmental Justice.* Ed. Richard Hofrichter. Salt Lake City: Univ. of Utah Press, 2002. 98–106.

Leopold, Aldo. *A Sand County Almanac.* 1949. New York: Ballantine Books, 1970.

MacDonald, Scott. "Toward an Eco-Cinema." *Interdisciplinary Studies in Literature and Environment* 11.2 (Summer 2004): 107–32.

Meeker, Joseph W. "The Comic Mode." *The Ecocriticism Reader: Landmarks in Literary Ecology.* Ed. Cheryll Glotfelty and Harold Fromm. Athens: Univ. of Georgia Press, 1996. 155–69.

Power: One River Two Nations. Dir. Magnus Isacsson. National Film Board, Video, Cineflix, 1996.

Reed, T. V. "Toward an Environmental Justice Ecocriticism." *The Environmental Justice Reader: Politics, Poetics, and Pedagogy.* Ed. Joni Adamson, Mei Mei Evans, and Rachel Stein. Tucson: Univ. of Arizona Press, 2002. 145–62.

Riverglass: A Ballet in Four Seasons. Dir. Andrej Zdravic, Canyon Cinema, 1997.

Rowe, Stan. "What on Earth Is Environment?" Originally published in *Trumpeter* 6.4 (1989): 123–26. Revised version at http://www.ecospherics.net/pages/RoWhatEarth.html. Retrieved 14 April 2007.

Rowe, Stan, and Ted Mosquin. "A Manifesto for Earth." Originally published in *Biodiversity* 5.1 (2004): 3–9. http://www.ecospherics.net/pages/ EarthManifes to.html. Retrieved 14 April 2007.

Suzuki, David. "The Nature of Things." *Life Stories: World-Renowned Scientists Reflect on Their Lives and the Future of Life on Earth.* Ed. Heather Newbold. Berkeley and Los Angeles: Univ. of California Press, 2000. 55–73.

Taylor, W. Paul. "The Ethics of Respect for Nature." *Environmental Philosophy: From Animal Rights to Radical Ecology.* Ed. Michael E. Zimmerman, Baird Callicott, George Sessions, Karen J. Warren, and John Clark. Englewood Cliffs, NJ: Prentice Hall, 1993. 66–83.

Ulman, Lewis. "Beyond Nature/Writing: Virtual Landscapes Online, in Print, and in 'Real Life.' " *Beyond Nature Writing: Expanding the Boundaries of Ecocriticism.* Ed. Karla Armbruster and Kathleen R. Wallace. Charlottesville: Univ. of Virginia Press, 2001. 341–56.

ECOCINEMA, ECOJUSTICE, AND INDIGENOUS WORLDVIEWS
NATIVE AND FIRST NATIONS MEDIA AS CULTURAL RECOVERY

JENNIFER A. MACHIORLATTI

Human beings are storytellers. Whether oral, written, or visual, narratives assist us in navigating our place in the world, guiding us on how to act and how to evaluate what goes on in the world (Hall 75). The stories of different people, therefore, are reflections of their worldview, that is, the complex web of interrelated beliefs, values, and practices. Worldview is part of our learned cultural orientation; it informs our social organization, our relationships to nature/environment, our beliefs about humanity, as well as cosmological or philosophical questions about the nature of the universe, reality, and the Divine. Culture—including music, written and oral storytelling, and visual art—emerges from and expresses a people's worldview. This essay explores, specifically, how film and video narratives by Native and First Nations peoples reflect shared expressions of Native worldview.[1]

Many traditional oral narratives of indigenous people are a direct reflection of their worldview that all creation is interconnected, with vast cyclical fluctuations and expressions of life, relationship, transformation, and renewal.[2] In fact, as Richard Hill reminds us, "Most Indian [Native American] languages do not have words for 'art' or 'culture.' The idea that these concepts were separate from each other was unknown to the native people of this land" (6).

Moreover, according to Paula Gunn Allen (Laguna-Pueblo Sioux), "The oral tradition is more than a record of a people's culture. It is the creative source of their collective and individual selves. . . . The oral tradition is a living body. It is in continuous flux, which enables it to accommodate itself to the real circumstances of a people's lives" (Sacred Hoop 224).

Tewa Diné filmmaker Beverly Singer writes that "today's [Native American] storytellers continue the practice of an art that is traced back countless generations and safeguard that the stories are being carried into the future" (3). At the same time, Singer feels filmmaking is "the white man's craft that betrayed Native Americans and promoted our demise" (33). I contend, however, that contemporary cinematic Native storytelling assists many Native peoples in recovering their cultural practices and in unifying them across time and place.

In the last three decades, First Nations people in Canada and Native Americans in the United States have established fluency with this storytelling technology. Contemporary Aboriginal storytelling in video and film has become vital to the recuperation and regeneration of personal and communal identity, language, cultural practice, and responsibility to/with the ecosphere, defined here as "the Life-giving matrix that envelops all organisms, intimately intertwines with them in the story of evolution from the beginning of time" (Rowe and Mosquin 3). Cinematic storytelling, I suggest, is operating on a much larger scale than traditional oral narratives: it is assisting in a global process of re/membering as a generative, evolutionary process.

Many of the film and video narratives by Native and First Nations peoples, expressed through an aesthetics of interdependence, are the cinematic extension of the oral tradition in which storytelling is seen as a living, changing entity, as suggested by Gunn Allen. Native media serve as a catalyst in the process of cultural recovery, remembering ancestral lineage, and (re)connecting the people to the full spectrum of unity, what Ivone Gebara in *Longing for Running Water* calls "a mystery that is associated with all that exists" (103). Moreover, from an ecocentric perspective, storytelling emerges from "the Earth Globe . . . [,] the generative source of evolutionary creativity" (Rowe and Mosquin 4). From this perspective, some aspects of Native worldview express an ecology of wholeness where separation and disconnection cause dis-ease, and where integration and connection foster vibrant health and abundance. First Nations and Native cinematic storytelling documents and preserves local tribal stories while serving an expansive ecospheric function that privileges trans-tribal relations. As Rowe reminds us, "The ecosphere is central and it constitutes the largest 'world community' " (2).

Drawing from two films, one produced in Canada and the other in the United States in the 1990s—a rich decade for indigenous cinema—this essay coalesces around three themes: (1) the disconnection that humans experience from each other and from the Earth's animal, plant, mineral, and spirit kingdoms; (2) the cultural remembering and recovery function of film and video storytelling; and (3) the relationship of individual media texts to an ecocentric worldview of interdependence. The growing body of Native filmmaking across the Americas offers the potential to weave larger possibilities of global connection. "This history of connectedness should not be underestimated in understanding the potential of indigenous communities to take advantage of the new technologies for communication," assert Smith, Burke, and Ward (8), for "in the not too distant future, it could emerge that indigenous peoples have more in common with each other at a global level than they do with the non-indigenous peoples who share the countries they live in" (19).

This analysis begins with the work of Shelly Niro (Mohawk) and Anna Gronau, whose interpretive-fiction film *It Starts with a Whisper* (1993) illustrates the importance of communicating accurate historical information, reconnecting to ancestral land, disrupting stereotypes, and questioning popular culture representations of Native peoples. The film demonstrates the trust required to receive information from ancestors—their gifts of compassion, knowledge, and humor, whether through dreams, visions, or other appearances of, and beyond, the material world. Films that feature rites of passage and learning about ancestral lineage as methods for reconnecting indicate the challenges that Native youth experience when living in a dominant culture that does not value their history, language, or culture. In this film a young woman struggles to live in a contemporary urban society where she lacks a connection to her ancestral past, until, that is, she meets her comical ancestral aunties.

When humans gain an awareness of our disconnection from self, from each other, and from the environments that sustain us, we may begin to experience a phase of remembering and recuperation. George Burdeau's *Backbone of the World: The Blackfeet* (1997), a self-reflexive documentary about his return "home" to the ancestral lands of the Blackfeet in northern Montana, signals this reunion of the human physical body and the Earth body. Moving from his well-established public life as a filmmaker, Burdeau physically walks the lands of his people and looks inward to rediscover himself as a Native person after years of separation from his ancestral home. Woven into this internal, personal story is also his outward journey, seen as the community's struggle to protect its sacred lands, an area called Badger Two Medicine in the northern U.S. Rocky Mountains. *Backbone* explores the inward journey of facing the emotional and spiritual effects of separation (from the land, from lineage stories, from ceremony) in order to move outward, toward seeing and being in the world in an ecocentric rather than egocentric and anthropocentric way.

Carried by remembering and reconnection, Burdeau's film presents an example of collectivity, where community activism unifies knowing and being in relationship with the endangered ecosphere. Here is where collective action occurs in order to raise awareness about the disrespect and disposal of the Earth's resources. The human has matured, moving through awareness, recollection, recuperation, and healing, into a place of full commitment to collective and (re)generative efforts. As Rowe and Mosquin warn us, without an ecocentric perspective that anchors values and purposes in a greater reality than one's own species, the resolution of political, economic, and religious conflicts will be impossible. Until the narrow focus on human communities is broadened to include Earth's ecosystems—the local and regional places where in we dwell—programs for healthy sustainable ways of living will fail (4).

THE AESTHETICS OF INTERDEPENDENCE: THE FIRST KNOWLEDGE IS THAT WE ARE ALL CONNECTED

Environmental cinema has been broadly defined as cinema about the environment or environmental issues. The films discussed in this essay, however, offer an understanding of "environment" that takes into account the relationships that are constitutive parts of an environment. These films express an ecology of interdependence that best defines them as instances of ecocinema. From this perspective, humans live symbiotically within and "compliantly as members of Earth's communities" (Rowe and Mosquin 8).

Indigenous cinema is, at its roots, an activist endeavor that looks to the past in order to make visible the enduring effects of colonization, to reclaim annihilated ways of being, and to envision an affirmative future for contemporary Native peoples. Through stories that communicate interrelatedness as authentic, balanced, and just, humans experience a kind of "return" from feelings of disconnection and dis-ease, moving through awareness, recovery, and back into wholeness. "How does a community heal itself from the ravages of the past?" asks Winona LaDuke, an Anishinaabeg/Ojibwe Green Party vice presidential candidate (11). Native cinema partially answers this question by communicating to audiences a multifaceted, intergenerational, and essential process of "recovering that which is sacred," that which holds ecological integrity, justice, and a sense of interconnectedness. Perhaps this is where people, those caught in the cycle of consumerism and resource depletion, might learn "relation-based rather than consumption-based, responsibility-based rather than right[s]-based" fundamentals of cooperation and community (Rowe 1).

One of the functions of a worldview, according to Porter and Samovar, is to help "us locate our place and rank in the universe" (15). There is a significant distinction between the Western, Northern, homocentric worldviews and indigenous worldviews. According to the colonizers' worldview, the universe is ordered as a hierarchy: God, humans (men, then women and children), animals (domesticated mammals), birds, fish, and others creatures, plants, and so on down the anthropocentric "evolutionary" ladder. This human-centered, divisive worldview inevitably leads to, for example, policy decisions on environmental resource use that benefit only the lives of humans. The damming of rivers creates electricity but changes an entire geographic region; the production of plastic makes it easy to haul groceries, but plastic seeps persistent pollutants into the soil and water for generations. Native-produced films such as *Blockade: Algonquins Defend the Forest* (1990), *Kanesatake: 270 Years of Resistance* (1990), *Lighting the Seventh Fire* (1994), and *Laxwesa wa: Strength of the River* (1995) document resistance to developing traditional lands and question worldviews that consider the Earth's ecosystem as "mere provisioners, valued only when they serve our needs and wants" (Rowe and Mosquin 3). Development and natural resource policies advantage some humans at the expense of other earth organisms.

An alternative way to think about worldview is in nonhierarchical terms, where all beings share the earth *and* the universal space. The ecological awareness that informs many of the films by Native peoples defines the environment as composed of *all* of the "worlds" of mother earth, the material and immaterial: land, sky, air, sea, as well as ancestors, spirits, and dreams. For Native peoples, ecology is the cosmology of interrelatedness. This interdependent orientation includes all things within the ecosphere (planet), as well as above and outside of it (sun, moon, stars, planets, spirits, and ancestors). Within the material realm there are humans and nonhumans such as plants, minerals, and animals—what we call "nature." The material realm also includes human cultural beliefs and artifacts, such as memory, communication styles, emotions, orientations of time, and values. According to Rowe and Mosquin, "Every person embodies an intelligence, an innate wisdom of the body that, without conscious thought, suits it to participate as a symbiotic part of terrestrial ecosystems" (5).

This expansive Native worldview does not stop with the planet but extends into the nonmaterial realm. This is the world of spirit and soul, known in some traditions as the fifth dimension, dreaming world, or *nagual/nahual*. Spirit animals, ancestors, guides, and dreaming occupy this realm.[3] In indigenous worldviews, the human experience is a balanced relationship of the physical presence in this lifetime with the soul and spirit realms, coexisting with the living and nonliving, the biotic and abiotic, the organic and inorganic. These relationships, in indigenous cosmology, are contained within Great Spirit, the great mystery.

Filmic texts contain multiple layers of meaning, those intended by their makers and those recognized and recuperated by viewers. Gaining an understanding of Native worldview helps expand the potential meanings of Native film and video for Western audiences. In this essay the concept of "meaning" recognizes multiple and simultaneous facets of interdependence. From this perspective, films are interactional, organic stories where audiences locate and confer meaning(s). Not only do these stories offer possibilities for looking at the material culture of particular nations (Navaho, Cree, and so on), they also enunciate shared themes and styles across nations. The films explored here are discussed from a textual, interactional perspective, with the understanding that meaning exists somewhere between film aesthetics and audience.

WHO AM I? WHERE DO I BELONG?
LISTENING TO THE ANCESTORS

Shelly Niro, Mohawk nation, Iroquois confederacy, Turtle Clan, Six Nations reserve, is a filmmaker, photographer, painter, sculptor, and installation artist. Niro's experience producing across multiple media influences her cinematic aesthetic tendency toward fragmentation. She explores non-mainstream narrative structures that mix history with fantasy, documentary with parody, as well as traditional images and sounds from her Iroquoian culture. In addition to offering a lyrical video form that includes a number of interrelated aesthetic elements or genre conventions, Niro presents content that emerges from the collision of Native identity and pop culture memories. It Starts with a Whisper (1993) is an amalgamation of history and contemporary representation, stereotypes and reality, self and other, that can all be understood as tensions of paradox. She has produced a number of short films that deal with themes of identity and tradition in contemporary society.[4]

It Starts with a Whisper (produced with Anna Gronau) is about a seventeen-year-old Iroquoian woman, Shanna, who lives in the in-between spaces: between adolescence and adulthood, the urban environment and her native homeland, the past and the present. She is disconnected from her ancestral people, the Tutelos, a band nearly wiped out by disease who eventually assimilated with the Cayuga near the Grand River in Ontario, Canada. Not only does the thirty-minute film correct inaccuracies regarding the past, it also focuses on a main character living in contemporary Canada who struggles to locate her "sense of self" between these worlds. On some level, all humans identify with that sense of loss and estrangement; it is a symptom of the human need for community but also of our disconnection from the ecosphere.

Shanna's character teaches us about multiple disconnections, not only the isolation experienced by youth but also the separation from the Earth and from one's ancestors. It is primarily through the ancestors that Shanna is able to reconnect with her history and her place in the world. Yet the ancestors are not of this three-dimensional world, thus linking the material and nonmaterial while at the same time deconstructing the Hollywood, colonized image of the elder.

Most of our mental images of Native elders have been shaped by western popular culture like dime novels or Hollywood movies. Mainstream western narratives often portray elders with long, gray, and braided hair. They wear traditional dress, have wise eyes, and are commonly shown with a medicine item like a rattle, a feather, or a sacred pipe. From the noble and dignified representations of Sitting Bull in Buffalo Bill's Wild West Shows of the late nineteenth century, to portrayals of Chief Dan George, Hollywood Native elders are stoic and quiet. It Starts with a Whisper, however, laughs at these stereotypes by presenting elders in new ways. The film makes them "real," that is, not always stoically noble. They are at times jokesters (tricksters) and thus remind us to laugh, even through our most challenging experiences.

Niro and Gronau introduce three of the four elders through a voice-over at the start of the film. Their narration, like murmurs from Shanna's dreams, immediately centralizes the earth community: "whispering waters, raging torrents, birth of bounty. Parched and starving land, breath of air, cyclone sting, fire that warms, flames that burn." Accompanying the voice-over is a close-up panning shot of beadwork, reminding us of women's work, of remnants of culture that survive through the passage of time. The beadwork does not merely "stand in" for the aunties who are not yet visually present. The beadwork itself is the ancestors, inanimate objects carrying the life story of their creators. As Niro explains, "If you try to retrace things you become aware that there are actual people that made the beadwork, that made the songs, and that these are organic creations. . . . Inspiration comes from something other than just the fact that you can do these things. It has to come from some place and that's what those voices are implying" (Abbott 7).

After the opening credits, the voices return during a montage of young Shanna in traditional dress, having discarded her blue jeans onto the ground, walking through a natural landscape, interspersed with cutaway shots of water, sky, and natural creatures from her homeland. The voices call to Shanna and urge her along her present journey:

Little one Shanna, don't be afraid, the voices of the past are calling you. The voices of the present urge you on. The voices of the dead tell you their sorrow. The sorrow inside you and beyond you. You're so young Shanna, what are your years across the centuries? Stumbling along your path, not knowing, never sure, which path to follow, which way to go. Shanna. Your grandfather has almost forgotten this water drum. So much has been lost, how do you go forward? Who knows what else has been forgotten?

A male voice narrates the story of the land and its people in Mohawk, and a woman translates into English. Two languages reinforce the paradox of two worlds, a space frequently occupied by colonized people and where incessant duality is made known to all of us. Shanna ponders the trauma of the past, drawing on the land, her ancestors and spirit moving onward and reconciling this fragmentation.

This is where the Tutelo people once lived. Tutelos. Tobaccos. Remember. Don't be afraid, Shanna. Don't be sad. We are with you on your journey. Voices of love. Voices of anger. Sometimes too many voices. Reach out to you, where you can't see us, we appear, from the silence we speak to you. Listen to the voice, Shanna, sing your own song, play your own drum.

Niro, however, does not settle for a simple representation of those who might offer guidance. This is underscored visually through a juxtaposition with the next scene in Shanna's black-and-white urban world. Shanna's aunties, who summon her over to their car at the curb, disrupt this monochromatic urban space. Color saturates the black-and-white image as Shanna enters the car of her elders, and we realize that these guardian angels/ancestors are unlike any we have seen in Hollywood cinema. Their round bodies are garishly dressed, the car windows are trimmed with fringe, and they chatter incessant jokes and advice as they offer snacks to Shanna. She is annoyed at them, self-conscious of their outfits and relentless verbal hovering. They take her on a journey to Niagara Falls, an ancestral land now occupied by kitschy tourist attractions and a multimillion-dollar gambling industry.

Niro and Gronau subvert cinematic realism by, for example, surrounding the car with looping, rear-projected scenery. Moments later, Shanna stumbles through an expressionistic set version of the tourist haven, disoriented by glaring neon signs. This is not the "real" (city) world, nor is it the "natural" world; it suggests the in-betweenness where Shanna lives disconnected from her people *and* urban contemporary culture. As Shanna moves along the expressionistic sidewalks of Niagara, the voices return—"Apache, Algonquin, Choctaw, Flathead, Hopi, Huron . . ."—and begin to echo into a mental commotion. In frustration she says, "I don't know what to do!" The scene transitions into Shanna entering a dream/vision with elder Elijah Harper (a *real*, recognizable elder to the film's regional/tribal viewers). Time and space are suspended in this dream sequence so that we might understand how to access information across multiple realms, underscoring the perspective of coexisting worlds.

Harper, represented as a visually familiar Native elder in traditional dress (feathered headdress, beads, and so on), is juxtaposed with young Shanna in her contemporary clothing. Niro evokes the iconic Native chief, mimicking and critiquing Hollywood. He appears serious and wise, compassionate and kind. He then breaks the imagined Native persona by launching into a lesson about mass media and stereotypes. To mainstream audiences raised on Hollywood stereotypes, this is out of character and awkward; to Native viewers, it is subversive and recuperative. Harper resists his own visual colonization. When Shanna says, "I feel defeated . . . I feel at times my heart and head could blow up," Harper responds, "Shanna, whatever you do, do not blow up!" Ancestors, it turns out, are funny and practical in their encouragement. There is no mysticism about him, even in this in-between environment. Niro places ancestors in the real and the unreal simultaneously to convey the ordinariness of their teachings. Time exists along a continuum where simultaneous experiences of past and present are not spectacularized nor mystified.

Later, a parodied Sandra Dee 1950s musical number, "I'm Pretty (I'm Pretty Mad at You)," merges a teen-picture genre ballad with Busby Berkeley-esque choreography. Niro, who grew up on musicals and Broadway shows, says, "The Hollywood medium has used the Indian, so now the Indian is using the Hollywood medium" (Abbott 8). The scene is a campy "girl power" moment, fully aware of Hollywood's misrepresentations. Shanna bonds with her auntie ancestors, takes them into her heart, and chooses to make the passage into adulthood. The film ends with a celebration at the Falls. It's December 31, 1992, marking the end of the quincentennial anniversary "celebrating" the arrival of Columbus in the Americas. Perhaps Shanna's transition into a strong and confident woman indicates hope for the people beyond the five hundred years since first contact. Images of fireworks over the Falls dissolve into an animated turtle, the Iroquoian origin/center of the world, with streams of light shooting up and outward from its back while on the soundtrack a song reminds us, "For as long as this land can last forever, I can see the circle grow."

Niro and Gronau present viewers with opportunities to understand the disconnection experienced by Native peoples, especially youth, within the confines of colonization. The first and most important separation is from traditional lands, held as the place where knowledge is remembered and accessed. The film begins with a confused, lost teenager whose rite of passage comes by walking on the land, connecting to the history and stories of her people (Tutelo), and recovering this for herself in the presence of her own ancestors. As Shanna embodies ancestral memory, she is able to bring them into her being no matter where she chooses to live, or how much pop culture surrounds her.

Story content alone is not what makes Niro's work interesting. She uses a postmodern, rebellious style that invites mainstream viewers outside of our comfort zone. Artwork by postmodern artists, suggests Steven Leuthold, "is more autobiographical than tribal," reflecting "the mixing of many traditions" (37). This style is accomplished through blending film genres, using parody, musical numbers, and documentary-inspired historical sequences, while also destabilizing our expectation of realism through unrealistic visuals and expressionistic locations. The result is that dominant genre conventions are fractured; in viewing such a work we (nonindigenous audiences) feel "othered" and detached. Among Native audiences, laughter fills the theater during the "I'm Pretty" number. With other audiences, there is silence. This may indicate how films address audiences at different levels, privileging certain ways of orienting ourselves. For example, one challenge that the film poses is its inaccessibility to a non-Native audience or an audience that is not pop culture savvy. They simply "don't get it."

Niro reappropriates familiar images and narrative strategies purposefully to investigate authenticity, identity, and the contemporary Native experience. Are these reappropriations meaningful for all audiences? And more important, do they have to be? The film clearly indicates divergence in worldviews, requiring cross-cultural knowledge to salvage its levels of meaning. The frustrations experienced by nonindigenous viewers are the sites of celebration for Native viewers who see their stories in central positions.

One function of experimental narrative is to contradict linear storytelling, presenting new ways of looking for meaning. Niro offers the possibility of an indigenous aesthetic, one that weaves multiple narratives and methods of narrating just like the beadwork in the film's introduction. The subversive parody of popular culture, combined with historical accuracy, makes this film an experiment in aesthetic formalism, one that disrupts our sense of three-dimensional space and linear understanding of time. The film not only communicates elements of an interrelated, multifaceted worldview, it embodies it. It is a story that validates particular Native experiences and simultaneously invites all viewers to expand the ways we see the world(s) around us.

The film speaks with a sense of responsibility to the past (ancestral wisdom) and knowledge of survival despite the influence of popular culture stereotyping. Shanna is confident and strong at the end of the film. She finally embraces her past through the ancestors' teachings, and accepts her place in the contemporary world. Rather than being trapped in the wounds of the (ancestral) past, Shanna negotiates her in-betweenness. The early Elijah Harper scene foreshadows the film's conclusion when he tells her, "You are here to live your life!"

WALKING THE BACKBONE OF THE WORLD: ALL OUR RELATIONS

If It Starts with a Whisper invites us to reexperience our concept of time and expand our understanding of the relatedness continuum, Backbone of the World teaches us about space, land, and the deep interconnections of all Earth beings. According to Karen Warren, many indigenous peoples share common beliefs about land, such as the knowledge that land is sacred and is a shared space. As Warren suggests, "Mother Earth was enspirited or ensouled" (86). Thus, the nonhumans (animals, trees, water, mountains) are regarded as eco-agents—acknowledged, respected, and often revered. A voice-over in Backbone of the World explains the Blackfeet connection to their surroundings as "an interrelationship, an interwoven-ness about Indians' view of the world around them that is uniquely different. . . . They saw the world as alive and they saw it as part and parcel of them, not as something separate from them, they were interwoven into the fabric of the land through their language."

Jeannette Armstrong (Okanagan) reminds us that "the Okanagan word for 'Earth' uses the same root syllable as the word for our spirit-self. It is also the word for referring to all life forces as one spirit in the same way as the human spirit capacity" (324). This worldview is based on a kinship model, a familial ecosystem that includes humans and nonhumans. "How one treats nonhuman natural beings is a matter of responsibilities owed to one's family members—a matter of kinship ethics" (Warren 87). Values of community, sharing, and reciprocity thought to imbue traditional ways are resurfacing in the words of contemporary First Nation activists such as Taiaiake Alfred (Mohawk). He calls for the restoration (remembering) of "selflessness and unity of being that are at the heart of indigenous cultural life; [those] that reject individualistic and materialist definitions of freedom and happiness, and that create community by embedding individual lives in the shared identities and experiences of collective existences" (187).

Alfred indicates the trajectory through which documentary film-maker George Burdeau moves while visiting his homelands, in what becomes a personal journey of recovering his sense of place on the tribal lands of his people. As film character and filmmaker, Burdeau progresses from an awareness of his own separation from the land and his people, into the arms of the community and an outward (collective) sense of responsibility. The film clearly indicates the interdependent relationships between humans and the natural world, and offers an example of ecocentric initiative though cinema.

Before making *Backbone of the World*, Burdeau was primarily known for his PBS productions *Forest Spirits* and *Surviving Columbus*, as well as for the Turner Broadcasting System (TBS) series *The Native Americans* (episodes that he directed include *The Plains* [1996], *Storytellers of the Pacific* [1994], and *The Pueblo People* [1991]). In making these mainstream films, Burdeau served as a "translator" of Aboriginal culture for white audiences.[5] While the TBS series was a necessary step in correcting historical record, it did not offer a uniquely Native perspective and focused more on the past than on current indigenous issues. Relegating aboriginality to the past, according to Ted Palys, undermines current treaty policies, land claims settlements, and movements of self-determination (13). Burdeau's work on this film fueled a movement toward more personal filmmaking in Native cinema, which is becoming common among emerging filmmakers today.

At the beginning of *Backbone*, Burdeau shares his intention for the film: "When I took on this project I knew that I wanted to do something different. I wanted to make a film that I could really say was from the Blackfeet point of view, from an Indian point of view." *Backbone of the World* is a distinctive visual and personal essay of returning home to walk the sacred lands and reconnecting to a worldview of relatedness; it is a self-reflexive, inward journey. Burdeau finds a sense of belonging among his people, generously sharing the stories of Blackfeet worldview and thus expanding our understanding of an ecocentric perspective.

The film weaves together several stories. One is Burdeau's own journey home to the Blackfeet region in the northern Rocky Mountains, and his reflective introspection during the production of the film. "For a long time it's been really important to me to come back to the Blackfeet reservation to find out about my cultural ways." Burdeau sits in a chair, turning the camera on himself as interview subject. "I've been making films for a long time and most of that time has been spent working with other Indian tribes. . . . I always envied people who had some sort of connection to their homeland and had the ability to connect to not only the community there and their family . . . but also that cultural connection."

The film cuts to Burdeau retrieving fresh water from a hole cut into the ice on a frozen lake as he continues, "Because I really didn't know much about my own heritage . . . I didn't even know what was Blackfeet." Burdeau speaks of his own disconnection from, and eventual recuperation of, traditional tribal history.

A second narrative woven into the film is the tribal story of Scarface, whose healing journey brought spiritual traditions like the SunDance to the Blackfeet, and is alternately told in Blackfeet by Mollie Kicking Woman and in English by Curly Bear Wagner. This narrative serves in the process of cultural remembering and recovery. It is the ancestral foundation of looking back for inspiration to continue forward. As in Niro's film, here too elders play an important role. They recollect tribal traditions, teach us about their relationship with the land, and share their concern for younger generations. The film intersperses interviews with tribal elders and Blackfeet people to emphasize the importance of "telling" one's stories. Storytelling is an organic being that sustains the society. The Scarface narration enters the film near the beginning, and again three times near the end of the film, indicating that Burdeau's filmic and personal journey is similar to Scarface's journey to the Sun, where he was required to practice honesty and courage. The visual accompaniment is what establishes Burdeau's aesthetics of interdependence—relating people to their geographic place.

In his analysis of earlier Burdeau films, Leuthold claims that the "landscape is central to Burdeau's visual repertoire" (110). This is evident in Backbone when the filmmaker repeatedly draws connections between the land and humans, linking aesthetics with content. For example, at the start of the film, the narrator tells us "the Blackfeet are a people unquestionably tied to the land, all of our spiritual traditions emerge from our relationship to the land, the earth is our mother." A montage sequence of a brilliant red, orange, and purple sky, combined with a slow panning long shot of the mountains, accompanies this comment. Hand-drawn images of Scarface, by Ed Spotted Eagle, dissolve slowly into and out of this landscape. Land, humans, and ancestors are woven together. Nonhuman entities are also given life: "You have to get permission from the Sun," the elders say, narrating the Scarface legend. Shots of the mountain range that includes Chief Mountain and the Badger region, along with sweeping long shots of Sweet Grass Hills' prairie space, are repeated throughout the film. Humans—represented by drawings, by black-and-white archival photos, or through footage of daily activity in the town of Browning, Montana—are placed within the expansive ecosystem. These sequences are numerous, serving as both transitions and narrative threads throughout the film. They fluctuate seasonally as well as with shifting sunlight patterns to evoke the cyclical processes of nature. The music and sounds accompanying the images are a fusion of instrumentals, voices, and natural sounds. Floating voices evoke the wind, the prairie, and the ancestors of the lands that they accompany on screen.

In addition to the return home to Blackfeet country and the elders' recounting of Scarface, a third story emerges in *Backbone*. This reflexive story parallels Burdeau's journey and features the Native male filmmaking team that the seasoned filmmaker mentors throughout the production. Not only does Burdeau document his "return home" but he also surrounds himself with a local crew of novice filmmakers—Darren Kipp, Joe Fisher, and Jay LaPlante—who went on to produce films of their own. Self-reflexivity holds up the narrative mirror to oneself and to others. One of these narrative mirrors is Burdeau's emotional and spiritual reflections. Another is the mirror of the cinematic apparatus itself. The filmmakers turn the camera on themselves to document the production process.

This narrative strand asks us to consider the question, What are Native people doing with this modern storytelling medium? In voice-over, a crew member explains, "What we're doing with bringing ourselves into this film and showing behind the scenes things; out there in the non-Blackfeet world it's not done that way. It's a different world and Indians don't see the world in the same way as American society or other peoples in the world." An example of this appears near the start of the film, when the crew experiments with the apparatus in order to create a feeling of chaos and disconnection from the outdoors. This helps establish the key theme of disconnection; the Blackfeet people are lost without their connection to the land. Burdeau and Fisher appear on screen from a steep, low-canted angle shot: "When we get out in the woods, it's really hard to know how we act anymore. We don't know who we are in the woods, we think we did, but we really don't . . . not like our ancestors. I don't know what to do sometimes . . . you get scared of the things that go on out here in the woods and you're even more likely to get caught up in violence in town . . . and you don't know where you are half the time."

Throughout this sequence, the men are framed from a variety of angles and distances, walking past the camera in and out of the frame. The camera sweeps upward to the treetops, whirls around, and pans back down. Overlaid are their voices: "voices of our ancestors calling you, talking to you and speaking to you and you can't understand them." A slow transition, evoking interrelationship, dissolves into a ceremonial structure with prayer flags on top, saplings bound to each other like bones of the mother, dissolving again into the mountain range, and zooming out to a lake. We are reminded, visually this time, that "the Blackfeet are a people unquestionably tied to the land, all of our spiritual traditions emerge from our relationship to the land . . . the earth is our mother."

A fourth narrative of the film is the community's story about a land-rights issue facing the Blackfeet region. This strand weaves lessons that correct historical inaccuracies and communicates a clear sense of eco-justice, often imbued in Native-produced films. The narration informs audiences of the encroaching materialist/capitalist interests onto a 130,000-acre track of Blackfeet land known as Badger Two Medicine, which was "opened" by the federal government (through the U.S. Forest Service) for oil and gas exploration. This land is one of the last places where Blackfeet can pursue spirit vision quests and, according to the film, is a sacred place gifted to them by Creator. According to Ted Andrews, the badger is the "keeper of stories," linked to the "word" of the people (246). "Sometimes a person needs a story more than food to stay alive. That is why we put these stories in each other's memory. This is how people care for themselves" (Barry Lopez, quoted in Andrews 246–47). Audiences are reminded that stories about the land are at the center of Native cosmology; therefore, land preservation is crucial for cultural and physical survival.

Burdeau reveals outsiders' ignorance of Native culture in two scenes where the Blackfeet share their experiences trying to explain sacred sites to representatives of the Santa Fe Mining Company and the Department of Forestry. One asks a Blackfoot man to "point out" the sacred sites and mark them on a map; another asks where the church is. "I'm looking for your church, where's your church? You say this is your spiritual area, where's your church," the Blackfoot man says, recounting his conversation. "Well, you're standing in our pew . . . this is our church," the man replies, adding "I'm sure this has stuck with this man for a long time, nature is our church." In a montage sequence, the mountain range, a close-up shot of a leaf resting silently on the water, local animals, and a bird in flight dissolve in and out. The film warns audiences about continued ecocide should the land be used for oil and gas exploration. Burdeau explains the relevance of this regional ecological issue to all people:

> If we as a tribal community have the ability to reach back and reclaim that [medicines, language, song, prayer, and land], then we also have the opportunity to share that with the rest of the world, and hopefully that will help us understand as a world population how we can live in better harmony, and take better care of the planet we're on . . . We have to change our way of looking at the world, and that's why Badger Two Medicine has become so critically important, not just to the Blackfeet people, but to all people.

The film teaches us about the relationship of the physical body to the land body. It suggests that we can learn by spending time on the land of the ancestors and hearing the stories from those lands. The film also provides a larger global perspective on the effects of destructive resource depletion like drilling and oil extraction.

As the film progresses through the complex tensions between modernity and tradition, economic development and preservation, ecosystem diversity and resource piracy, we see moments of hope. But there is also a haunting sense that it is only a matter of time before the sacred lands are depleted through development and materialist greed. When the elders die, taking their stories with them, will the people, their culture, and their history become extinct? The efforts by Native filmmakers to recuperate and reinvigorate these stories in a new medium are even more urgently needed.

Much like Niro's film, Backbone is instructive, celebratory, and hopeful in its approach. Rather than trying to address all of the concerns of Native peoples, Burdeau's film focuses on the positive experiences of homecoming, and on the solidarity of the community in honoring the ancestors and protecting the land from development. The film also mentions contemporary social problems facing Native Americans. On camera, Joe Kipp tells Burdeau (now behind the camera) "that society [150 years ago until present] was basically destroyed. We were encouraged, forced, coerced to build a new society based on the concept of the white American family. It's not working, at least for the Indian people, it's not working. We have a dysfunctional society today." This voice-over is accompanied by a montage of shots of the town: stray dogs, rundown signs, old cars and roads make up the environs where locals spend their time. "We don't have those sacred objects or many of them left to carry on. If those sacred areas are lost then there will be complete genocide. . . . We will not exist as a Blackfeet nation." The images slowly dissolve into the comforting mountain range on which the survival of the Blackfeet rests.

Sustained oppression results in generational poverty, unemployment, and flight from the reservation. Alcoholism, drug abuse, and suicide are current crises facing Native community leaders. The recuperation of cultural ways is vital to the present efforts of recovery, healing, and self-determination.[6] The cycle of cultural extinction has been clearly documented: first the land is seized and occupied, then original languages diminish, followed by a waning of stories and cultural traditions. Ecocentric films remind audiences of the cosmological wheel of life: if the Earth is relentlessly abused, cultural traditions will be lost, regional peoples' ways of being will vanish, and, inevitably, our bodies will fail to be sustained in a physically and spiritually diminished planet.

Calling attention to environmental responsibility and documenting responses to particular environmental threats cannot be the sole focus of ecocriticism and of ecocinema. In another essay, "Children, Welcome to Your Past," I suggest that one of the greatest challenges for humans in the current (tech)knowledge regime is to relocate our relationship to, and within, the planet's complex ecosystem. As a result of Western/Northern conquest through capital acquisition and control over nature, many humans have forgotten that we rely on our relations with and within communities for survival. Overcoming our estrangement from each other and from the land is where we might learn from traditional peoples. Moreover, expanding our worldviews provides new possibilities for ecocriticism and ecocinema. The films and video works of Aboriginal peoples are visionary forms of storytelling toward this effort.

NOTES

1. Breaking out of our learned cultural beliefs, values, and behaviors requires learning and living across multiple worldviews. This essay is constructed for readers who are starting their journey of cross-cultural awareness; therefore, many concepts are generally defined. I understand the complexities of differing worldviews and the power circulating between and among such diverse ways of seeing and knowing the world. Writing in generalizations is not meant either to essentialize or to perpetuate simplicity; rather, it helps to introduce complex concepts to readers who perhaps are thinking for the first time beyond what they consider "normal" and "natural."

2. The politics of naming and being named is an important aspect of this work. For example, Native American, Indian, Aboriginal, and indigenous are terms used to describe the "original" inhabitants of particular regions. Métis is the distinction for peoples of mixed ancestry, and those living in northern/western regions of Canada and the United States are called Inuit. First Nations

is the dominant/official label in Canada, just as Aborigine/Aboriginal is in Australia and New Zealand, and Native American in the United States. Where possible, I will refer to specific nation, tribal, or lineage affiliations (e.g., Diné, Navaho, Dakota). I will refer to United States original peoples as Native Americans or Native, and to Canadian original peoples as First Nations. I will also use the terms Aboriginal and indigenous to indicate a pan-Aboriginal sentiment. The term Indian is used only when the source text employs the term.

3. See Thunder Strikes and Orsi, *Song of the Deer,* and Forest, *Dreaming.*

4. See Native Networks. Retrieved 20 November 2009. http://www.nativenetworks.si.edu/nn.html.

5. Burdeau has also produced or directed *Great Bear Rainforest* (2001), *Who Owns the Past?* (1999/2000), and *Surviving Columbus: First Encounters* (1990).

6. There are other films that directly deal with the generational effects of colonization (residential schools, substance abuse, and poverty), such as *Richard Cardinal: Cry from a Diary of a Métis Child* (Obomsawin, 1986), *Foster Child* (Cardinal, 1987), *Healing the Hurts* (Lucas, 1991), *Backroads* (Ceechoo, 2000), *Patrick's Story* (Cuthard, 2000), and the recent film debut by artist Nadia McLaren, *Muffins for Granny* (2006).

WORKS CITED

Abbott, Larry. "A Time of Visions: Larry Abbott Interviews Shelly Niro." Retrieved 21 March 2001. http://www.britesites.com/native_artist_interviews/sniro .htm.

Alfred, Taiaiake. *Peace, Power, Righteousness: An Indigenous Manifesto.* Oxford: Oxford Univ. Press, 1999.

Andrews, Ted. *Animal Speak: The Spiritual and Magical Powers of Creatures Great and Small.* St. Paul: Llewellyn, 1995.

Armstrong, Jeannette. "Keepers of the Earth." *Ecopsychology: Restoring the Earth, Healing the Mind.* Ed. Theodore Roszak, Mary E. Gomes, and Allen D. Kanner. San Francisco: Sierra Club Books, 1995. 316–324.

Backbone of the World: The Blackfeet. Prod. Pamela Roberts. Dir. George Burdeau. Rattlesnake Productions, 1997.

Drumbeat for Mother Earth: Persistent Organic Pollutants Threatening Indigenous Peoples. Prod. Joseph DiGangi, Amon Giebel, Tom Goldtooth, and Jackie Warledo. Dir. Joseph DiGangi and Amon Giebel. Greenpeace/Indigenous Environmental Network, 1999.

Forest, Ohky Simine. *Dreaming the Council Ways: True Native Teachings from the Red Lodge.* York Beach, ME: Samuel Weiser, 2000.

Gebara, Ivone. *Longing for Running Water: Ecofeminism and Liberation.* Minneapolis: Fortress Press, 1999.

Gunn Allen, Paula. *Grandmothers of the Light: A Medicine Women's Sourcebook.* Boston: Beacon Press, 1991.

——. *The Sacred Hoop: Recovering the Feminine in American Indian Traditions.* Boston: Beacon Press, 1986.

——, ed. *Spider Woman's Granddaughters: Traditional Tales and Contemporary Writing by Native American Women.* New York: Fawcett Columbine, 1998.

Hall, Bradford. *Among Cultures: The Challenge of Communication.* Belmont: Thompson/Wadsworth, 2005.

Hill, Richard. "Introduction." *Native American Expressive Culture* 9.3–4 (Fall/Winter 1994): 6–7. Ithaca, NY: Akwe:kon Press.

It Starts with a Whisper. Prod./Dir. Shelly Niro and Anna Gronau. Bay of Quinte Productions, 1993.

LaDuke, Winona. "The Growing Strength of Native Environmentalism: Like Tributaries to a River." *Sierra Magazine* (November–December 1996): 38–45.

Leuthold, Steven. *Indigenous Aesthetics: Native Art, Media, and Identity.* Austin: Univ. of Texas Press, 1998.

Machiorlatti, Jennifer. "Children, Welcome to Your Past: Native and First Nation Video as the Enunciation of Interdependence." *Ethnic Media in America: Building a System of Their Own.* Ed. Alice Tait and Guy Meiss. Dubuque: Kendall Hunt, 2005. 128–151.

Masayesva, Victor, Jr. "The Emergence of Native American Aesthetic." *Independent Film and Video Monthly* 10.17 (December 1994): 20–27.

Niro, Shelley. "Biography." *Women Make Movies.* Retrieved 10 September 2009. http://www.wmm.com.

——. "Biography." *VTAPE.* Retrieved 10 September 2009. http://www.vtape.org.

——. "Biography." *National Museum of the American Indian: Native Networks.* Retrieved 10 September 2009. http://www.nativenetworks.si.edu/eng/rose/niro_s.htm#open.

Palys, Ted S. "Histories of Convenience: Understanding Twentieth Century Aboriginal Film Images in Context." Retrieved 3 May 2006. http://www.sfu.ca/~palys/yorkppr.htm.

Porter, Richard E., and Larry Samovar. *Intercultural Communication: A Reader.* 7th ed. Belmont, CA: Wadsworth, 1994.

Rowe, J. Stan. "Ecocentrism and Traditional Ecological Knowledge." Retrieved 7 May 2007. Ecocentrism Homepage. http://www.ecospherics.net/pages/Ro993tek_1.html.

Rowe, J. Stan, and Ted Mosquin. "A Manifesto for Earth." *Biodiversity* 5.1 (2004): 3–9. Retrieved 22 April 2007. http://www.ecospherics.net/pages/EarthManifesto.pdf.

Singer, Beverly. *Wiping the War Paint Off the Lens: Native American Film and Video.* Minneapolis: Univ. of Minnesota Press, 2001.

Smith, Claire, Heather Burke, and Graeme K. Ward. "Globalisation and Indigenous Peoples: Threat or Empowerment?" *Indigenous Cultures in an Interconnected World.* Ed. Claire Smith and Graeme K. Ward. Vancouver: UBC Press, 2000. 1–24.

Thunder Strikes and Jan Orsi. *Song of the Deer: The Great SunDance Journey of the Soul.* Malibu: Jaguar Books, 1999.

Wagamese, Richard. *Keeper'n Me.* Toronto: Doubleday, 1994.

Warren, Karen J. *Ecofeminist Philosophy: A Western Perspective on What It Is and Why It Matters.* Lanham, MA: Rowman and Littlefield, 2000.

PART II
BODIES THAT MATTER
ENVIRONMENTAL JUSTICE IN FICTION AND DOCUMENTARY FILMS

TESTIMONIAL STRUCTURES
IN ENVIRONMENTAL
JUSTICE FILMS

. . . .

CORY SHAMAN

One of the most chilling scenes of Steven Soderbergh's *Erin Brockovich* (2000) involves a young mother who learns that her legal dispute with a corporate energy utility has inadvertently brought to light a correlation between her family's illnesses and environmental contamination. The title character, played by Julia Roberts, explains that the water supply contains dangerous chemicals linked to the array of health problems the family has experienced. Facing such overwhelming news, the young woman, Donna Jensen, sits silently as she comprehends her naïveté regarding corporate deception and the implications of her family's continued exposure to toxic material. The silence of her dawning recognition gives way to panic as the camera cuts to her children playing innocently in a backyard pool, then back again to Jensen who quickly turns, dashes outside, and anxiously insists they leave the no longer benign pool.

Such scenes of awakened consciousness typically constitute the political *point d'appui* for those who suffer from environmentally related disease. No star is born in this scene; rather, environmentally related sickness, a politicized but ailing subject in a polluted world, and a sympathetic mediating figure who models a variety of lay epidemiology all materialize on screen in the initial stages of environmental justice (EJ) activism. Jensen's physical turn echoes her altered ideas of environment, but her initial silence indicates the difficulties in knowing how to speak about disease, poisoned water, and corporate abuse. Likewise, the viewer is oriented to the shifting meaning of bodies and nature within intimate domestic spaces, a form of radical consciousness frequently associated with such alternative health paradigms as environmental illness (EI) and multiple chemical sensitivity (MCS). Within this rich patch of physical and ideological space, the film addresses testimonial problems by foregrounding the role of mediators to facilitate and communicate narratives of damage.

Erin Brockovich's account of politicized bodies and spaces helped bring EJ concerns to mainstream cinema with a fictionalized narrative of real socio-environmental damage. Just as important to the history of representing EJ issues, though, have been documentary films like Slawomir Grünberg's *Fenceline: A Company Town Divided* (2002), broadcast on the critically acclaimed PBS series *P.O.V.* These films function within a trajectory of increased public attention to the causes and outcomes of environmental injustice, a consequence of advocacy work in the 1980s and '90s outlined by pioneering EJ advocate Steven Bullard: "After more than a decade of intense study, targeted research, public hearings, grassroots organizing, grassroots network building, and leadership summits, environmental justice . . . is out of the closet" (xvi). Out of the closet but also in front of the camera, I argue, EJ activism has gained significant visibility through the proliferation of EJ films.

In the context of such "new social movements" focused on politicized recognition, attention to sick bodies and damaged environments figures prominently in advocacy work when individuals (like Jensen) and groups (like the one featured in *Fenceline*) are radicalized and compelled to seek legitimate standing in communities, courts, and corporate boardrooms. Both films are cautionary in their exploration of such visibility in the multiple and contradictory forces involved in developing authoritative knowledge, mobilizing EJ actors toward political action, and effectively communicating to those who hold the power to make substantive change—what I am calling testimonial structures of the EJ movement.

Phil Brown's study of popular epidemiology supplies a detailed explanation of such activist struggles in what he calls a new "public paradigm" of environmental disease, one that I argue can be mapped onto the politicized structures of recognition highlighted by these films. Brown identifies these key stages: the initial formation of EJ consciousness arises out of an "illness experience"; those who are ill make the cognitive link between human and environmental degradation through "social discovery"; building consensus in communities takes place as groups understand their shared concerns about healthy people and environments in "collective" and "politicized" "illness experience[s]"; and citizens join forces with institutional professionals to develop hybrid forms of knowledge while mediating agents aim for change through "popular epidemiology, citizen-science alliance, community-based participatory research" (25). Brown suggests that these collective actions are a direct challenge to the "dominant epidemiological paradigm (DEP)," an instrument of mainstream knowledge that does not adequately comprehend socio-environmental damage (17).

In a similar critique, Michelle Murphy and collaborating EJ theorists Steve Kroll-Smith and H. Hugh Floyd have elaborated an analysis of this new public paradigm's articulation through specific spaces—built and natural—and across bodies where visibility is necessary to create opportunities for justice (Kroll-Smith and Floyd 11). *Erin Brockovich* and *Fenceline* model this effort to "reframe" bodies and places by representing how frequently unrecognized dimensions of threatened bodies and environments become intelligible in activist formation and advocacy contexts. More important, these films investigate how citizens and mediators negotiate this process when internal division, community disagreement, and the increasing invisibility of persistent human and environmental degradation threaten to undermine EJ campaigns.

In answering Giovanna Di Chiro's foundational question about strategic EJ activism, "How do people mobilize through action in order to sustain or transform certain relationships with 'nature' and their environment?" (299–300), these films show that recognizing, valuing, and foregrounding embodied knowledge and the materiality of place is a critical and contested dimension of successful movements. Specifically, the Hollywood production *Erin Brockovich* focuses on the conflicts of embodiment in creating effective mediation and mobilizing citizens to action, while the documentary *Fenceline* uncovers the complicated demands inherent in forming consensus and representing environmental damage in advocacy situations. These films' insistent attention to testimony through social transactions explicitly involving bodies, place, and awareness suggests a constructive framework for understanding cinematic representations of EJ activist efforts to remedy human illness and damaged environments.

Erin Brockovich is famously based on the experiences of a real working mother who took a leading role in the fight against Pacific Gas and Electric (PG&E) in Hinkley, California. By agreeing to an arbitration settlement, PG&E accepted responsibility for polluting the community's water supply with hexavalent chromium (an anti-rusting agent), and they paid a record $333 million to compensate for the host of human illnesses associated with this contamination. The film examines the role of laypeople in bringing attention to criminal environmental activity, specifically Brockovich's mediating position and, to a lesser extent, the citizens she encourages. Yet the film wrestles with questions of environmentally endangered bodies and places by privileging negotiations that highlight the visually appealing and healthy body of Brockovich, a tactic that threatens to obscure real EJ concerns.

Most contemporary reviews of *Erin Brockovich* pointed to the obvious importance of Roberts's sexual appeal in gathering otherwise inaccessible information necessary for the prosecution of the case. In a well-known exposé of the film's historical inaccuracies, Salon.com writer Kathleen Sharp explains that "the foul-mouthed, full-cleavaged Brockovich travels to the town on her own initiative, investigates the case with the help of dogged smarts and a few low-cut dresses and persuades her employer to take on the case." Most famously, Brockovich describes her manipulation of an immature clerk at the rural Hinkley Water Board by explaining to her boss, Ed Masry (Albert Finney), the reason for her investigative success: "They're called boobs, Ed." This brief scene with a nervous teenager clarifies the importance of her embodiment; sex sells movies, but its effectiveness in selling environmental causes displaces attention from damaged people and degraded environments.

Brockovich's own health issues tend to obscure audience awareness of disease and its treatment, and her rapidly healing body presents a model of well-being generally unavailable to citizens of Hinkley. Before the environmental case even arises in the film, Brockovich takes legal action stemming from a physical injury in a car accident. Though she wears a neck brace in court and in several ensuing scenes, she is highly mobile and pain-free for the rest of the film. Her later hospitalization for aggravated exhaustion is merely a minor setback; she experiences a remarkable recovery and perseveres despite lingering effects of her exhaustion. This blueprint for quickly resolved health issues masks the more intractable and pervasive chromium poisoning that is the basis for EJ action.

Brockovich's sexuality and physical wholeness is problematic as her mediating role between the legal arena and the blue collar setting of the town threatens to derail the case. Inasmuch as Sharp's assessment is correct about the advantage Brockovich gains through her body, those accomplishments typically occur outside the context of professional legal work. A large part of the film presents Brockovich in the unfamiliar territory of lawyers, judges, and legal negotiation where her brash attitude and all-too-fleshy appearance are amusing and titillating to those experts, but just barely tolerated. Kurt Potter, an experienced environmental lawyer who is brought into the case after Brockovich has done a great deal of "leg" work, suggests to Masry that her status as sexual "secret weapon" is most valued in developing the case.

Plainly cast by these men as a "bombshell," Brockovich is excluded from their negotiations—and thus the fate of the plaintiffs—behind the glass walls of a conference room. The mise-en-scène makes Brockovich's limitation acutely evident, since this proverbial glass ceiling, turned on its axis and made literal, physically blocks Brockovich from their discussion while allowing the two men to view her openly. As a consequence, Brockovich's representative power as mediator is greatly reduced, and the knowledge she has gained through intimate contact with citizens is increasingly lost to the legal process.

Potter's misperception of Brockovich's body, a suggestion that secret (sexual) weapons only produce suspect or incomplete information, extends to a dismissive approach toward the bodies of claimants as well. In attempting to create a corporeal *cordon sanitaire* around the case, Potter appoints a surrogate for Brockovich, Teresa Dallavale, to gather citizen's affidavits. Dallavale, whose muted attire and manner overdetermine a desire for unsexed, incorporeal legal work, attempts to collect "appropriate," disembodied testimony from members of the Hinkley community. When Dallavale asks for objective facts free of personal details, one family physically withdraws into the shadows and subsequently threatens to pull out of the case. The play of light and dark in this meeting forecasts the subsequent rift between legal representatives and claimants.

Though bodily excess threatens to push Brockovich and the litigants out of the case, she is able to salvage a minor mediating role because of her extensive familiarity with the case histories, a familiarity expressed through the intimate corporeal knowledge that Dallavale refuses. In another meeting, a bristling Brockovich proves that her apparent faulty research is actually grounded in the specific materiality of more than six hundred litigants, including Annabelle Daniels, whose illness and family circumstances she describes in detail from memory, not from a case file: "She had a tumor on her brain stem detected last November, an operation on Thanksgiving, shrunk it with radiation after that. Her parents are Ted and Rita. Ted's got Crohn's disease. Rita has chronic headaches and nausea and underwent a hysterectomy last fall." Brockovich's knowledge of diseased bodies mitigates the dangers of her own body, but this compensation is severely limited, since her success relegates her to a small office away from Hinkley. Moreover, such exclusion based on her overdetermined sexuality is disabling, since Annabelle, Ted, and Rita appear only descriptively as the camera insists that the viewer encounter Brockovich's righteous indignation at the moment when we might otherwise see the crippling effects the chromium has had on the Daniels family.

Although attention to human disease and the damaging effects of toxins on the body generally requires the physical presence of those who are most affected, this drama of injustice shies away from displaying the illnesses of Hinkley's residents in favor of investigating the formation of Brockovich's mediating role. The film explicitly addresses Brockovich's bodily damage and the sexual discrimination she fights. Such misogynistic attention and exclusion is not a surprise, though, and the film's privileging of gender as the narrative endpoint of injustice regrettably tends to foreclose awareness of the more inclusive and wide-ranging crime, environmental injustice.

While it is important to consider what is lost with Brockovich's liabilities as mediator, real opportunities for EJ awareness become available as she contends with these limitations. That is, Soderbergh frames Brockovich's efforts to facilitate testimony through her repeated attempts to control the representational terms of her own body. This political struggle activates a familiar narrative of disenfranchisement for the viewer through which citizen efforts to manage the EJ meaning of diseased bodies and environments are clarified. Hinckley residents similarly encounter debilitating forces and must renegotiate the possibilities for healthy bodies and spaces. In forging common cause, what would otherwise constitute divisiveness in an EJ setting "becomes less important in shaping thought and experience, increasingly displaced by the production of knowledge among confederates" (Kroll-Smith and Floyd 10). Toward this end, Brockovich's usually damaging sexual availability gets recoded when her reproductive health galvanizes Donna Jensen's resolve to fight PG&E, and her all too visible health and reproductive ability help to recruit a resistant community member to the cause against PG&E.

Jensen's resolve to seek justice for the environmental illness she suffers is not yet completely forged in the scene described at the beginning of this essay, but she has begun to understand how the vectors of corporate power, toxic pollution, and the mediating figure of Brockovich combine to produce her understanding of health and illness, the environment, and the possibilities for reinhabiting a contaminated body. The viewer, progressively conscious of these determining factors and aware of how body and place play a role in constituting that dense material and ideological position, begins to see the complex set of social and environmental forces that determine her health and the social, medical, environmental, and legal choices available to her. Just as Brockovich's body is a site for many competing forces, Jensen is "multiply materialized," a category of subject formation Michelle Murphy uses to designate "the assumption that there is no singular, unacculturated body to unearth" (92).

Murphy associates this politicized body with the coordinates of "self, body, and illness," where the subject is produced "by acts of abjection, but also by a tide of contingencies, a sea of gestures, a stream of interruptions that pull on these lines to create other knots for inhabiting the world" (92, 97). Murphy's work with MCS examines ways of becoming that are important to understanding how a series of such activations take shape in the development of new, environmentally oriented social movements seeking to reverse the unintelligibility of abject positions. This dense materialization provides a new way of understanding damaged environments, human disease, and political advocacy. Through this structure we can envision the forces that frustrate the full materialization of environmental justice, a way of seeing facilitated by the film— in short, a critique of the "dominant epidemiological paradigm."

Brockovich's effort to recruit citizens requires an insistence on her own bodily availability and a more sensitive awareness of the dangers of embodiment for others. Her already complicated position increases in complexity as she mediates expert and lay forms of environmental experience and knowledge; representing multiply materialized bodies through her own heavily coded healthy and reproductive body, she clarifies viewers' understanding of the shifting corporeal indicators that produce the bodies of environmental injustice victims. From this perspective we see her body in the context of miscarriages, breast cancer, and hysterectomies, but also accusations of child abuse—circumstances that form the physical history and environmental trauma of women who live at the site of contamination. When citizens cannot or will not see the full significance of their bodies, Brockovich steps in to foster and authorize that recognition.

Donna Jensen's initiation into EJ awareness seems improbable without the guiding hand of Brockovich. The film shows how explicit knowledge of illnesses, a physically oriented consciousness, does not necessarily lead to an awareness of the causal links between environmental pollution and human disease. Brockovich catalyzes Jensen's transformative recognition when she attaches technical information about toxic chemicals to the family's illnesses. Her mediation bridges the scientific and lay perspective through what EJ theorist Sylvia Noble Tesh describes as the "citizen-expert" position, a role that connects subjective and scientific or "expert" knowledge (105). Jensen comes to recognize her body's vulnerabilities to environmental dangers (as opposed to some sort of flaw in herself) through the mediation of Brockovich; but the film suggests that it is only through Brockovich's physical wholeness and reproductive integrity that Jensen is able to muster the will to fight. When Jensen receives a grim diagnosis regarding tumors that had usually tested benign, she asks Brockovich, "You think if you got no uterus and no breasts, you're still technically a woman?" Turning to Brockovich as friend and defender, she pleads, "We're going to get them, Erin, aren't we?"

Jensen's determination to act depends on Brockovich's "wholeness" when her own body fails, demonstrating the corporeal basis of her testimony. In this context the film argues that Brockovich's openness is not an invitation for sex, but a call to the citizens of Hinkley to be open about their own intimate bodily knowledge. The beauty-queen-turned-advocate recuperates her pledge to "the creation of a peaceful earth for every man, woman, and child." To be fair, the overdetermined physical presence of Roberts overshadows Jensen's trauma—one that we quite reasonably do not see on screen—yet such trauma etches an indelible trace on our view of environmental injustice.

The film also takes up instances where such openness does not yield citizen trust so easily. The plight of the plaintiffs and the plot of the film turn on convincing an influential (read gossipy) member of the community, Pamela Duncan, to join the ranks of those suing PG&E. When Brockovich attempts to recruit Duncan to the community's cause, she is met at the front door with sneering accusations of meddling and legal profiteering. The physical space of such encounters undermines Duncan's complete defiance of this advocacy work, however. Soderbergh's reverse shots through a screen door deliberately underscore the division between the two women across the literal threshold of the home. This classic symbolic barrier between characters is visually complicated, though, because the main door at Pamela's back further entraps her in a terrible limbo, neither in nor out of her own home. While the closed door may be seen as a defensive measure against Brockovich's intrusiveness, it suggests that Duncan is protected yet not a legitimate part of the space that would normally create safety and comfort. Indeed, this image suggests the larger thematics of the film in demonstrating the vulnerabilities and forms of alienation that accompany the most cherished and protected domestic spaces. The scene expresses a real desire to inhabit an uninhabitable space/body, a need to negotiate the impossible "elsewhere within here," a description of a condition Murphy borrows from Trinh Minh-Ha to characterize EJ subjectivity (96).

The full meaning of this ambiguous space is deferred until Brockovich finally reaches Duncan by presenting her own fully articulated motherhood. Near the end of the film, the camera adopts Duncan's perspective when the door opens to reveal Brockovich surrounded by her three children, a performance of motherhood that allows her immediate entry. Once they reach the backyard, Duncan gives her a pointed lesson in the vulnerabilities of damaged bodies in the domestic settings of poor people. Their conversation occurs across a clothesline demarcating a still-lingering division between the two, but the line is far thinner as the two put their most sincere cases forward. Before Duncan tells her story, Brockovich preaches the virtues of speaking out against PG&E's abuses, suggesting that "it doesn't matter" if she will "win, lose, or draw" as long as she speaks out in defense of her children.

But Duncan explains exactly how much she really has to lose in bearing the bodies of her children in public places: "I'd bring the kids into the hospital with towels soaked from their nosebleeds. They called county services because they assumed the kids were being abused." The nosebleeds were actually the result of chromium in the water, and the misinterpretation of her children's illness shows Duncan's wariness in exposing herself to such social risks. Duncan enacts a process of "'reframing' problems" suggested by environmental health scholar Jason Corburn through which "holders of local knowledge can 'create value' by identifying additional considerations and options for action unseen by others" (69). The film withholds any graphic presentation of the bloody towels or the emergency room scene and so suspends the potential for a fully transformative effect on both Brockovich and the audience. Yet the scene does address the toxic nature of public discourse that discriminates along class lines, and Duncan's testimony reveals the necessity of "reframing" the problem of bodies in this case.

Duncan demonstrates how easily the bodies of her children—connoting various forms of abuse by the toxic environment or domestically at the hands of a parent—and thus her own testimony can be turned and read against her. This exchange between Brockovich and Duncan stages the striking question "Why not speak up?" in instances where there is apparently clear and obvious injustice. More precisely, the film asks what happens when the women who inhabit toxic domestic spaces do not see or will not admit to the correlation between illnesses and chemical contamination through their own lack of awareness, because of corporate deception, or because to do so would be too compromising. *Erin Brockovich* offers a fundamental challenge to the charge that such recognition comes easily through embodied and emplaced knowledge. The scene shows how difficult problem-solving processes can be with even the best form of citizen-expert mediation, but Duncan's ability to connect to Brockovich as a mother secures community solidarity, a bodily whole.

Again, while the film suggests that legal success and activism depend on recognizing how embodiment can be simultaneously an asset and a liability for citizens and mediators, the sustained focus on Brockovich frequently works against the very critique offered to viewers, since it tends to obscure the bodies that matter most. Although the film does explicitly chasten Brockovich's mediator status, these critical insights must be measured against the losses incurred by focusing on her body. However, attention to the multiple materialization of bodies, including the crucial formative role of mediation, begins to mitigate claims that her dominating presence only supersedes the experiences of Hinkley citizens, those who have suffered injustice. The body—and the female body, especially—constitutes the conflicted origin of activism in the film for both mediators and citizen-experts.

The importance of making both human and environmental damage visible to those who hold decision-making power is similarly a primary focus of Slawomir Grünberg's *Fenceline: A Company Town Divided*. The film investigates how place functions in testimonial constructions, particularly when community members disagree over the environmental and health implications of industrial activity. In such instances of testimonial contestation, place appears to broker environmental justice disputes, yet such success again depends on reconstituting the terms of visibility—in this case, continuing to bring damaged environments into view in important decision-making contexts. Set in the "Cancer Alley" town of Norco, Louisiana, the film examines claims against Shell Oil for its airborne release of such known carcinogens as methyl ethyl ketone and benzene, which are involved in the manufacture of petroleum products. Described as a "flash point" of the EJ movement by activist Denny Larson, the Diamond case became a significant national test case in the fight against corporate abuses of people and the environment. This leading effort drew support from major environmental groups such as Greenpeace and the Sierra Club, becoming the focal point for Grünberg's film (Lerner 153).

The residents of the Diamond community, an exclusively African American neighborhood within Norco, have long demanded a just and fair relocation away from the refinery owned by Shell. The name of the town and the neighborhood bear the roots of the conflict between citizens depicted in the film; Norco, literally a company town, is derived from the New Orleans Refining Company while the name Diamond is a holdover from the plantation that existed there until the 1920s.

The specter of historical injustice suggested by the slave past explains the persistence of racial divisions in the town, but more importantly it shows the interpretive differences regarding industrial emissions and natural environments. For residents of Diamond, the airborne emissions constitute toxic exposure, simply one of many destructive legacies for African Americans that include the usual litany of high illiteracy rates, high unemployment, and low income, all factors that compound their health vulnerabilities. Alternatively, the film explains how Shell has created jobs and security for the white community—including extensive medical protections—and a very real sense of family, as one woman succinctly explains: "Shell takes care of you." These radically differing versions of "home" illustrate the key role of place in EJ struggles; inhabitants are enmeshed in historical land use patterns that determine prevailing attitudes about environments and place-based decisions. The film represents EJ advocacy efforts to validate testimony through environmental materiality as a way to oppose conflicting claims about the meaning of poisoned landscapes.

As the town is sharply divided along class and color lines, Grünberg self-consciously alternates equally between the two communities for the first three quarters of this hour-long documentary to see how environmental conditions mirror those socioeconomic divisions on the ground. The leading EJ activist in the film, Margie Richard, is contrasted with a retired Shell worker from the white community, Sal Digirolamo, who opposes the environmental litigation. Like *Erin Brockovich,* this film confirms that embodied, experiential knowledge is formed and solidified in intimate, local, and domestic settings, as the camera introduces us into the living rooms and front yards of a number of Norco residents. Grünberg also interposes shots of Shell's incineration flare throughout the film to show how the entire town exists in the shadow of this significant touchstone of corporate presence. The documentary reveals how citizens come to know and speak about the ever-present physical manifestation of the chemically intensified environment, how they claim meaning under the potent sign of the industrial flare.

One of the most telling juxtapositions between narratives of place comes with the guided tours led by Richard and Digirolamo. Richard drives slowly through her neighborhood describing numerous deaths and illnesses; while the homes of the sick and dead glide slowly across the screen, her narration is punctuated by constant references to asthma and cancer. The camera frequently cuts to industrial facilities across the street from these homes, demonstrating the "fenceline" proximity of Diamond residents to the source of pollution. When Richard's own home comes into view, she lists a sister who died from sarcoidosis, a grandson who almost died of asthma, and her mother who is dependent on oxygen. More hospital ward or morgue than neighborhood, the picture of community that emerges in Richard's story is a toxic site where family and friends experience unusually high rates of industry-related illnesses.

Digirolamo gives his own tour on foot, walking the viewer to the homes of older citizens whose advanced ages suggest longevity and apparent well-being. He points to homes and people driving by in cars, explaining, "That person's 80 and her husband died at 82. This man's about 83, 84. I'm sure we've had a few of them die of cancer. I'm not aware of any recently. I wouldn't know how many." Digirolamo's emphasis on community health excludes the more formal accounting that Richard clearly has undertaken, and his concluding remark, "We don't die too often in Norco," suggests a utopian community space eerily free of any signs of human illness, much less industrial contamination. The more affluent suburban neighborhood is the setting for an interpretation of environmental and human health that is reflected in the tidy appearance of physical space. Clearly, the very different physical perimeters drawn by Richard and Digirolamo define the understanding each uses to develop narratives of the community's socio-environmental health.

Yet the sincerity and authority of both Richard and Digirolamo are perfectly evident as both speak from direct knowledge of their surroundings and their own experiences. In fact, Digirolamo explains his deep admiration for Richard while articulating one of the defining problems addressed in the film, a statement that characterizes a central tension in many EJ struggles: "I stand for what I think is right, she stands for what she thinks is right." The apparent impasse demonstrated here defines the limits to bodily, experiential knowledge—I take the use of "stand" to be a literal expression of embodied belief—attached to place in advocacy testimony, and it highlights their diametrically opposed interpretations of the industrial emissions. As Jason Corburn suggests, these disagreements "over such things as which stories and evidence count, how they should be appropriated, and who in the community ought to narrate history and make authoritative claims" are not uncommon (63). Such a deadlock is precisely the strategy of industry to pit competing claims against each other in order to produce reasonable doubt regarding industry-related illness and environmental degradation.

In the context of developing citizen knowledge before it reaches professional settings, bodies have long mattered in EJ advocacy efforts.

They are, most obviously, the site of physical debilitation or disease, and as Barbara L. Allen explains, bodies are the source of a very specific kind of understanding: "Local knowledge deriving from experience differs fundamentally from cosmopolitan or universal conceptions of knowledge and science. Local experience is embodied rather than disembodied" (19). The movement's emphasis on knowledge grounded in embodiment and experience is meant to grant the legitimacy of claims made by ordinary citizens as empowering corroboration of scientific, corporate, or other "authoritative" and "reputable" forms of knowledge. But when such knowledge competes with equally authoritative forms of embodied knowledge, the burden of proof shifts dramatically toward the ability to further augment or corroborate the body's experience. EJ theorists traditionally identify this competition as a "struggle over who will control the privilege to officially define the boundaries between safe and dangerous environments" (Kroll-Smith and Floyd 195). In Grünberg's film, Richard requires authoritative corroborating evidence of environmental damage when neighboring citizens deny the caustic effects of industrial emissions. The remainder of the documentary explores her attempt to do so by making the intersection between bodies and place newly visible.

It follows, then, that in order to complete the logic of environmental justice advocacy, local experience must yield material evidence of environmental damage that correlates with human illness. In arguing that women historically have been at the center of the EJ movement, Robert R. M. Verchick suggests that a "local context" specifically "allows them to better identify such [environmental] harms when they appear" because "residents of polluted communities, who every day tend the gardens, do the laundry, and care for their children, are much more likely to notice the first clues of environmental threat" (67). *Fenceline* dramatizes the EJ idea that an awareness of human illness, the self's knowledge of body, is incomplete unless it is measured against toxic environments that can demonstrate comparable damage and common points of origin.

As *Erin Brockovich* so forcefully demonstrates, mediating figures are important in developing the kind of critical knowledge that underwrites effective testimony; in *Fenceline,* such work comes through an environmental advocacy group based in California. The Refinery Reform Campaign (RRC) trains the citizens of the Diamond community to collect air samples in order to document contamination, forming what is known as the Bucket Brigade. This brigade is not immune to contradictory efforts, though, as the unusual images used by RRC trainers reveal how the slippery vocabulary of embodiment connected to air quality analysis risks obscuring socio-environmental damage.

RRC representative Denny Larson describes the air collection tool in terms of lungs breathing in, and he goes on to identify the chemical signature of the air as "a criminal fingerprint." This metaphoric language clearly is meant to give citizens a foothold on unfamiliar scientific practices, acknowledge the credibility of citizens' bodily knowledge, and recognize the seriousness of violated environments. Yet Larson's terms also function within a discourse of advocacy to grant ultimate legitimating authority to simulated lungs instead of those human lungs that suffer from breathing toxic air; likewise, such terms foreground the human mark (fingerprints) over and above environmental damage. Mediating figures in this case, not unlike Erin Brockovich, threaten to eliminate the very basis of EJ concern through such seemingly innocuous talking points. Branding environmental outlaws is dangerous work.

Nevertheless, Larson's attempt to connect existing local embodied knowledge with knowledge generated outside the community marks an important turn in mediating efforts; his involvement shows the significance of transporting place beyond the confines of its locality in order to gain technical corroborating authority. The idea that exporting place is required, that the air samples are sent away to be tested, forecasts the need for explicit intersections between places in producing credible EJ testimony. The film explores how citizens struggle to give presence to the insubstantial toxins in the air to prove claims about human and environmental degradation.

Armed with the corroborating evidence that validates their claims of environmental pollution and chemically related illness, the community members appear to have succeeded in making a case that supersedes the contestation by Digirolamo and others. Yet, in a series of testimonial venues, Richard is generally met with inaction and a deferral of responsibility. Sherry Arnstein identifies these as the pitfalls of the "ladder of citizen participation" where local activists are able to participate, but their views are only accounted for in dismissive and perfunctory ways (quoted in Corburn 42). Unable to make headway with Shell representatives at the site of the oil refinery, Richard travels to Washington, DC, with Wilma Subra, a scientist who has been documenting the community's air quality. At an EPA hearing, bureaucratic malaise merely absorbs such compelling information without making active and immediate change. In an attempt to provide vital information, Subra presents data collected that day following Richard's prepared statement. The inactive response demonstrates minimal government will to leverage corporate responsibility. But these scenes also suggest that while Richard's physical presence is important, the abstraction of place in statistical figures—even ones that are clearly emerging daily, as the proceedings show—may be a significant reason why her testimony is ineffective.

To gain standing in this case against Shell requires presenting the socio-environmental damage in its fullest materiality outside the Norco community. Ultimately forced to approach the polluters themselves with concrete evidence of damage to nature and people, Richard travels to a UN conference on climate change attended by Shell executives. In order to articulate the intersection of bodies and environment more materially, Richard brings a bag of polluted air to the conference. She explains to a friend that she wants to "put it in the hands" of those responsible for destroying her "good town." Richard's desire to hand over the responsibility of toxic criminality entails literally relocating the damaged environment to the spaces occupied by Shell's power brokers.

Grünberg goes to considerable lengths to follow Richard, traveling over great distances carrying the contaminated air, with several scenes devoted to a view of this radical transfer of body and place. Richard's easy movement through airport security with the unusual air-capturing contraption is surely an uncanny experience for post-9/11 viewers hypersensitive to biological agents and air travel in the age of terrorism. This unruly advocate makes her way through the tightly guarded spaces of airlines, international travel, and the X-ray security checkpoint at the conference. The film explicitly develops an alienating effect necessary to reframing physical space as Richard checks her bags and the bucket of air before she hurtles through the earth's atmosphere in the pressurized and conditioned air of the jet. The portability of such highly toxic environments through sanitized and apparently safe environments testifies to a common insensibility to the coexistence of poisoned environments and otherwise seemingly safe environments. The X-ray's inability to spot danger confirms the limitations of institutional authority in bringing environmental hazards into clear view, a view that is reoriented by the documentary.

After arriving at the conference, Richard is barely given the chance to speak at the end of a session where Shell is represented. Suffering the kind of parochial dismissiveness so common in these situations, she perseveres to speak by bearing the knowledge of a citizen-expert and, just as important, the material evidence of toxicity captured in the bucket. The bagged air acts as the literal proof that legitimizes her voice in the newly formed role of expert; the graphic and tangible nature of her evidence lends apparent scientific and material authority that substantiates the otherwise merely subjective testimony she offers. Ironically, though, the Shell representative takes the bag from her and jokingly asks, "Can I breathe it?"

Once again, the film brings the viewer face-to-face with how utterly and willfully disconnected corporations are from the specific sites of contamination. Executive "bodies" too easily miss the point of those bodies suffering because of toxic exposure and corporate neglect. This anonymous representative of corporate power goes to the brink of exposure with his joking but ultimately refuses to set lips or lungs on the air. His refusal is an explicit admission of the EJ connection between place and body that Richard makes clear. The unnamed Shell officer blushes at his own response, an apparent unwitting acknowledgment of what he and his company cannot help but repress. His body expresses what the viewer hopes must be his newly formed recognition.

Michelle Murphy uses the concepts "personal ecosystems" and "mutual embrace" to explain the often unacknowledged connection between bodies and environments, an interface Richard achieves by restaging place when she makes the case for socio-environmental illness. Supplementing the content of her testimony, which in this corporate context is controlled and actively disciplined, the materiality of place/body substantiates her narrative and attaches power to the advocacy role she presents. While she does not speak the discourse of corporate stakeholders in their meeting, Richard's body, its visible difference—a kind of toxicity in this commercial space—and the presence of a poisoned and poisonous environment in this venue bear such unmanageable testimony that the Shell delegation and the viewer must respond to her and to the causes of such injustice. To his credit the representative meets with Richard after the session and promises to make her grievances known. The documentary concludes by showing that being in the presence of damaged environments and imperiled people has created the basis for change; activist narratives are married to the materiality of bodies and place, and they collaborate in what amounts to the most persuasive EJ methods, the most convincing "mutual embrace" represented in the film.

Richard took her body, her story, but most important the toxic air to the front lines of corporate power in an effort to draw attention to the causes and consequences of what she and the members of the Diamond community believed to be destructive environmental policies. Ultimately, the film shows that binding body and place materially into the testimonial venue—and just as important, showing the refusal to bind healthy bodies to certain environments—is crucial in making substantial change. The film's final scenes explain that Richard's trip created a substantive response to the community's demand for a just and fair relocation, confirming the effectiveness of her testimony.

Through both *Erin Brockovich* and *Fenceline,* viewers become aware of the limitations and possibilities of embodied knowledge and embattled environments in testimonial confrontations with networks of power, a strong indication of the need for critical visibility in environmental justice negotiations. This awareness is brought about most effectively by film, I argue, since awareness is necessarily dependent on the direct materialization of those bodies and places most affected. Both films focus on the way bodies and environments are ignored or marginalized; though *Erin Brockovich* may permit as many gaps in recognition as it bridges, these two films open up a space to consider the way bodies and places function in testimonial situations. While EJ claims of damage are convincing to sympathetic audiences, this form of "witnessing" is particularly effective in demonstrating the authenticity of claims to those who are otherwise resistant to the critiques engendered by environmental justice studies. These are not the exclusive limits of testimony, but they do provide the outlines of advocacy efforts that continue to be addressed on the ground by activists and theorists.

Issues of evidence and testimony are increasingly relevant to those historically disadvantaged and disenfranchised people who have suffered environmental injustice. Both films illustrate how ostensibly powerless people attempt to secure the rights "to live unthreatened by the risks posed by environmental degradation and contamination, and to afford equal access to natural resources that sustain life and culture" (Adamson, Evans, and Stein 4). These films show that theatrical performance—in this case, documentary and popular film—creates the context for a fuller recognition of the embodied and emplaced testimonial structures of environmental justice politics.

WORKS CITED

Adamson, Joni, Mei Mei Evans, and Rachel Stein. *The Environmental Justice Reader: Politics, Poetics, and Pedagogy.* Tucson: Univ. of Arizona Press, 2002.

Allen, Barbara L. *Uneasy Alchemy: Citizens and Experts in Louisiana's Chemical Corridor Disputes.* Cambridge: MIT Press, 2003.

Brown, Phil. *Toxic Exposures: Contested Illnesses and the Environmental Health Movement.* New York: Columbia Univ. Press, 2007.

Bullard, Robert D. *Dumping in Dixie: Race, Class, and Environmental Equality.* 3rd ed. Boulder, CO: Westview Press, 2000.

Corburn, Jason. *Street Science: Community Knowledge and Environmental Health Justice.* Cambridge: MIT Press, 2005.

Di Chiro, Giovanna. "Nature as Community: The Convergence of Environment and Social Justice." *Uncommon Ground: Toward Reinventing Nature.* Ed. William Cronon. New York: W. W. Norton, 1995. 298–320.

Erin Brockovich. Prod. Danny DeVito, Michael Shamberg, and Stacey Sher. Dir. Steven Soderbergh. Universal Pictures, 2000.

Fenceline: A Company Town Divided. Prod. Jane Greenberg and Slawomir Grünberg. Dir. Slawomir Grünberg. Log In Productions, 2002.

Kroll-Smith, Steve, and H. Hugh Floyd. *Bodies in Protest: Environmental Illness and the Struggle over Medical Knowledge.* New York: New York Univ. Press, 1997.

Lerner, Steve. *Diamond: A Struggle for Environmental Justice in Louisiana's Chemical Corridor.* Cambridge: MIT Press, 2005.

Murphy, Michelle. "The 'Elsewhere with Here' and Environmental Illness; or, How to Build Yourself a Body in a Safe Space." *Configurations* 8 (2000): 87–120.

Sharp, Kathleen. "Erin Brockovich: the Real Story." *Salon* 14 April 2000. http://www.salon.com/ent/feature/2000/04/14/sharp/index.html. Retrieved 8 August 2006.

Tesh, Sylvia Noble. *Uncertain Hazards: Environmental Activists and Scientific Proof.* Ithaca, NY: Cornell Univ. Press, 2000.

Verchick, Robert R. M. "Feminist Theory and Environmental Justice." *New Perspectives on Environmental Justice: Gender, Sexuality, and Activism.* Ed. Rachel Stein. New Brunswick, NJ: Rutgers Univ. Press, 2004. 63–77.

DISPOSABLE BODIES
BIOCOLONIALISM IN
THE CONSTANT GARDENER
AND DIRTY PRETTY THINGS

RACHEL STEIN

Environmental justice calls for the strict enforcement
of principles of informed consent and a halt to the
testing of experimental reproductive and medical
procedures and vaccinations on people of color.
—Principles of Environmental Justice

The grassroots environmental justice (EJ) movement that arose in the 1980s addressed the disproportionate environmental hazards and deprivations suffered by poor and people of color communities in the United States and around the world. While mainstream environmental groups had defined the environment as a pristine wilderness that needed to be defended from human depredation, environmental justice groups defined it instead as "where we live, play, work, and worship." These activists focused their attention on the interactions of communities with their natural and built environments, questioning why the environmental health of the poor and of people of color was being sacrificed so that wealthier, usually whiter communities could be situated in less toxic environments and enjoy more abundant natural resources. Their emphasis upon human/natural interactions made it clear that environmental injustices encompass a wide range of urban and rural issues: land claims, clear-cutting of forests, radiation exposure from uranium mining and nuclear wastes, dumping of toxic industrial wastes, conflicts over water rights and water quality, hazardous work sites and underemployment, substandard housing, toxic schools, transportation, economic disinvestments, deteriorating infrastructure, as well as numerous other social/physical ills that put the bodies and lives of the poor and people of color at risk (Adamson, Evans, and Stein 3–14). Biocolonialism further extended these exploitative practices by seeking vulnerable human bodies as natural resources to be consumed for the profit and pleasures of those with greater social and economic power, as evidenced by the transnational organ trade and testing of pharmaceuticals.

Dirty Pretty Things (2002) and *The Constant Gardener* (2005) are examples of recent films that warn us against the biotechnological colonization of vulnerable third world people who, driven by the stringencies of poverty, politics, illness and/or immigration, exchange their bodily integrity for the possibility of improved survival. Fernando Meirelles's *The Constant Gardener* exposes the abuse of impoverished Kenyan AIDS and tuberculosis patients who are forced into risky drug trials conducted by transnational pharmaceutical corporations hoping to reap profit from such deadly epidemics. Stephen Frears's *Dirty Pretty Things* focuses on the illicit transnational trade in human organs, wherein undocumented refugees to England are coerced into trading their kidneys for forged identity and immigration papers. The radical commodification of third world bodies into biomaterials to be consumed in the service of wealthier, and often whiter, bodies is an insidious form of biocolonialism and environmental injustice that these two films call into question. While the films are fictional, they illuminate actual contemporary instances of using third world persons' biomaterial for first world consumption.

The Principles of Environmental Justice adopted at the First National People of Color Environmental Leadership Summit, which convened in Washington, DC, in 1991, included a thirteenth principle, quoted above, that called for a halt to such biomedical misuse of the bodies of people of color (Di Chiro 309). Both of the films under discussion in this chapter expose instances of environmental injustice and biocolonialism, and thus draw public attention to issues that are often of too little concern to those outside affected communities. However, simply drawing our sympathies to environmental injustices is not sufficient for creating effective understanding and positive change.

Environmental justice movements foregrounded intersections of social justice issues and environmental ills, and made evident the race and class assumptions that had permeated mainstream "nature talk" (Di Chiro 310–20). In response to those detrimental ideas, environmental justice groups insisted that local communities needed to articulate their own particular relationships with their environments, as proclaimed by their motto, "We speak for ourselves." Furthermore, environmental justice groups promoted the agency and activism of communities on their own behalf, as survivors of environmental ills collectively struggled to redress wrongs, to alter the status quo, and to positively reframe human relations to our environments.

When we examine *The Constant Gardener* and *Dirty Pretty Things* within this ideological framework, it becomes evident that Meirelles's film remains safely within a colonialist viewpoint even as it exposes the assumptions of the colonizers, while Frears's film ventures into an environmental justice vantage point that helps viewers to understand the ravages experienced by those who are the targets of biocolonialism. By analyzing the perspectives of both films toward biocolonial consumption of third world bodies, viewers may become aware of the contours of our own "nature talk" and of the ecocritical stances through which we produce and consume film images of environmental struggles.

The Constant Gardener and Dirty Pretty Things feature detective/thriller plots in which a female and male protagonist uncover and challenge biocolonialism; in both films the man becomes motivated to oppose biopiracy because the woman is already involved, either as a victim of such practices or as an activist trying to halt them. Despite these plot similarities, the films represent different forms of biocolonialism from opposite perspectives and gazes that shape viewers' understanding of biopiracy. While The Constant Gardener exposes the travesty of using Kenyan people as test subjects for dangerous experimental drugs without their informed consent, the film is told from the vantage point of a British civil servant unknowingly complicit in this practice. Here, Africans are mostly represented as tragic "others," passively suffering from an array of irremediable ills. Although the protagonist does come to understand how colonial forces are implicated in this suffering, he never really engages with or even understands the perspectives of the native peoples he is attempting to protect. This limits the vision of the film.

Dirty Pretty Things comes closer to the environmental justice assertion that affected communities must speak for themselves. Its protagonists are the refugees themselves, pressured to participate in the illicit organ trade in London. We see the trade through their eyes, understanding the stringencies that cause them to exchange organs for legal identity papers, or to subvert the exchange entirely, as happens at the conclusion of this film. While The Constant Gardener exposes the corruption of governments and medical corporations practicing biocolonialism, Dirty Pretty Things approaches the topic from the vantage point of those whose bodies are sought as biomaterials. Both films address important issues, but the social/political perspective of Meirelles's film is clouded by colonial assumptions, while Frears's film has the clearer focus of insiders.

As diseases such as HIV and tuberculosis spread around the globe, assuming epidemic proportions especially in impoverished third world nations, pharmaceutical companies rush to create effective drug treatment regimes for desperate markets. Competition among pharmaceutical companies means that speed in new drug production is of the essence in gaining patents and national approval for distribution of new, hugely profitable medications. Stringent drug trial regulations in first world regions such as the United States and Europe, and the unwillingness of citizens in those areas to participate in risky medical tests, have prompted pharmaceutical companies to seek elsewhere for more accessible drug test populations. Pharmaceutical companies now regularly conduct drug trials in African, Middle Eastern, and Eastern European countries with little regulation of medical testing, and large populations of vulnerably ill patients receiving scant treatment leap at opportunities for any sort of medical care.

This surge of drug trials in the third world raises serious concerns about biomedical colonization of patients by pharmaceutical giants from the developed world, who are now "trading in people" (Flaherty, Nelson, and Stephens). Anna Romany of Johnson and Johnson explains that "foreign patients with little exposure to medicines offer a blank slate for experimentation. Medical deprivation makes patients 'better for our purposes'" (Flaherty, Nelson, and Stephens 3). This disparity in knowledge of medical practices between testers and test subjects often leads to ethical breaches, such as the failure to obtain genuine informed consent; the trial of risky drugs, with serious side effects, that are not approved for testing in the developed world; the failure to provide effective treatments available in the first world to third world patients involved in drug trials; and a final outcome of corporate medical profits achieved at the expense of patients in impoverished countries. For example, pharmaceutical tests may enroll patients unfamiliar with Western standards of medical care without explaining the nature of the trial or the medication, and without any attempt to obtain genuine informed consent from them. Such patients do not realize that they have any alternative to signing an incomprehensible form, perhaps even in a foreign language; and if they live under authoritarian national regimes, consent itself may be a foreign concept (Flaherty, Nelson, and Stephens).

Nor are test subjects informed that they may be given drugs with adverse side effects deemed too risky for testing in the developed world. Pfizer regarded a 1996 spinal meningitis epidemic in Nigeria as the perfect opportunity to test its new antibiotic on a pool of children. To conduct the testing, Pfizer monopolized Nigerian medical facilities and personnel, thus disrupting the treatment of patients. Of the two hundred children in the drug trial, eleven died and many others developed side effects, but Pfizer did not stop the testing even when lives were clearly at risk. "It could be considered murder," commented a physician working with Doctors without Borders (quoted in Stephens 2). Additionally, patients in drug trials are sometimes deprived of existing drugs so that pharmaceutical companies can study the course of illnesses or test new treatments. In 1997 in Thailand, HIV-positive pregnant women were denied the drug AZT once it became available in that country, so that the U.S. Army could study transmission rates of HIV from mother to child; as a result of this, many more children with this disease were born to women in the study (Flaherty and Struck 2). Similarly, in 2000, HIV-infected people in ten Ugandan villages were observed but not treated in a study of this illness (Boseley). While pharmaceutical companies may argue that their third world drug trials provide treatments to patients who have little other medical care, the companies stand to reap huge financial profits by using these populations to test experimental drugs quickly and with very little regulation or responsibility. Clearly, these transnational drug trial practices are a form of biocolonialism in which third world bodies serve as guinea pigs for first world medical ventures: "Rich countries have drugs and hypotheses, while poor countries have vast numbers of patients" (Flaherty and Struck).

The Constant Gardener, based on the novel of that title by John Le Carré, exposes film viewers to this misuse of third world patients taking risky pharmaceuticals rife with dangerous side effects, without informed consent. Focusing on an English couple stationed in Kenya, the film presents their contrasting stances toward this medical practice as they uncover the unscrupulousness of the drug trials. Justin Quayle is a British diplomat who, throughout much of the film, appears naively sheltered from the harsh realities of colonial corruption that his impassioned and politically radical young wife, Tessa Quayle, uncovers during her work with local African people. As Tessa visits African communities, accompanies her doctor friend, Arnold Blum, to local health clinics serving native people suffering from HIV and TB, and gives birth in a hospital serving Africans, she becomes increasingly disturbed by evidence that European pharmaceutical firms are testing an experimental tuberculosis drug called Dypraxa on the Kenyan populace, without asking for their informed consent nor warning them that the drug has deadly side effects and is killing numbers of native test subjects. Tessa documents these questionable testing practices, sending reports of her findings to British diplomatic officials and European watchdog groups monitoring drug testing around the globe.

Justin continues to serve the British government that has brokered the deal to promote illicit drug testing in Kenya, while taking refuge in the English garden he has created by transplanting British flowers in his African compound. A "constant gardener," Justin devotes himself to his English plants, blinded to the ironies of his own biocolonization of this patch of African soil. While his gardening may appear harmless or even nurturing to viewers, it reinforces the theme of biocolonization and his own colonial superiority and domination of the African landscape and the indigenous flora. More important, Justin's gardening distracts him from attending to Tessa's discoveries about the human costs that colonization and biocolonization extract from the subject population. Only after Tessa is murdered in order to bury her findings does Justin leave his supposedly innocent refuge in the garden, to investigate the more violent biocolonization forces that have killed his wife and scores of African drug trial subjects.

As *The Constant Gardener* veers back and forth between Tessa and Justin's perspectives on the drug trials, their contrasting stances are borne out by the filming itself. Oftentimes, when Kenyans are represented in the film, it is through panoramic shots that sweep over city crowds and landscapes, giving us almost a blur of images and bodies, a technique that reflects Justin's detachment from the Kenyan populace. Only when Tessa immerses herself within local communities does the lens zoom in to focus on individual faces of Kenyans interacting with her. In such scenes, the filming emphasizes that Tessa regards Kenyans as distinct individuals, worthy of attention, respect, and bodily integrity. Once Tessa dies, this perspective mostly vanishes from the film, to reappear only occasionally as Justin tracks Tessa's investigation.

While Justin tends to view the Kenyans as a large suffering mass to whom he owes no personal allegiance or compassion, occasionally an individual child looms into focus for him: in particular, Wanza Kilulu's brother, Kioko Kilulu, and Dr. Lorbeer's child assistant, Abuk, whom Justin tries to rescue from marauders. In the closing scenes of the film, at Justin's funeral, when Tessa's cousin, Ham, is accusing British diplomats and European pharmaceutical companies of murdering the Quayles and numerous Kenyans, the film cuts away to close-ups of smiling Kenyan children. This may imply that viewers, too, should see only Kenyan children as worthy of our sympathy and protection, while the rest of the population remains a hopeless blur. This filmic perspective allows viewers to remain detached from the Kenyan population, rather than identifying with their suffering and according them the full human status and rights that an environmental justice stance demands of us.

Justin's continuous attention to Tessa also keeps the film, and consequently the viewers, pointed toward concern for European characters rather than focused on the harsh consequences of drug testing of the local population. Even as Justin retraces Tessa's investigation and confirms her findings, his focus remains on uncovering the work that she kept secret from him; even as he comes in closer contact with individual Kenyans and learns more of their plight, his attention is on understanding his dead wife, rather than on the dangerous drug tests that she tried to expose. He does the work for her sake, in her name, rather than out of a burning desire to halt the deadly drug trials; we might interpret his desire to understand Tessa posthumously as another form of colonization in which men conquer the mysteries that women embody for them. How does Justin's focus affect viewers of this film? Do we see the limitations of his view when we compare him to Tessa? Does Justin's perspective remain a barrier to viewers coming to understand the impact of biocolonization, or does our sympathy for his loss bring us further into the emotional costs of the issues? Through Justin's devotion to Tessa's memory and to completing her work, the film emphasizes the consequences of her death, far more than the loss entailed in the similar death of Wanza Kilulu, the young Kenyan woman who dies after giving birth as a result of taking Dypraxa in the drug trial. While the film does show us glimpses of Wanza's younger brother, Kioko, tending her and her baby, our attention is soon directed back to Tessa, and to Justin's attempts to care for her after their child is stillborn. The death of Tessa, the white English woman, is emphasized throughout the film—framing the entire story—while the death of Wanza, the African woman, is presented as a minor detail, proof of the deadly side effects of Dypraxa rather than a personal tragedy.

Another way that The Constant Gardener misdirects viewers' attention away from the Kenyan population affected by the trials is through the sexual rumors that the diplomatic/pharmaceutical authorities spread about Tessa, Arnold, and Justin in order to discredit their investigations into drug trial malpractices, and to influence public attention away from government and corporate roles in their murder. The corrupt authorities mask the political, economic, and moral questions raised by Tessa's and Arnold's investigations by planting scandalous rumors of an extramarital and interracial relationship between the two friends, recasting them as adulterous lovers instead of political allies. These sexual allegations are also used to frame Arnold for Tessa's murder, thus pointing all eyes away from those truly responsible.

Because Arnold's homosexuality has been closeted, due to Kenyan criminalization of same-sex behaviors, his sexual identity can't be used to refute these dangerous rumors, and so heterosexism masks the corporate and governmental agents who are the actual villains here. When Justin takes up Tessa's investigation of Dypraxa after her murder, the sexual scandal is also used to discredit his findings, painting him as the cuckolded husband, crazed by grief at Tessa's betrayal of their marriage, instead of as a loyal spouse seeking justice for the murder of his wife. While the plot of *The Constant Gardener* does later reveal the falseness of these allegations, viewers are initially drawn into the scandal—since this is the explanation that we hear first—and only later do we learn the truth. Viewers experience the force of misdirection that characters must also overcome and, therefore, may gain some understanding of how sexual scandal is being used to undermine radical challenges to the corrupt regime; however, the film often leaves our attention embroiled in the smoke screen of sexual rumor rather than focused on the underlying truth; it thus reinforces the public's tendency to pay more attention to personal behavior than to corporate and governmental malpractice.

Similarly, the film remains ambivalent about the first world view of Africans as disposable people, to be subsumed by foreign interests. As the woman at HIPPO (a European agency keeping watch on illegal transnational drug testing) explains to Justin, there is a huge profit in producing drugs to treat epidemics. She says, "If the TB market performs as forecast, billions and billions of dollars are waiting to be earned. And the way to earn them is Dypraxa, if, of course, the preliminary trials in Africa have not thrown up any disturbing side effects." She explains that any delay in the drug trials, or any time spent redesigning the drug, would cut down those profits; and it is cheaper to "fix" the drug trials by covering up deaths and hiring murderers to silence those who ask too many questions.

In this colonial economics, third world people are sacrificed in cold blood to assure first world profits. Sandy Woodrow, the director of the English diplomatic department in Kenya, justifies using African people as disposable test subjects: "We're not killing people who wouldn't be dead otherwise. Look at the death rates." And Dr. Lorbeer, who invented Dypraxa and then went into seclusion once people began to die in the drug trials, condemns transnational pharmaceutical companies that donate expired drugs to Africa: "Disposable drugs for disposable patients. Big pharmaceuticals are right up there with the arms dealers. This is how the world fucks Africa. It's how they expiate their guilt." The first world offers futile attempts at humanitarian aid to mask their interests in profiting from African illnesses and deaths. As Bernard Pellegrin at the British home office states candidly in a letter, "The issue here is deniability. If nobody told us Dypraxa was causing death, we can't be held responsible."

We see Europeans such as Tessa, Arnold, and Justin taking action to halt the drug trials that prey upon third world patients; but we see almost no sign of activism/agency among Africans, beyond one brief television sound bite in which Justin glimpses a Kenyan woman speaking about her women activists organization. Unlike other instances of postcolonial art and activism in which affected communities "speak for [themselves]," *The Constant Gardener* relies upon European characters to tell the story from the outside; therefore, while we do end up with an indicting portrayal of the colonial corruption that implements dangerous drug trials without informed patient consent, we are given no sense that African peoples are resisting these practices, nor that they have the human agency to halt biocolonialism. Ultimately, through this weak portrayal of Kenyans, the film unfortunately reinforces the first world view that Africans are "disposable" people rather than citizens capable of acting in solidarity and resistance in their own collective interest, refusing biomedical colonization.

The human organ trade that occurs both legally and illegally in many parts of the globe is a transnational exchange in which wealthier, often whiter persons in need of organ transplants arrange to purchase organs from donors who are frequently poor people of color, especially women in dire circumstances. Nancy Scheper-Hughes, director of Critical Studies of Medicine, Science, and the Body at Berkeley and also an officer of Organs Watch, an organization that monitors the international organ trade, notes that

> sanctions in one country may stimulate organ sales in a neighboring one. Wealthy patients have shown willingness to travel great distances to secure a transplant, even in areas where the survival rates are quite poor. And with the globalization of the economy, the circulation of bodies and body parts increasingly transcends national boundaries. In general, the movement and flow of living donor organs —mostly kidneys—is from South to North, from poor to rich, from black and brown to white, and from female to male bodies. (Scheper-Hughes)

Given this situation, Japanese sociologist, T. Awaya comments that "we are now eyeing each other's bodies greedily, as a potential source of detachable spare parts with which to extend our lives," a perspective which he calls "social or friendly cannibalism" (Scheper-Hughes).

In fact, the *Christian Science Monitor* has termed this global gray market, in which buyers and sellers of organs cross national boundaries to conduct this bodily exchange, "transplant tourism" (McLaughlin and Prusher). The phrases used to describe the exchange of body parts, such as "organ harvesting," "social or friendly cannibalism," and "transplant tourism," point to the process of transnational biocolonialism in which the body parts of poor third world persons will be literally absorbed into the bodies of the richer and more powerful denizens of the first world who can afford to travel the globe in pursuit of extended health.

A few examples illustrate the dynamics of this new, transnational form of biocolonialism that now transpires around the globe. In Chinese prisons, kidneys, corneas, liver tissue, heart valves, and skin are systematically harvested from executed prisoners—minutes after they are shot —and prisoners are often respirated until this surgery is complete. Between 2,000 and 5,000 prisoners are executed each year, and organs from such prisoners are reputed to have been given to recipients in the government elite and sold to foreigners ("Habeas Corpus"). India became a huge market for kidneys, whose sale was legal until 1996 but has now been driven underground and managed by crime gangs expanding from drug trade to organs trade. Most of these kidneys are transplanted into persons from the Middle East, Europe, and the United States. The medical anthropologist Lawrence Cohen talks of the Indian "kidney for dowry" trade in which villagers sell organs to obtain dowries for daughters (Scheper-Hughes). In Brazil a large transplant practice is supported through an "unofficial" system of encouraging donations through "compensated gifting"—offering money and protection, housing, and so on for organs (Sheper-Hughes). In South Africa most donor bodies are township blacks and coloreds who were the unfortunate victims of violence and other traumas (Scheper-Hughes). In these instances, poor people of color driven by poverty, political/social forces, or desperation sell their organs and jeopardize their future health and well-being. Ironically, in this global market their body parts are tradable commodities, worth much more economically than the persons themselves or their labor.

Within this context, Stephen Frears's film *Dirty Pretty Things* is a canny portrayal of the transnational organ trade that focuses on the political and economic forces driving vulnerable persons to exchange health and body parts for greater opportunities of survival and security. The film also portrays the resourceful resistance of the refugee community. Set in contemporary London, the story focuses on two refugees seeking asylum in England from political discord and violence in their home nations: Okwe, a Nigerian doctor who has fled from the corrupt regime that has framed him for their murder of his wife, and Senay, a Muslim Kurdish woman seeking a better life than that of her female ancestors, presumably fleeing harsh sexism and ethnic persecution.

Dirty Pretty Things explores intersections and parallels between refugee migration and the illegal organ trade, as these immigrants become prey to this illicit transnational exchange of body parts across national, racial, class, and gender boundaries. In contrast to *The Constant Gardener*, this film concentrates on third world individuals coerced into relinquishing bodily integrity to the forces of biocolonialism, and through this focus *Dirty Pretty Things* reveals the insidious social pressures that drive refugees into the trade. More important, the film also presents the immigrants' cleverly strategic teamwork to successfully subvert the organ exchange for their own ends, thus emphasizing the intelligent agency of third world characters who resist the powerful tide of biocolonialism. Unlike the mass helplessness and hopelessness of the Africans presented from a first world perspective in *The Constant Gardener*, *Dirty Pretty Things* portrays the ugly realities of the organ trade from the point of view of individual refugees, leaving viewers with a more complex understanding of third world responses to biocolonialism.

Okwe and Senay work as a desk clerk and chambermaid at the London hotel that serves as a vector in the illicit organ trade. The hotel manager harvests the organs of illegal aliens in exchange for forged passports and citizenship papers. As the manager explains to Okwe, the trade offers each party "happiness": the alien trades his or her kidney for forged identity papers, the manager gets $10,000, and the buyer gets health. During the course of the film, Okwe and Senay will be pressured by their political and economic situations to participate in this illicit and subterranean organ trade. The film makes very clear how transnationalism drives organ markets as "alien" bodies are encouraged to sacrifice their organs in order to gain political, economic, and social protection. In one scene in the film, the child of an African man who had his kidney removed in a botched surgery explains the situation to Okwe: "He is English now. He swapped his insides for a passport." In this ultimate form of objectification, the foreign body becomes a natural resource, harvested for those empowered by the market economy.

The fact that *Dirty Pretty Things* begins and ends in an international London airport and is primarily based in the hotel emphasizes the dynamics of "transplant tourism." We learn that a number of the staff, many of whom are undocumented "aliens," are sources of organs, along with other third world persons who come to the hotel for this surgery. The hotel functions as a vector of this trade, representing transience and transnational consumption, and highlighting the class, ethnic/racial, and gender differential between those who are employed there and those who are guests. The manager says, "Strangers come to the hotel in the night to do dirty things, and it's our job to make things look pretty again." His philosophy both sanctions and masks the "dirty" or ugly realities that permeate the illicit organ trade: poverty, lack of citizenship rights and civil protections, as well as many sorts of objectification that will permit refugees to be cannibalized by more privileged, wealthy, whiter, mostly male citizens. The job of the hotel is to host and then hide this inequitable process of consumption, as it does with other sorts of prostitution.

Dirty Pretty Things also emphasizes the way that sexual objectification reinforces biocolonialism, not as a distracting smoke screen as in *The Constant Gardener,* but as an additional form of sexist social coercion that drives targeted women into the organ trade. As someone seeking political asylum, and as a Muslim Turkish woman in a predominantly Christian country, Senay is vulnerable to the men in positions of authority over her. She is not permitted to find legal employment, so she works under the table as a chambermaid until immigration officers discover her deception. When she loses her job in the hotel, she seeks work in a sweatshop, where the owner repeatedly forces her to perform oral sex on him as payment for not reporting her to Immigration. After biting his penis during an oral rape, and therefore forfeiting her job, Senay sees no other way to support herself and protect her body from sexual violation; she desperately accepts the hotel manager's invitation to sell her kidney for a false passport and papers so that she will be able to escape to the United States.

Ironically, to seal this deal, the manager also forces Senay to have vaginal sex with him, although her virginity is sacred to her. The film makes it clear that men in power view Senay only as a physical, sexual object and bio-donor, and so her identity, her culture, and her well-being are totally disregarded. Paradoxically, Senay sees the sacrifice of a kidney as her only means of escaping these forms of objectification and attempting to gain a better life; but, as Ogwe warns Senay when he hears about her plans for the organ exchange, "Because you are poor, you will be gutted like an animal."

The film also presents successful resistance and subversion of the organ trade dynamics as Okwe, who is being blackmailed by the manager into performing the organ harvesting surgeries, successfully withstands these pressures and fights back in order to save Senay and himself from being consumed by this trade. Okwe, who was a doctor in

Nigeria, uses his medical knowledge and ethics in order to investigate and resist the organ removal trade based at the hotel. He first learns of the trade when he finds a human heart blocking the toilet in a hotel room; he informs the corrupt manager about it and also tries to call the police, until the manager suggests that Okwe would risk being deported if he contacted them. Later, Okwe is summoned to treat a foreign man whose wound from kidney removal has become septic, and he learns more about the exchange of organs for citizenship papers and new identities. The hotel manager tries to lure him into the trade, suggesting that Okwe could better remove organs without butchering the donors, but Okwe resists the manager's bribes as well as his threats about immigration authorities. It is only Okwe's concern for Senay's health and life that finally pulls him into the organ removal process, and, crucially, Okwe is then able to use his medical knowledge and ethics to subvert the dynamics of the trade.

Instead of first world cannibalization of third world bodies, the refugees team up to reverse the flow of body parts and resources. Okwe, Senay, a black prostitute from the hotel, and a Chinese friend from the hospital morgue remove the manager's kidney; the two main characters then use the money from this sale and the forged passports the manager has provided them to migrate once again in search of their dreams. When the go-between who is transporting this kidney asks Okwe why he hasn't seen them before, Okwe sums up the unequal dynamic at play in the organ trade when he describes the way that refugees, ethnic/racial minorities, and women service those in power, even to the extent of providing new body parts: "Because we are the ones you don't see. We drive your cars and clean your rooms and suck your cocks." While those who purchase these vital organs will never "see" or comprehend the forces that have driven the donors to this illicit, bloody, financial/biomedical exchange, viewers of this film have encountered the issues from within the perspectives of undocumented immigrants whose desperate situations make them perfect targets for this trade.

Fittingly, Dirty Pretty Things ends as it began, in the London airport where Senay will fly to New York City, a city that she hopes will fulfill her dreams for freedom and opportunity; Okwe will return to Nigeria to be reunited with the daughter whom he had to abandon when he fled for his life. The Constant Gardener ends with the hopelessly romantic death of Justin, who sought out the spot where Tessa was killed so that he, too, would be murdered by the same hired thugs and thus join her in death. Instead of the ineffective solution offered by the other film, Dirty Pretty Things ends on a note of tempered hope that Okwe and Senay have momentarily thwarted the pressures of biocolonialism; even though they love each other, they are each choosing to pursue an individually meaningful new life. *Dirty Pretty Things* leaves viewers with an optimistic appreciation of the resourceful agency of third world persons who must struggle collectively to break free from the coercive powers of the first world.

Both *The Constant Gardener* and *Dirty Pretty Things* show viewers the insidious operations of first world consumption of third world bodies, revealing instances of biocolonialism that are often carefully hidden from sight. As a pair, the films mirror each other, each illuminating one axis of the exchanges: first world greed and corruption along with first world exposure of these dynamics; third world desperation and suffering along with resourceful agency and collective resistance. While we need to understand both aspects of this global phenomenon, we should also be canny viewers, able to question the vested interests even of a stirring film such as *The Constant Gardener*. While *The Constant Gardener* might leave us feeling despair before the enormities of the problem, the hopeful conclusion of *Dirty Pretty Things* is likely to inspire more belief in the power of third world outrage and subversive action.

WORKS CITED

Adamson, Joni, Mei Mei Evans, and Rachel Stein, eds. *The Environmental Justice Reader: Politics, Poetics, and Pedagogy.* Tucson: Univ. of Arizona Press, 2002.

Boseley, Sarah. "U.S. Drug Tests on Third World Poor Leave Some To Die." *Guardian* 4 May 2000. http://www.commondreas.org/headlines. Retrieved 14 October 2005.

The Constant Gardener. Dir. Fernando Meirelles. Focus Features, 2005.

Di Chiro, Giovanna. "Nature as Community: The Convergence of Environment and Social Justice." *Uncommon Ground: Rethinking the Human Place in Nature.* Ed. William Cronon. New York: W. W. Norton, 1996. 298–320.

Dirty Pretty Things. Dir. Stephen Frears. BBC Films, 2003.

Flaherty, Mary Pat, Deborah Nelson, and Joe Stephens. "The Body Hunters: Overwhelming the Watchdogs." *Washington Post* 18 December 2001. http://www.washingtonpost.com (Archives). Retrieved 14 October 2005.

Flaherty, Mary Pat, and Doug Struck. "Life by Luck of the Draw: In Third World Drug Tests, Some Subjects Go Untreated." *Washington Post* 22 December 2000. http://www.washingtonpost.com (Archives). Retrieved 14 October 2005.

"Habeas Corpus—Asseveration—Organ Harvesting from Executed Prisoners in China." *Harper's Magazine* February 2002. http://www.findarticles.com/p/articles/mi_1111/is_1821_304/ai_82743065. Retrieved 4 August 2004.

McLaughlin, Abraham and Ilene Prusher. "What Is a Kidney Worth?" *Christian Science Monitor* 9 June 2004. http://www.csmonitor.com/ (Archives).

Scheper-Hughes, Nancy. "The New Cannibalism." 24 May 2004. http://sunsite
.berkeley.edu/organswatch.

Stein, Rachel. *New Perspectives on Environmental Justice: Gender, Sexuality and
Activism*. New Brunswick, NJ: Rutgers Univ. Press, 2004.

Stephens, Joe. "As Drug Testing Spreads, Profits and Lives Hang in the Balance."
Washington Post 17 December 2001. http://washingtonpost.com (Archives).
Retrieved 14 October 2005.

ENGAGING THE LAND/ POSITIONING THE SPECTATOR

ENVIRONMENTAL JUSTICE DOCUMENTARIES AND ROBERT REDFORD'S THE HORSE WHISPERER AND A RIVER RUNS THROUGH IT

BETH BERILA

This essay brings together feminist theory, environmental justice scholarship, and feminist cultural geography to analyze the implications of particular portrayals of our relationship to the land. Specifically, I juxtapose two Hollywood films touted as revering the western landscape with two environmental justice documentaries that interrogate different communities' responsibility for addressing environmental degradation. I am particularly interested in how these different portrayals construct a gendered and racialized relationship to the environment by positioning viewers differently in relation to the land, thus shaping our perceptions of the land and our living relationships to it. The contrast raises some useful questions about the value and limitations of the different filmic genres for environmental movements.

Specifically, the juxtaposition of these distinct film genres helps illustrate the larger question of how films situate spectators in relation to the environment and to environmental issues. Whereas the two Robert Redford films I discuss position viewers in a dominating and colonizing relationship to the land, the two environmental justice documentaries emphasize our lived relationship with it and demand much more accountability to the ecosystems it supports. Some of this difference results from the distinct genres, rhetorical and political purposes, aesthetic conventions, and target audiences that distinguish mainstream fiction films from documentaries. Most major mainstream films deploy the established convention to draw the viewer into the storyline, while documentaries often refuse that suspension of disbelief. The Redford films foster an admiration for the western landscape while allowing viewers to abdicate responsibility for protecting it. The documentaries offer what feminist critic bell hooks has called an "oppositional gaze," through which filmmakers and community activists "talk back" to the dominant colonizing gaze. In doing so, the documentaries produce counternarratives around environmental degradation and challenge viewers to read against the grain of dominant representations of nature in film (hooks 309–13).

The juxtaposition of these four films, then, raises valuable questions about the types of environmental interventions open to visual narratives. While the Redford films create useful emotional connections to the land, they do so precisely by obscuring the effects of human interventions in ecosystems. If ecocentric ideals are to be achieved, it is not enough for humans to admire the beauty of nature while still portraying it as a one-dimensional "object" to be possessed. Instead, environmental justice is best fulfilled when humans position themselves in a dynamic and mutually interdependent relationship with nature.

Robert Redford's *A River Runs Through It* (1992) and *The Horse Whisperer* (1998) have garnered critical acclaim for their stunning cinematography of the U.S. West. Redford's films are also informed by his star persona as a staunch advocate both of environmental preservation and of independent cinema. Because of Redford's status as a prominent environmentalist and a filmmaker who foregrounds the beauty of the western landscape, his films readily open themselves to an ecocritical analysis.

Specifically, the films discussed here illustrate the problematic gendered and racial power dynamics in the portrayal of land. Redford's films feature scenic vistas and panoramic shots of mountains, forests, and water, usually uninhabited by humans. The films espouse a kind of conservationist relation to the land by invoking its pristine beauty. They offer shots of stunning western landscapes, but they also encourage viewers to see the vistas merely as objects of beauty. They do little to encourage viewers to locate themselves, and their lifestyles, in relation to the land and its ecosystems. For instance, the camera usually pans from above so that the spectator is surveying the land from a high position, in a kind of colonizing gaze. Alternatively, the camera shots hone in on close-ups of fields shown glowing in the twilight sun, or water gently rippling in the wind. Both kinds of shots portray the land as an aesthetic and untouched space, to be appreciated, admired, and even preserved for its beauty, but not as a living ecosystem of which humans are a part and on which we depend.

In his critique of certain aspects of environmentalism, and even of ecocriticism, the scholar T. V. Reed has noted that "pretending to isolate the environment from its necessary interrelation with society and culture has severely limited the appeal of environmental thought, to the detriment of both the natural and social worlds" (146). The representations of nature in the Redford films reflect and encourage this isolation, or alienation, of humans from nature. While the films glorify the beauty of the West, and so are touted as environmentally friendly by mainstream audiences, they work to obscure some of the implications of aestheticizing the land. To some extent this simple glorification is the result of the conventions and rhetorical goals of many major feature films, which often do not have the overt political or educational bent of documentaries. However, this dynamic perpetuates the colonizing impulse that has historically fueled western expansionism, and the gender and racial formations that have accompanied it. Redford's films revere the West by emphasizing a doctrine of preserving untouched landscape; by extension they reaffirm the myth of the rugged American West in which that philosophy is embedded.

While Redford's films work to reinforce hegemonic appropriations of the land, the two environmental justice documentaries discussed here interrogate these appropriations. Kate Raisz's *Toxic Racism* (1994) and Joseph Di Gangi and Amon Giebel's *Drumbeat for Mother Earth* (1999) reveal how poor communities of color bear the brunt of environmental abuse such as toxic dumping. They offer an explicit analysis of the racial, gender, and class power dynamics that shape our relations to nature. Such overt political analysis is much more typical of the documentary genre than it is of feature films, while, perhaps not accidentally, the latter appeal to much broader audiences than most documentaries. Taken together, these films help us raise provocative questions about how human relationships to the land are represented and thus produced by the culture. What gets erased, or masked, when films construct the landscape as something to be gazed at from afar, or to be seen as an untouched object of beauty? How does a film's portrayal of the western landscape as a retreat for healing and recuperation, or as a wilderness in need of taming, shape our perception of the actual living land? How can these portrayals obscure gender and racial relations toward the land, and toward women and communities of color? What different possibilities emerge when spectators are positioned as a part of a living and diverse ecosystem that includes humans but extends well beyond us? What kinds of portrayals create more accountability for "preserving" the land?

THE CONSUMING GAZE

The Horse Whisperer and *A River Runs Through It* portray the landscape of Montana as a visual spectacle meant to be admired and protected, at the same time that the cinematography works to appropriate the land.

The camera angles reveal Montana's spectacular natural beauty, but they also create sweeping panoramic shots that enable the spectator to "consume" that land visually. The camera embodies a kind of touristical gaze that defines a particular consuming relationship to space and the environment (Pratt 1–14). This type of imagery is likely to support the tourist industry in the West, but it does little to examine critically the costs of such tourism on the ecosystems themselves. The visual spectacle offers audiences an appealing escape into beauty that is popular in feature films set in the West.

This carefree enjoyment without responsibility, however, is less helpful to the advancement of environmental consciousness than it may seem; it invites a recreational consumption that renders invisible the exploitation of land and peoples that historically has made possible the western mystique. Both Redford films portray a longing for an American way of life now lost: the relative simplicity, and the rugged cowboy ranch life that is uniquely "western." Given the role of the U.S. western cowboy narrative in fostering the American dream of western expansion, this nostalgia appears to support environmental protection while simultaneously upholding the ideologies that often enact environmental degradation (Carmichael 3–6). Because the mythic U.S. West is such a valorized component of hegemonic U.S. history, films that recreate and privilege western beauty can muster support for protecting national parks and preserving mountain scenery. However, that same mythic western ideology has fueled the pioneer move to conquer the West, to tame the open space; in doing so, it has often done violence not only to the ecosystems of the West but also to Native American and Chicano/a communities who already inhabited that supposedly untouched space. As Reed has noted about the limits of an environmentalism that idealizes and isolates nature, "What are left out, of course, are human beings as connected to nature, not only as appreciators but also as destroyers" (150).

By glorifying the western landscape as an untouched beauty to be appreciated, Redford films reflect and reinforce an anthropocentric rather than an ecocentric perspective. The films nostalgically set the western lifestyle apart from the hyper-driven, fast-paced urban life. In *The Horse Whisperer*, for instance, Annie's fast-track New York City urban existence is portrayed in stark contrast to the more mellow and simple "natural" rhythms of the Montana cowboy life. While viewers are clearly meant to identify with the latter, the two lifestyles remain neatly distinct as Annie returns to her New York life and family at the end of the film. By setting them as opposites, the film fails to interrogate how the two are interconnected; how, in effect, a consumption-driven lifestyle might threaten the ecosystems on which that very lifestyle depends. It perpetuates a perception of the West as a pristine yet rugged landscape that idealizes a simpler way of life, but one that, as scholar Mei Mei Evans suggests, is most readily available to heterosexual white men.

Indeed, women and people of color are often conflated with the land and perceived as closer to nature, and thus in need of being tamed, domesticated, and controlled; as such, they are not given access, as heterosexual white men are, to the mythic West as a site in which to test their identity (Evans 184). In a scene from *A River Runs Through It,* for example, the shot pans acres of trees, canyons, and rivers; on the soundtrack, Norman MacLean's voice-over praises the beauty of the Montana landscape and recounts the challenges of entering the forest firefighting team, an activity that both helped define his masculinity and allowed him to help tame nature at those moments when "she" became unruly.

In another shot, the two MacLean brothers and the father are shown fly-fishing in the Blackfoot River. While Norman struggles to recapture his fishing skills after having spent time in the East attending college, Pitt's character elevates fishing into an art as he lets his line caress the surface of the water, like a lover and an artist. As his fishing line strokes the surface of the river, nature is gendered feminine and passive, as scholar Gillian Rose theorized in another context, while the camera aligns viewers with this feminization of the river. In this scene the water lies still, in wait of Paul's artistic touch; Paul is portrayed as deeply connected to nature while also able to master it. The shot emphasizes the beautiful light on slow-moving water, stunning mountains on the horizon, and tree-lined shores. The bird's-eye views and high camera angles encourage viewers to inhabit the "master of all I survey" gaze, enacting Mary Louise Pratt's notion of an "imperial eye." As they swoop from above and survey the landscape from a distance, these shots construct a relationship between the spectator and the landscape that fails to locate the viewer as a part of the ecosystem.

The Horse Whisperer makes this issue more evident. One scene shows Annie on her first visit to the Booker ranch, following a hastily sketched map on the back of a postcard. As she rounds the bend in her vehicle, she faces a stunning panoramic shot of the Rockies, still and uninhabited, but stormy with winter clouds. This shot further reinforces the tension between a connection with the landscape (although still a voyeuristic one) and the imperial gaze. The scene alternates between point-of-view shots of mountain vistas through Annie's gaze from inside the vehicle and shots from above and behind the vehicle that position her as traversing nature. The scene shows Annie moving into the natural scenery, gendering the landscape as feminine by blending the woman with the natural space.

Later in the film, when Annie and Tom are riding horses in the mountains, the camera sweeps the terrain until the two riders stop and sit overlooking a canyon. The camera shot features another high-angle glimpse of the quiet, untouched mountain scenery, swirling with storm clouds. The dialogue accompanying these images centers on finding peace in knowing one's role in the world, something that Annie imagines the Booker family has out West and she lacks back East; the implication is that solace and a clear sense of identity can be found in the western land. The film's status as a major motion picture with Redford's star persona as actor and director lends credibility to this claim. These shots, however, once again construct an agrarian landscape that is sharply juxtaposed with the fast-paced technological life that Annie leads in New York (Brown 283), without suggesting any of the interconnectedness of the different ways of life, or their implications for the environment.

Moreover, just as women have been objectified through the filmic male gaze, as feminist film scholar Laura Mulvey theorized, the landscape is here reduced to scenery, rather than a living ecosystem. According to Mulvey, faced with this objectification, the white woman spectator has either to align herself with the patriarchal filmic gaze or to actively resist it (Mulvey 62–65). Similarly, either Annie must learn to view nature as Tom Booker does, or she must be purged from the landscape.

REPRESENTING SPACE AS GENDERED AND RACIALIZED

Edward Soja and Henri Lefebvre have theorized that our perceptions and experiences of space and time are cultural constructions that also shape the social relations of the people who inhabit this space. Feminist cultural geographers, such as Linda McDowell, Doreen Massey, Daphne Spain, and Gillian Rose, have analyzed how cultural constructions of space also shape gender identities. Spatial constructs inform gender relations, as particular spaces, such as the home, are gendered feminine while others have historically remained unavailable to women. Moreover, spatial constructs reflect and produce gendered and raced relations, as individuals learn how to interact with each other in particular ways. Visual culture plays a key role in shaping our understandings of spatial constructs and gender and racial identities; thus, cinematic portrayals, in terms of both content and production elements, help shape our relationships to nature.

Visual culture has the power to transcend space and at the same time inform our perceptions of space. If viewers' primary relationship to the western landscape is mainly cinematic, films can work to alienate us from nature. As Willoquet-Maricondi notes in the introduction to this volume, the camera becomes the filter that shapes our perceptions and relations to land. Feature films offer the possibility of artistic and emotional experiences, often with a suspension of disbelief and an escape into the narrative. That emotional connection is useful in environmental movements, but it has its limitations if it doesn't also create a sense of interconnectedness and responsibility. In the case of the myth of a pristine, wild, and untamed West, these portrayals have important implications, particularly if we understand the function of space in helping shape gender and race relations. If our relationship to space is socially constructed, then how Hollywood films construct the spectators' relationship to the land can reveal how gender and racial ideologies are maintained, in part, by perpetuating a colonizing relationship with the land.

Both Redford films present aesthetically appealing images of the Western environment in ways that reinscribe the ideological role of the American West in our national consciousness. This relationship pervades the American western genre; it is deeply engrained in our national consciousness and is imbued with violence (Slotkin 1–28; Carmichael 1–19). Indeed, as Evans points out in her article, " 'Nature' and Environmental Justice," these representations of nature construct an ideological paradigm of the "natural" that shores up white heterosexual masculinity in its colonizing relation to the land and, by extension, reveals who is and who is not authorized to inhabit that space. Evans writes,

> This ideological paradigm creates a representational paradigm whereby heterosexual white manhood (i.e. "real men") is construed as the most "natural" social identity in the United States: the "true American," *the* identity most deserving of social privilege. . . . Those who have been socially constructed as Other (i.e. not white, and/or not straight and/or not male) are viewed as intruders or otherwise out of place when they venture into or attempt to inhabit Nature. (183, emphasis in original)

This ideological perception defines the land as wild and dangerous, marking it as the purview of heterosexual white men to tame and possess. The tamer controls the land, which is now fetishized as an object of beauty, gendered, and racialized. The gendered and racialized portrayal of nature informs how women and people of color are situated in the films. Both films help perpetuate the subordination of women and the exoticization and marginalization of communities of color. In doing so, they also reproduce the exclusionary aspects of mainstream western environmentalism as a social movement. To reshape the environmental movement is hardly the films' rhetorical purpose, but given their widespread exposure and popularity, they invite questions about the productivity of certain strategies.

In *A River Runs Through It,* the mother in the MacLean family is relegated to the margins of this patriarchal world; while she cooks, cleans, and expresses her need for love from her sons, her authority and presence are consistently displaced. The most notable scene in which this occurs takes place in the family kitchen where the two brothers are fighting over a dangerous canoe ride on the rapids that Paul has pressured his younger, terrified brother to undertake. This scene exemplifies the tension that exists between the two brothers and the forms of patriarchal masculinity that they each represent.

Paul is the wild renegade who revels in shocking the white middle-class Presbyterian community in which he lives, while simultaneously being deeply connected to the Montana landscape through fly-fishing. Norman is the upstanding scholar who is shown repeatedly recoiling from Paul's rebellious risk-taking. Norman embodies the moral values of his father, fulfilling his expected role as professor and husband, while Paul embodies the values of the wild, rugged West. While Norman is pressured into participating in the canoe ride out of fear of disappointing his brother, the shot following their ride on the rapids shows him reacting negatively to Paul's rowdy celebrations with a look of resentment and fear.

The prodigal son, the attractive-looking but uncontrollable Paul, will ultimately die so that his legacy as a rebel might remain untouched while Norman's more "proper" masculinity is reinscribed. The film thus ushers in a new form of masculinity that validates Norman's role as a husband and an urban-dwelling professor, but it also keeps alive the myth that Paul's life embodies. The film thus suggests that the form of masculinity that Norman embodies is the one that is required in contemporary society, but that it is founded upon the myth of the wild West that Paul embodies. Both forms of masculinity, however, are formed in relation to a feminized and domesticated nature.

When the long-standing rivalry between these two versions of mas-

culinity explodes into a fistfight, the mother tries to intervene by step-
ping between them but falls before she can separate them. After a telling
pause during which the boys do not bother to help the mother up, they
resume fighting, accusing each other of causing the mother's fall. To
stop the fight, the mother insists that she slipped, and puts her bent
glasses back on. The matronly martyrdom she displays, combined with
the preeminence of the masculine bravado overriding any expressions
of concern for their mother, reveals just how patriarchal this environment is. The focus of the scene remains on the fight between the two
boys and the mother's inability to control them. The fight erupts because
of a test of the two brothers' masculinity in running the rapids, illustrat-
ing the tension between Paul's rugged impulse to test himself against a
nature he must conquer, and Norman's reluctant participation in a role
to which he will never fully measure up. The mother remains marginalized, useful only as a means through which the boys prove their dominance and masculinity.

As Annette Kolodny points out, there is a long tradition of portraying
nature as a feminine wilderness in need of taming; for a man to do so is
to develop his masculine identity. This scene, paired with several other
instances in the film in which the mother is portrayed as maternally
invasive, passive, and ineffectual, helps link all that is feminine with the
threat of emasculation that must be overcome. The fight in the kitchen
becomes a continuation of the test on the rapids, so that the mother
comes to stand in for the river, further emphasizing the gendering of
nature. The fact that the boys continue fighting until she accepts full
blame for their fighting makes that link even clearer. The portrayal of
the land and the portrayal of the mother reflect the interconnected gender ideologies that reinscribe patriarchy as dominant over both.

The more disturbing portrayal of the woman's link to nature as a wild
"other" in need of taming occurs with the character of Mabel, Paul's
girlfriend. As a Native American woman, Mabel is clearly exoticized and
patronized through repeated comments about her wild hair and her
rebellious nature. The camera shots, coupled with her wardrobe and
behavior, portray her in a sexually objectifying way, in stark contrast
with Norman's more "proper," conservatively clothed white girlfriend,
Jessie. The scene where Paul and Mabel crash a white bar and insist on
being served shows them dancing in a public display that is meant to
unsettle the white onlookers; they are horrified by a white man dancing
in sexually suggestive ways with a Native American woman. The camera gives us a view of Mabel through Paul's own gaze of her dancing

sexually or passed out drunk. She has very little agency in the film, and we do not see the world through her eyes.

The clear contrast between her and Jessie, Norman's girlfriend, highlights the degree to which she is turned into an exotic object of attraction in the film. This scene is indicative of the very real racism in Montana at that historical moment. But Paul's motivations for bringing her to the bar are far less about battling racism than they are about building his masculine bravado and rebelliousness. She seems to be a token of his persona throughout the film.

Mabel's portrayal offers her character little agency or self-determination but sends very clear messages about who controls and who belongs in this western, "natural" space. The film's nostalgia for this time period and the matter-of-fact perpetuation of exoticized stereotypes of Native American women do little to further more equitable race relations in contemporary times.

Women in *The Horse Whisperer* are marginally better represented than those in *A River Runs Through It,* although it is also clear that certain kinds of behaviors in women are not appropriate in the West. *The Horse Whisperer* tells the tale of a young woman, Grace, and her horse, Pilgrim, who are seriously injured in a horse accident. The girl, her mother (Annie), and the horse travel to Montana to seek the help of a horse whisperer, Tom Booker (played by Redford), who will heal the horse physically and emotionally.

Annie, the main female protagonist, is the editor of a women's magazine based in New York. Repeated notice is made in the film about her direct, authoritative, and "aggressive" New Yorker behavior. Her editorial staff chaffs at her abrupt orders; her husband challenges her need to control everything; the veterinarian is frustrated that Annie refuses her suggestion to put the horse down; and the Booker family appears shocked at her sudden appearance at their ranch and at her presumption that Tom Booker will care for her horse.

This character's urban ways are shown to be out of place in Montana and in stark contrast to the rancher's wife, Diane Booker, who is shown to be warm, maternal, and able to handle ranch life and physical labor. Viewers are meant to like Diane, as she takes care of her family and of Grace, displaying a protective maternal domesticity that is lacking in Annie's "harsh" Eastern aggressiveness. Indeed, Diane Booker is ultimately the one who remains in the West with her family and ranch, while Annie returns to her life in the East, leaving Tom Booker heartbroken.

It is telling, of course, that the West is used as a recuperative space that is no longer needed once Annie and her heterosexual white family are healed. For Annie, the West becomes an escape mechanism whereby the reality of her marital problems can be avoided, while the retreat to the ranch allows her daughter and the horse to recover from their psychological and physical traumas. It is an admirable space where a close and caring family takes in strangers to help them heal. But it is also a place where nature straddles a fine line between threatening and domesticated, as rugged storms blow in over the mountains and fences are neatly built. Once Annie decides to return to being a wife and mother, rather than break up the family and stay with Tom Booker, the West has served its re-domesticating role and is no longer needed. Rather than instilling a sense of responsibility for human impact on the land, the film's narrative reinforces the idea that the West and its landscapes are available to be used for meeting the needs and pleasures of humans.

Whereas the feminist cultural geographer Joanne Sharpe argues that women's bodies often become symbolic of the nation state, or a part of the national identity, even as they are denied agency, in these films the West has only a passing need of women or people of color. Women and people of color are used to shore up national identity, but they are also often denied a voice in shaping that identity or what is done in its name. Similarly to A River Runs Through It, The Horse Whisperer centers on white characters and promotes patriarchal values. While there are a couple of characters of color in the New York magazine office where the female protagonist works, they play minor roles. One of the more explicit references to people of color occurs in a story Tom Booker tells Grace about a boyhood friend of his from the Blackfeet Nation who hit his head on a rock while swimming and incurred serious damage. The story, which is meant to encourage Grace to address her psychological trauma in response to the horse riding accident and the death of her best friend, is a tale of a young damaged man from the Blackfeet Nation who "disappears" emotionally and psychologically from this western world. He is not shown visually in the film, and thus is not physically present to the audience, being represented only through the words of a white character. Once again, only certain parts of the U.S. western landscape and myth are portrayed and idealized, thus rendering invisible the hostile race relations and the lived reality of many people of color in the West, which are rarely as idyllic.

Given how formative the mythic West has been in the construction of American national identity, the role of women in that myth is significant. Both Redford films make clear that this construction of the western landscape is the purview of white heterosexual males, revealing the cultural ideologies that inform the claiming of land as a commodity to be owned and consumed. White women and women and men of color are integral parts of this national ideology as they are aligned with nature, but they are ultimately marginalized and purged as patriarchal masculinities are upheld.

DISRUPTING THE CONSUMING GAZE

Of course, there is nothing inherently problematic in suggesting that finding a connection to nature can create a sense of peace and clarity. Indeed, feature films such as these, with the prominence of Redford's name and talent, offer the possibilities of connecting with the mystery and beauty of western space in ways that can fuel the environmental drive to preserve that land. But the nostalgia with which the West is portrayed in these films also serves the larger purpose of positioning the spectator in a dominating and consuming relationship with the landscape, instead of locating humans as part of a larger ecosystem. The ideological implications of this portrayal become clearer when it is juxtaposed with the portrayal of the environment in environmental justice documentaries. Documentaries that examine the policy decisions and economic disparities of environmental hazards, and the communities that are most affected by them, confront viewers with a different relationship to nature by demanding accountability to both people and ecosystems. The genre serves different functions than feature films and therefore offers productive insights into the relative efficacy of alternative visual strategies for environmental movements.

The environmental justice documentaries *Toxic Racism* and *Drumbeat for Mother Earth* put in evidence the power relations that make certain communities, particularly poor communities of color, vulnerable to toxicity. Both films foreground the racial, gender, and economic power dynamics that infuse relationships between human beings and nature. They illustrate that communities can have a harmful or a beneficial effect upon the land, thereby creating the sense of interconnectedness and responsibility that the two Redford films lack. These documentaries illustrate how local residents are mobilized into protecting themselves and their neighbors when they are faced with unjust exposure to health contaminants. The choice of images and camera angles in these documentaries are much less celebratory of the landscape as a spectacle to be enjoyed from a distance; instead, they serve to implicate viewers in the issues portrayed in the films and force us to reflect on our own relationship to the land and to the communities affected by the issues.

Because they present communities that have become activist out of necessity, and because they tend to reveal the far-reaching nature of environmental justice issues, these documentaries challenge viewers to interrogate our own roles in creating or redressing environmental damage. They thus demonstrate the kind of "ecojustice pedagogy" that this volume calls for.

Both documentaries reflect the basic principles of environmental justice, including redefining the concept of environment so as to include both urban and wilderness spaces; taking responsibility for the health and preservation of the land; and undertaking a structural analysis of the racial and class dimensions of environmental degradation. Environmental justice scholars such as Robert Bullard and Vandana Shiva have theorized the sociopolitical hierarchies, both nationally and internationally, that place a disproportionate burden on the world's poor, particularly poor communities of color. *Toxic Racism* and *Drumbeat for Mother Earth* trace the linkages between the marginalization of certain communities and their exposure to toxic hazards. In doing so, they highlight the structural inequalities that make some communities bear the brunt of environmental degradation. They also reveal that cultural inequality, as Homi Bhabha notes, is not a natural and inevitable power dynamic, but a socially constructed one; it can take us out of ourselves in ways that alter how we relate to the environment as the borders are displaced and redefined. Bhabha is referring primarily to the ways that marginalized counternarratives are embedded within ideologies about western national identity. This western identity, which has defined itself against those "Others," is then radically destabilized when marginalized people and their histories are revealed as internal to it.

In *A River Runs Through It,* as we have seen, Mabel's character illustrates the racialized exoticization of women of color that pervades much of mythic western ideology. She is constructed as an "Other" who does not have a voice but whose sexuality and nonconformity to Presbyterian morals become a tool for Paul's rebellion. However, far from being something external to the mythic West, her otherness is an inherent part of the myth; while she must be purged from the myth, as must Paul, her presence is necessary to justify it: she must be tamed, as must unruly nature, in order for Norman's more "proper" patriarchal masculinity to succeed.

The environmental justice documentaries discussed here present a counternarrative to this hegemonic view of women and land, and of viewers' relationship to them, thereby encouraging us to cultivate a more responsible sense of our connectedness with the environment.

These documentaries place women and people of color at the forefront of the fight to protect their communities, including the natural environment on which they depend. These films portray the resident activists as citizens who are well informed about the environmental hazards that affect their community, thereby positioning them, rather than scientists, as "experts." As environmental justice scholar Giovanna Di Chiro points out, women of color tend to be leaders in the environmental justice movement because their socially constructed gender roles as mothers and caretakers place them closest to the issues. They are often the ones best positioned to see the effects of the hazards because they are the ones most likely to bear the brunt of them. By featuring the strength, knowledge, and community-organizing skills of these activists, the two documentaries present a much more empowering picture of women and communities of color, and a much more mutually enriching relationship between humans and the environments in which they live.

Toxic Racism examines the effects of toxic dumping, large-scale hog farming, and lead poisoning on three communities. The racial and economic makeup of the communities makes them particularly vulnerable to environmental hazards and contamination. In each community, local residents challenge the corporations and governmental officials responsible for the decisions to dispose of hazardous materials in their community without adequate input from residents. The documentary presents a structural analysis of the racial and economic disparities that place a disproportionate burden on marginalized communities.

Drumbeat for Mother Earth tells a similar tale of exclusion from key decision-making processes by focusing on several Native American Nations that have been exposed to persistent organic pollutants. Citing the pollution of waterways, land, fish, and caribou in these communities, Native activists argue that current environmental practices are a contemporary form of cultural genocide; not only are people becoming ill from exposure to polluting chemicals but the contamination of land and waterways is also harming traditional practices, such as hunting, fishing, and canoeing, that are central to their respective Native cultures.

In Toxic Racism, the camera shots bring viewers close to the unattractive and dangerous environmental sites by giving us close-ups of contaminated streams and cesspools, animal pens jammed with squealing pigs, and deserted urban blocks and projects filled with lead paint hazards. The camera angles in these shots do not provide idealized sweeping vistas; instead, they bring the viewer uncomfortably close to unattractive sights as they hone in on landscapes damaged by toxins and inhabited by people who often have little option to relocate. In these shots, viewers are not removed from the land, enjoying it at a safe distance from above, but rather are closely implicated in the environmental degradation. If, as Chandra Talpade Mohanty and Biddy Martin suggest, perceptions of reality and the relationship between one's identity and one's relationship to space is shifting, contextual, and fluid, then forcing viewers to experience those shifts through camera angles that bring us face-to-face with environmental degradation can prove productive (165).

Similarly, the camera angles in *Drumbeat for Mother Earth* bring viewers face-to-face with the consequences of persistent organic pollutants on Native communities. While *Drumbeat* does include sweeping high angle shots, these shots depict grazing caribou and water contaminated by corporate plants. Viewers, therefore, cannot so easily "consume" the landscape as idyllic because the underlying pollution is revealed. The nostalgic beauty that might have been portrayed, as in Redford's films, is disrupted by the documentary's discussion of the threats facing the land and the communities that inhabit it.

Indeed, both *Toxic Racism* and *Drumbeat* depict the land as a vibrant, complex ecosystem, as local activists insist on the need for a responsible and ethical treatment of the land. By juxtaposing shots of natural features, animals, and people, the documentaries reveal the interconnection between the three, highlighting how the health of all living beings in ecosystems is affected by environmental toxins. These toxins ripple through particular communities made vulnerable by economic, gender, and racial politics. Indeed, *Drumbeat* highlights the central role of the environment—including caribou, water, air, and fish—in indigenous cultural identities: they are not simply "natural resources" to be consumed; they are also sacred, both because they are part of the Earth and because native cultural practices and beliefs have developed from fishing, canoeing, and hunting caribou in these lands.

Thus, the portrayal of the land in this documentary renders visible a point that is neatly obscured by the gendered and racialized imperial gaze of the Redford films: that the destruction of ecosystems is, for Native peoples, an extension of the historical genocide they have suffered. While some of this revelation can be attributed to the difference in rhetorical and aesthetic conventions between feature films and documentaries, not all of it can; it is revealing that we do not see feature films offering a moving fictional account of the effects of these toxins on Native communities. Such films can be made, but they rarely find Hollywood support. It is telling, then, that many of the activist leaders in this documentary are Native women who are depicted in significantly different ways than Mabel in *A River Runs Through It*. The women in *Drumbeat* present the kinds of counternarratives mentioned earlier that reveal how the oppression of land and people have allowed the western myth to flourish. The structural link the documentaries draw between the historical and contemporary genocides of Native communities and cultures renders unavoidable a confrontation with the violence such environmental hazards enact.

Moreover, the two documentaries address issues of identity in very different ways than the Redford films. In the latter, masculine identity is shored up through the domination and domestication of nature; both white women and women of color, in different ways, are aligned with the feminine landscape that must be tamed as a threat to patriarchal order. The documentaries, on the other hand, link the racial and economic identities of affected communities to the environmental degradation they experience. They reveal how institutional racism has historically robbed people of color of economic wealth and the freedom to make decisions over their lives and communities. Consequently, both documentaries demand an analysis of how racial and economic conditions determine who is most affected by environmental hazards.

These environmental justice documentaries implicate viewers in a vexed relationship to the environment, troubling the nostalgic view perpetuated by the Redford films. In doing so, these films demand an accountability on the part of viewers for the environmental degradation the films depict and to the communities that experience that toxicity.

WORKS CITED

Adamson, Joni, Mei Mei Evans, and Rachel Stein, eds. *The Environmental Justice Reader: Politics, Poetics, and Pedagogy.* Tucson: Univ. of Arizona Press, 2002.

Bhabha, Homi. *The Location of Culture.* New York: Routledge, 1995.

Brown, Timothy J. "Deconstructing the Dialectical Tensions in the Horse Whisperer: How Myths Represent Competing Cultural Values." *Journal of Popular Culture* 38.2 (2004): 274–95.

Bullard, Robert, ed. *Confronting Environmental Racism: Voices from the Grassroots.* Boston: South End Press, 1993.

——. *Unequal Protection: Environmental Justice and Communities of Color.* San Francisco: Sierra Club, 1994.

Carmichael, Deborah A., ed. *The Landscape of Hollywood Westerns: Ecocriticism in an American Film Genre.* Salt Lake City: Univ. of Utah Press, 2006.

Drumbeat for Mother Earth. Dir. Joseph Di Gangi and Amon Giebel. Prod. Joseph Di Gangi, Amon Giebel, Tom Goldtooth, and Jackie Warledo for Greenpeace and Indigenous Environmental Network. Bullfrog Films, 1999.

Evans, Mei Mei. " 'Nature' and Environmental Justice." *The Environmental Justice*

Reader: Politics, Poetics, and Pedagogy. Ed. Joni Adamson, Mei Mei Evans, and Rachel Stein. Tucson: Univ. of Arizona Press, 2002. 181–93.

hooks, bell. "The Oppositional Gaze: Black Feminist Spectators." *Feminist Film Theory: A Reader*. Ed. Sue Thornham. New York: Routledge, 1999. 307–20.

The Horse Whisperer. Dir. Robert Redford. Touchstone Pictures, 1998.

Kolodny, Annette. *Lay of the Land: Metaphor and Experience in American Life and Letters*. Univ. of North Carolina Press, 1984.

Lefebvre, Henri. *The Production of Space*. Trans. Donald Nicholson-Smith. Cambridge, MA: Blackwell, 1991.

Massey, Doreen. *Space, Place, and Gender*. Minneapolis: Univ. of Minnesota Press, 1994.

McDowell, Linda. *Gender, Identity, and Place: Understanding Feminist Geographies*. Minneapolis: Univ. of Minnesota Press, 1999.

Mohanty, Chandra Talpade, and Biddy Martin. "Feminist Politics: What's Home Got to Do with It?" *Femininity Played Straight: The Significance of Being a Lesbian*. New York: Routledge, 1996. 163–84.

Mulvey, Laura. "Visual Pleasure and Narrative Cinema." *Feminist Film Theory: A Reader*. Ed. Sue Thornham. New York: Routledge, 1999. 58–69.

Pratt, Mary Louise. *Imperial Eyes*. New York: Routledge, 1992.

Reed, T. V. "Toward an Environmental Justice Ecocriticism." *The Environmental Justice Reader: Politics, Poetics, Pedagogy*. Ed. Joni Adamson, Mei Mei Evans, and Rachel Stein. Tucson: Univ. of Arizona Press, 2002. 145–62.

A River Runs Through It. Dir. Robert Redford. Sony Pictures, 1992.

Rose, Gillian. "As If the Mirrors Had Bled: Masculine Dwelling and Masculinized Theory, and Feminist Masquerade." *Bodyspace: Destabilizing Geographies of Gender and Sexuality*. Ed. Nancy Duncan. New York: Routledge, 1996. 45–55.

Slotkin, Richard. *Gunfighter Nation: The Myth of the Frontier in Twentieth-Century America*. Norman: Univ. of Oklahoma Press, 1998.

Soja, Edward. *Thirdspace: Journeys to Los Angeles and Other Real-and-Imagined Places*. Cambridge, MA: Blackwell, 1996.

Spain, Daphne. *Gendered Spaces*. Chapel Hill: Univ. of North Carolina Press, 1992.

Toxic Racism. Dir. Kate Raisz. Prod. Laurie Donnelly. PBS by WGBH Boston, 1994.

PART III

POSITIONING ECOSYSTEMS IN FICTION, DOCUMENTARY, AND ANIMATION

THE LANDSCAPE'S LIE
CLASS, ECONOMY,
AND ECOLOGY IN
HOTEL RWANDA

HARRI KILPI

In 1988 Western cinema audiences were treated to a small spectacle of primatologist Dian Fossey (played by Sigourney Weaver) hectoring a Rwandan government official in *Gorillas in the Mist*. After being told that protecting the gorilla sanctuaries and other park lands is expensive, she retorts, "That's your problem: make new laws, raise taxes, but give *my* gorillas the protection they are entitled to" (my emphasis). Although the film provides us with a fleeting glimpse into the problems of the local human population—the official contrasts the decreasing number of gorillas and the increasing number of people—it is mostly preoccupied with its American heroine. The gorillas depicted in the film are, as David Ingram notes, "idealized figures possessing the redemptive innocence typical of the Hollywood wild animal movie" (135–36), while misty mountainscapes of northwestern Rwanda are portrayed as paradisiacal, pristine spectacles of unspoiled nature, places that are, in Fossey's words, "as close to God as you can get."

Yet, already during the time of the film's shooting, the Rwandan people inhabiting and living off similar nearby landscapes were plagued by constantly increasing population, chronic land disputes, famines, a growing AIDS epidemic, border warfare, and a corrupt dictatorial government. All these features would not only put mountain gorillas in danger but also feed into the horrific genocidal pogrom of 1994, mostly against the Tutsi minority of the population, that left nearly one million people dead in the space of just 100 days (Diamond 313).

Although eyewitness testimonials, reports issued by nongovernmental organizations, autobiographical accounts, academic articles, and novels have been published in steady stream, ten years on, *Hotel Rwanda* (2004) remains the only widely circulated film about the Rwandan disaster.[1] Based on true events, the film recounts the story of Paul

Rusesabagina, a hotel manager in the capital, Kigali, who bribes and plots his way through the bloodbath and saves the lives of over a thousand people huddling in his hotel.

In this essay I want to investigate how this film portrays and explains the events of 1994. My approach is an ecocritical one in that it focuses on the representations (or lack thereof) of nature, ecology, and land-related economic issues in *Hotel Rwanda,* and on how they are used or not used in the process of comprehending the genocide.[2] I will focus on ecological and economic accounts of the conflict in order to form a composite framework of history, economics, and nature against which the film can be assessed. I argue that *Hotel Rwanda* deploys a set of relatively conventional rhetorical devices used by Hollywood in its depictions of war, atrocities, and Africa. As a result the proper representation of ecological and economic causes of the conflict are left undeveloped. The analysis shows how the film's anthropocentric and individualistic discourse obscures or at least hinders a more complete understanding of a conflict that has its roots in the region's environmental problems and specificities.

Two important caveats are in order. First, my ecocritical approach does not seek to replace the argument that "this genocide resulted from the deliberate choice of a modern elite to foster hatred and fear to keep itself in power" (Human Rights Watch 1–2). While I acknowledge this view as correct, I also believe, following Jared Diamond, that other causes contributed to these events as well (318). In the case of *Hotel Rwanda,* an ecocritical reading can bring those causes and the absence of their portrayal back to the spotlight. Secondly, to focus on the macro levels of ecology and economy is not to absolve individual agents of responsibility, neither is it to sympathize with them as helplessly predetermined victims of cruel circumstances. It is to examine the larger causal framework that might have created a fertile ground for the agitators and that might help explain the genocide's unforeseen ferocity. Since *Hotel Rwanda* presents, at least so far, a rare and widely distributed representation of the genocide within the popular culture, it lends itself to critical inquiry in these terms. I will therefore start by showing why one might argue that the film has a special claim to truth and remembrance—how it seeks both dramatic and informational impact on its audiences—and is thus liable to the reading proposed above. I will then outline the factual background to the genocide and situate the film's story in this context. The bulk of the essay will analyze *Hotel Rwanda* in terms of its representation of the genocide and its perpetrators, its dominant places and characters, and the sense of normality it creates through these components. All these themes are related to the real-world environmental, ecological, and historical framework of Rwandan society. How the film does or does not make these connections, and what these choices signify for the critical portrayal of the genocide, form the key points of my analysis.

HOTEL RWANDA'S CLAIM TO TRUTH

Some might object to this venture simply because *Hotel Rwanda* happens to be a film. It is "just" entertainment. However, entertainment products do carry important and deconstructable ideological messages that rely on, mediate, and rework the *doxa*, or the generally held beliefs of their audiences, whether they be about race, class, gender, society, or nature.

Hotel Rwanda, especially, cannot be let off the hook of ideological critique for four reasons. First, rather than being "just" entertainment, the film is based on the recent history and true events of exceptional violence and poignancy that give it an inherent call for seriousness. Accordingly, *Hotel Rwanda* bears all the hallmarks of a serious art house film: the brand image of the ascending independent company Lions Gate Films; realist aesthetics; repertoire actors with award potential; relatively modest production values; slow, platformed release planned to coincide and peak with the post-Christmas festival season and, in this case, with the tenth anniversary of the genocide.[3] Therefore, the assumptions of seriousness and "high quality" (implying also epistemological reliability) underpin its making and its intended reception.

Second, since one of the most conspicuous aspects of the Rwandan crisis was the willful negligence of the international community and the continued ignorance of Western audiences, there seems to have been an implied need to address these facts by recounting some of the events that really took place behind these epistemological smoke screens. The promotion of *Hotel Rwanda* takes up these facts and makes them and the veracity of their portrayal the central themes framing the film's critical and consumer reception. The opening screens on the film's official Web site state that "when a country descended into madness and the world closed its eyes he [Paul] opened his arms and created a place where hope could survive. Hotel Rwanda: A True Story." Director Terry George notes that this "was a story that had to be told, a story that would take cinemagoers around the world inside *an event that, to all our great shame, we knew nothing about.* But more than that, it would allow audiences to join in the love, the loss, the fear and the courage of a man who could have been any of us—if we ever could find that courage" (my emphasis).[4]

Thus, a keen passion for reminding and educating audiences about what happened, to produce a real impact on audiences' ideas and attitudes about the Rwandan conflict, was among the driving themes of the film and its promotion. It is therefore not surprising that, third, the promotion was explicitly extended to the educational level with the Teacher's Guide designed to "engage students with activities and lessons." While the tradition of teaching guides accompanying entertainment films goes back at least to the 1950s, in this case it boosts an already powerful claim for truthfulness and credible representation of the past, and elevates the film to the position of authority of a bona fide historical commentary accurate enough to be used for didactic purposes. Like all other historical accounts, *Hotel Rwanda*'s arguments and representations of the nature and the history of the genocide thus become liable for peer review and criticism.

Finally, meta-statistical evidence on *Hotel Rwanda*'s reception in the press indicates that the film was nearly universally acclaimed by the critics.[5] For example, Roger Ebert of the *Chicago Sun-Times* called it a "riveting drama"; the *New Yorker*'s David Denby could "hardly think of another movie in which sheer intelligence and decency have been made to seem so attractive or effective"; *Newsweek*'s David Ansen admitted that "ultimately, one's reservations are overwhelmed by the story's urgency; it's impossible not to be shattered"; while *Empire*'s Dan Joli concluded that "it's a weighty message movie, but it's a message worth delivering." Neatly confirming the arguments I have made above about the film's nature and educational motives, Mick LaSalle of the *San Francisco Chronicle* indicated that *Hotel Rwanda* is "important, in that it *documents* for a mass audience what it [the genocide] was like. It's useful, in that it *shows how it can happen*" (my emphasis).

This reception increases the film's prestige and can create an image of added credibility around the claims made in the film and its promotion. This, in turn, raises the question of how well deserved that image really is. Together, these four reasons present a powerful case for interrogating *Hotel Rwanda* in terms of its ecological and historical representations and call forth the following questions: How and what are we taught to know about the genocide? How do the conventions of Hollywood storytelling bias this knowledge and learning? What is emphasized and what is bypassed in the portrayal and explanation of the events? What kind of impact does it have on knowledge and attitudes about the conflict and its causes?

Before addressing these questions, it is useful to recall some of the events that immediately preceded the genocide. Since the space does not allow for a longer historical perspective, I will limit my references to its various key moments as they emerge during the discussion of the film's key themes below.

Taking advantage of Rwanda's increasing economic, social, and political turmoil in the late 1980s and the early 1990s, the Tutsis, exiled in Uganda and Burundi, and organized as the Rwandan Patriotic Front (RPF), renewed their guerrilla attacks on their home country in 1990. The former Hutu general and the dictatorial leader of the country since 1973, Juvenal Habyarimana, retaliated by ordering summary pogroms of the Rwandan Tutsi communities, and a sporadic civil war ensued. On top of the already existing economic hardships, the countryside was terrorized and many people were displaced into settlement camps. However, in August 1993 Habyarimana and the RPF agreed to a fragile ceasefire, followed by the Arusha Peace Agreement, which called for power sharing. At the same time, a 2,000-strong UN peacekeeping force, UNAMIR (the United Nations Assistance Mission in Rwanda), was dispatched to Rwanda under the leadership of Canadian general Romeo Dallaire.

Opposing the peace process, the Hutu extremists in the government and military continued to demand harsher measures against the "Tutsi invasion," and although Habyarimana did not implement the articles of the treaty, the proponents of Hutu Power saw his policy as appeasement and treachery, and instigated his assassination on April 6, 1994. The murder was, of course, pinned on the Tutsis and was used as a signal to launch a meticulously preplanned extermination campaign, first in the capital Kigali and then in the whole country.

Dallaire, who had known about these plans for at least three months in advance, was consistently given orders not to intervene (see *Shake Hands with the Devil*; Human Rights Watch 18–19). The international community was evacuated from the country, but any opportunity of quick containment of the violence having been lost in the bureaucracy of the Western states and the UN, mass killings in Rwanda continued unabated. In three months, 800,000 to 1 million people, or over 10 percent of the population, were killed in what was finally being acknowledged in the West as a genocide. The slaughter ended only with the advancement and the final victory of the RPF (July 18, 1994), which in turn dislodged two million people, mostly Hutus, fleeing the Tutsi army in fear of reprisal killings. These people ended up in the massive refugee camps on the Congolese and Tanzanian borders, whose thronged conditions riddled with volcanic smoke produced some of the iconic images of the conflict, such as those taken by photojournalist Sebastião Salgado (168–223; Diamond 315–17). Less well known was the fact that these camps ended up accommodating many militia members and other culprits of the genocide, becoming bases for guerrilla activity across the border (Gourevitch chap. 1).

MARGINAL IMAGES OF A MAD, ELEMENTAL FORCE: REPRESENTING THE GENOCIDE AND ITS CAUSES

Hotel Rwanda is mainly set in the Hotel des Mille Collines, situated in a wealthy suburb of Kigali. The story starts in late March 1994 and with the first signs of the coming atrocities. Paul, the black manager of the hotel, feels safe, as the UN seems to be set for protecting the site as the refuge of the capital's Western community. A few days after Habyarimana's assassination, however, the UN withdraws and leaves Paul to his own devices. He calls in all favors, uses all the connections he has, and bribes and negotiates away the waves of aggressive militiamen bent on "cleaning the hotel" from "cockroaches." He manages to save around one thousand people from the slaughter and finally gets his own family to safety in a refugee camp in the Tanzanian border.

The opening credits of *Hotel Rwanda* are seen against a featureless black background. At the same time, on the soundtrack, radio channels and static keep changing until they settle on "RTLM, Hutu Power Radio," pouring forth blatant anti-Tutsi propaganda. This discourse, which comes with no historical explanations or intertitles, becomes the first explanatory framework for the genocide and is reproduced many times in the course of the film. During the first few sequences, the propaganda is connected to Paul's business associate, George Rutaganda, preparatory Hutu rallies, and *interahamwe* militia and their colorful uniforms.

This set of features will define the perpetrators and the procession of genocide for the rest of the film: the killers are frequently incited to action by the radio messages, they are clearly distinguished from the hotel's inhabitants and other people by their military or militia uniforms, and, apart from Rutaganda and General Bizimungu, they are usually seen as unindividuated and herdlike mobs. The violence and massacres they visit on their victims are limited to a handful of very short or mediated scenes. For instance, the daylight carnage is seen only once as a shaken Western cameraman shows his footage to his producer and Paul. In another scene, as Paul's family leaves their home for the hotel, he tells his son not to look at the roadside lawns which are littered with corpses. Later, as Paul drives home after buying supplies, his car bumps into dozens of bodies, only just visible through the early morning mist.

This strategy of "tasteful," restricted portrayal of mass murder might have had a reasonable economic cause—the low amount of violence guaranteed a lower rating from the Motion Picture Association of America (MPAA) and therefore larger audiences—but, as I will argue later, it also contributes to a false sense of Westernized normality that can be found in the film. In any case, the ratings system and other structural reasons like it could be criticized for their propensity to sanitize the atrocious nature of any war.

Even if the atrocities had been depicted in their true horror, the representation of their background and culprits in *Hotel Rwanda* is also severely limited. RTLM (Radio Télévision Libre des Mille Collines) did fan the flames with its hate-mongering, and the *interahamwe* did carry out the first killings in many areas, especially in Kigali. However, the militias and the killings did not emerge from a black featureless void, nor did they constitute an elemental, weather-like force that pounds the hotel time and again in the film. By ignoring any background before the immediate events in April 1994 and forgoing a more complete depiction of the events, the film trivializes the full ecological framework of the genocide and thus limits its scope of impact on our understanding of the subject.

Perhaps most important, by singling out the *interahamwe* both in dialogue and in the images as the sole perpetrators, the film misses the ubiquity and the true scale of the genocide. This is because it was not just the militias and soldiers who carried out the murders, but huge chunks of the ordinary populace, from young teenagers to men in their sixties. As Mahmood Mamdani notes, "Though planned from above, [the genocide] was executed by sections of civilian population" (19). This fact leads to an uneasy question well formulated by Gil Courtemanche:

> Studiously, methodologically, coolly, a few hundred men were planning the elimination of a segment of humanity. . . . How could they believe, as did the Nazi leaders, that the majority of the population would follow and join this small number and agree not only to point the finger at suspect houses but also incite the rabble to kill their neighbours and comrades at work? How could they seriously believe that the people would agree to turn into killers by the thousands? Most of all, how could they have been so sure of it? (163–64)

As *Hotel Rwanda* seems to argue that only crazed militiamen carried out the rarely seen murders, there are only two occasions when explicit speculations are aired in an attempt to answer this question. When Paul tells about his experiences on the supply trip, his aide wonders, "Why are people so cruel?" to which Paul replies, "Hatred. Insanity." This answer again addresses only the most immediate state of affairs—the killers might well have been in some state of insanity when they did their deeds—but surely it cannot exhaust Courtemanche's question, which is also implied in the aide's wonderment. Although many people killed only under the threat of their own life, why was it that so many others joined the *interahamwe* in the first place, and in the impromptu killings, even without the militia membership (Mironko 163–64)?

In another, earlier scene a historical explanation is offered. A "local specialist" tells a Western cameraman that the Belgians started the Hutu Tutsi division. They canonized the alleged physical differences between the "tribes" and installed the Tutsis in power. But while they left after the decolonization process in the 1950s and the 1960s, they switched the power to the Hutus, who then embarked on reprisal massacres. "Am I telling the truth, Paul?" he asks at the end his half-a-minute lecture, and Paul replies, "Yes, unfortunately." Although this account contains true facts, such as the humiliating phrenological measurements of the native population, the claim that the Belgians created Hutus and Tutsis is not true (compare Burr; LaSalle). The precolonial Rwandans used this division in the early nineteenth century, while the Belgians later exploited and sharpened it by institutionalizing the differences and consolidating the power of one of the sides, the Tutsis, in a classic exercise of divide and conquer (see Mamdani 11). This distinction may appear as so much sophistry as far as the colonial victims are concerned, but it is an important one, as it will help outline the long-term ecological context of the conflict and explain the contemporary willingness to kill.

THE LAND AND ITS POPULATION:
THE CAUSAL FRAMEWORK MISSING FROM HOTEL RWANDA

Rwanda is situated in a high mountainous plateau with moderate rainfall and an altitude too high for malaria and tsetse flies. These geological circumstances allow for a larger population growth relative to Central and other African regions; as Diamond notes, the areas of Rwanda and Burundi were densely populated already before the arrival of the Europeans (319). This situation could also be seen as one of the main reasons calling for advanced administration, laws and customs of land ownership and inheritance, and the complex hierarchies that this entails. In the case of Rwanda, one of the basic outcomes was a class distinction between cattle-raising pastoralists and agriculturalists. The former were mostly Tutsis and formed the ruling aristocracy of the nascent Rwandan state, while the latter were, in Mamdani's words, "subject population" and mostly Hutus (9).

Despite the fact that there were few actual differences between these "tribes"—after all, they "spoke the same language, lived on the same hills, and had more or less the same culture"—the Belgian colonialists authorized the division with the powerful tenets of racist physical anthropology, and froze it into a caste-like structure for the purposes of governance (Mamdani 9, 11). Right from the start the Belgian rule, both in itself and through its Tutsi middlemen, was severe and bloody; when it was being dismantled during the decolonization process in the 1950s and the early 1960s, anti-Tutsi pogroms emerged, most notably in 1959 and 1963. These acts were finally legitimized by the Belgians, who, as their parting shot, installed Hutus into the leadership of independent Rwanda (Mamdani 11–5). The conflicts between the Hutu military and the Tutsi guerrillas organized in Uganda and Burundi continued with regular and bloody intervals during the 1970s and the 1980s, and maintained the culture of violence.

At the same time, thanks to fertile volcanic soils, New World cash crops such as coffee, Western medicine, improved public sector health care, and relatively stable foreign borders, the population continued to grow at an annual rate of 3.2 percent between 1960 and 1992. Yet at the same time the economy grew only relatively slowly in Rwanda and therefore, by the 1980s, Rwanda was one of the most densely populated areas in Africa and one of the twenty poorest and least developed countries in the world (Diamond 319).[6] For the subsistence of its numerous people, the whole country had been cultivated using mostly old-fashioned, relatively low-yielding methods. The national park lands were the only exception to this countrywide rule (André and Platteau 4, 6). Therefore, when cinemagoers saw Dian Fossey doing research on gorillas in the paradisiacal, preserved landscapes, in reality the people living just beyond the mist-shrouded horizon were on the verge of an ecocatastrophe due to overcultivation, deforestation, and soil erosion (Diamond 320). The ubiquity of fully gardened hillsides and banana plantations may have had the almost clichéd look of a biblical paradise to General Dallaire (see *Shake Hands with the Devil*), while in reality they were the indexes of ecologically unsustainable agricultural practices and a Malthusian population time-bomb about to blow up.

This situation is vividly illustrated by Catherine André and Jean-Phillippe Platteau's meticulous field research on land relations in a hill village in Gisenyi, northwestern Rwanda. The area was almost totally Hutu, which is why the racial hate-mongering against the Tutsis cannot account for the killings that affected this area as well (1–47). André and Platteau show how during 1988–93, as the area's already large and dense population kept growing, the hill and the village experienced rising inequality of land endowments and landlessness, increasing incidence of absolute poverty, a growing number of land disputes and litigation, and an increasing number of young thieves and delinquents (28–30, 37). They conclude that "the prevailing state of extreme land hunger created a troubled environment which made the most desperate people (particularly young people with only bleak prospects) ready to seize any opportunity to change their present predicament or reverse the present order of things" (38).

Therefore, the fact that the landed and successful people figure in disproportionately large numbers among those killed in the area during the genocide "suggests that the 1994 events provided an unique opportunity to settle scores, or to reshuffle land properties, even among Hutu villagers, a well-known but ugly feature of all civil wars" (40; see also Mironko 164, 168–69). In a footnote André and Platteau remark that "it is not rare, even today, to hear Rwandans argue that a war is necessary to wipe out an excess population and to bring the numbers into line with the available land resources" (40). Mironko, who interviewed several convicted killers for his research, notes "how ordinary these killings seem to the perpetrators and how casually the speakers still seem to regard their participation in them" (184).

Needless to say, *Hotel Rwanda*, committed as it is to the ethos of altruism, humanity, and courage, cannot include these (to Westerners shocking) features of ordinary people in its portrayal of the seemingly elemental, mad, weather-like evil. The rhetorical register it has chosen and is unwilling to disrupt cannot accommodate the fact that "hundreds of thousands of others [in addition to the militias] chose to participate in the genocide reluctantly, some only under duress or in the fear of their own lives. Unlike zealots who never questioned their original choice, these people had to decide repeatedly whether or not to participate, each time weighing the kind of action planned, the identity of the proposed victim, the rewards of participating and the likely costs of not participating" (Human Rights Watch 2; see also 10–12).

On the one hand, in Hollywood's discourse on humanity, this kind of "weighing" is necessarily either dehumanized and transformed into cold-blooded calculation, as exemplified by George Rutaganda's character, or reduced to simple madness that labels the actions of militiamen.

On the other hand, the Hutu extremists willing to hang on to power might instinctively have known the answers to Courtemanche's question revisited in these paragraphs; they thus knew that they could count on their countrymen's nearly inhuman, nihilistic desperation brought on by several factors, all converging toward a Malthusian ecocatastrophe. Even if the architects of the genocide did not plan this part with any conscious intent or knowledge, or indeed worry of the state of the country, the same factors can still help explain the pace and magnitude of the events unleashed by the acts of agitators and the *interahamwe*.

"AN OASIS OF CALM":
SPACE, IDENTITY, AND THE FALSE SENSE OF NORMALITY

By focusing too closely on the extraordinary—and in itself certainly heroic—story of Paul Rusesabagina, the film constructs through him and his hotel a sense of normality that is problematic in two ways. First, his notably Westernized perspective has very little to do with the ordinary Rwandan experience in the 1980s and the 1990s and thus skews the larger aim of educating us about the genocide outlined in the film's promotion. Second, and more generally, it can be argued that Paul's view, while accurate and truthful in relation to his immediate surroundings, fails to take into account the environmental factors shaping the history of the region and the people.

Again, it could be argued that to examine *Hotel Rwanda,* a story mainly interested in an individual act of heroism, in terms of history and ecology is to miss the focus and point of the film. This might be formulated as follows: the acts of altruism are possible even in the face of atrocities that can be reduced in representation in order to concentrate on the human, emotional, and rational stress felt by the main protagonist. Counterarguments would include what I have said above—that the filmmakers and promoters set an explicit agenda for themselves, which was to remind and educate the public about the genocide in general—and the fact that Paul's exceptional story is universalized in no uncertain terms. The film's Web site informs us that it was the remarkable human element of the story that struck a chord with *Hotel Rwanda* producer Alex Ho. "This story is very close to my heart, and it's the kind of story I really appreciate," he says. "It's about a *normal* man who, when prompted by his wife, is able to use his position to help others" (my emphasis).[7]

In similar fashion, director Terry George states that "it was a perfect story to be told on film—a riveting political thriller, a deeply moving romance, and, most of all, a *universal* story of the triumph of a good man over evil" (my emphasis).[8] Although the filmmakers might be right about the general human aspect of the story, there is no going around the fact that this concentration on the representation of Paul normalizes and universalizes not only his benevolent behavior but also his social status and lifestyle. Because of his occupation, upper-middle-class wealth, and Western lifestyle, Hotel des Mille Collines becomes only a very partial Hotel Rwanda, that is, an unrepresentative microcosm of the country—and one that is relatively easy on the eye of the Western cinemagoer.

How does this work in cinematic practice? First of all, as I have already noted, the scenes at the hotel dominate the screen time, while the landscapes, slums, and roadsides outside the hotel are seen only fleetingly. Furthermore, Hotel des Mille Collines was not any old hotel, but a luxury establishment frequented by tourists, diplomats, aid workers, journalists, wealthy Rwandans, UN peacekeepers, Western soldiers, and high-class prostitutes. Accordingly, the film's mise-en-scène consists of well-kept and spacious lobbies, rooms, lawns, courts, and pools. Although the customers are seen only in short vignettes, it is clear that they are professionals and other well-off people at the top of the Rwandan society, or Westerners who are by default at least as rich and wealthy as their domestic counterparts. As the pressure from the *interahamwe* mounts, this customer profile is confirmed when Paul gathers them, acknowledges that "many of you know influential people abroad," and urges them to use their contacts. This network, which is only available to Paul and his social peers, results in many safe exit visas and staves off attacks on the hotel, which remains, according to two minor characters, "an oasis of calm" and "an oasis in a desert." Later, when the Westerners and the wealthy are evacuated, poorer people trickle in, but their representation is even more marginal than that of the original clientele of the hotel. Of course, in picking up Paul's story, the filmmakers had to include the hotel, but to focus on it and on its wealthy clientele so exclusively obscures the real normality of the Rwandan experiences outside the hotel's walled enclosure.

Second, Paul's demeanor might seem normal or even average when judged by Western standards. His well-articulated speech, immaculate suit and tie, and stoic yet stylish and relaxed wine nightcap with his wife fulfill all the usual bourgeois criteria that are familiar to an average member of advanced consumer society. Paul outlines his lifestyle himself in a short, bitter outburst after the evacuation of the Westerners: "I am a fool. They told me I was one of them and I . . . Wine, chocolates, cigars, style, I bought it. I swallowed it, I swallowed all of it. And they handed me their shit. I have no history, I have no memory. I am a fool, Tatiana."

Although this is a poignant and deserved reminder of the racism, cowardice, and willful ignorance of the West, what is left unsaid is that even this fraudulent, deceptive, and shallow form of wealth was out of reach for the vast majority of Rwandans. It thus follows that in no way can Paul represent normal, average Rwandan experience in the hands of postcolonial powers and ecocatastrophe. That experience was characterized by a decade of chronic abject poverty, famines, disease epidemics, callous economic policies, and civil war—all features unseen in Hotel Rwanda.

And yet Hotel Rwanda is seen as offering a representative view on the country. The Washington Post's Ann Hornaday writes that "plunging viewers right into Paul's world as he provides the hotel's powerful guests with Scotch and Cuban cigars while dealing favors and inside knowledge that make so much of the world go round, George vividly limns the quiet post-colonial beauty of Paul's Rwanda, even as the forces of discord encroach." What is left unsaid here is the fact that "Paul's world" and "Paul's Rwanda" signify the wealthy elite of the country who, unsurprisingly, look quite familiar to Western audiences in terms of their lifestyle.

Paul himself is also a familiar figure for Western cinemagoers who can identify and sympathize with him as a bourgeois peer. Like him, Western audiences live in similar conditions and are used to using luxury hotels when abroad. Like him, Western audiences received the information of the genocide in tasteful, decently restricted packages overridden by other news. And perhaps like Paul—who explicitly detaches himself from politics—Western, or at least American, audiences might have grown used to hearing politics laid out in simple, absolute binaries, such as good and evil, madness and sanity, hatred and love, that allegedly need no further analysis. Claudia Puig's review in USA Today echoes this attitude as she writes that "the focus here is an ordinary man, a hardworking hotel employee named Paul . . . an apolitical man who summoned the courage to shelter more than 1,000 people as the slaughter raged around them" (my emphasis; see also LaSalle and Oppenheimer).

HOLLYWOOD CONVENTIONS VERSUS
WIDER ECOLOGICAL FRAMEWORK

Paul's actions remind Western viewers that we should have intervened in 1994; but while the snippets of human suffering he witnesses as our proxy push our emotional buttons, they are not persistent and complex enough to demand that we understand why everything happened in the first place. Therefore, Paul's story, Hotel des Mille Collines, and its microcosmic Rwanda emerge as a sanitized, easy version of the genocidal war, and Africa in general, described by Courtemanche:

> On the balcony of room 312 [of the Hotel des Mille Collines], perched on Kigali's highest hill, a soul at peace with itself could easily think it was in paradise, looking down on these tattered clouds that hide the thousands of oil lamps being lit, the babies and old people coughing their lungs out, the stinking cooking fires, and corn and sorghum cooking. This mist, which little by little takes on all the colours of the rainbow, acts as a protective Technicolor cushion, a filter that lets only shadows, sparkles, and faint and fleeting sounds pass through from the real world. This . . . is how God must see and hear our constant activity. As if on a giant movie screen with Dolby quadraphonic sound, while drinking some kind of mead and nibbling celestial popcorn. An interested but distant spectator. This is how the Whites at the hotel, instant minor gods, hear and figure Africa. Close enough to talk about it, even to write about it. But at the same time so isolated with their portable computers in their antiseptic rooms, and in their air-conditioned Toyotas, so surrounded by little Blacks trying to be Whites that they think Black is the smell of perfumes and cheap ointments sold in the Nairobi duty-free shop. (44)

Similarly, Western spectators of Hotel Rwanda, protected by their first world wealth and comforted by the cinema seats, globally branded "meads," and popcorn, are doubly distanced from the real Rwanda: they are watching a film that focuses on and normalizes the privileged spaces and persons "perched on Kigali's highest hill." Finally, Paul's renunciation of his Western lifestyle fails to address the core issue of that lifestyle, namely its wastefulness. Had this point been made and connected to the urgent land scarcity and resource depletion in real Rwanda, the film could have constructed a powerful epiphany and warning about the possible consequences of neglected problems relating to human ecology and living beyond our resources. Instead, Paul's recantation only touches the surface and reduces the complexity of the Rwandan situation. Therefore, his character perpetuates a general attitude of anthropocentrism and its myopia toward slow-burning ecological issues, an attitude that is, regrettably, cross-cultural and not confined only to modern, Western societies (see Diamond 79–178, esp. 137, 152).

Because of its choice of subject, its restricted representation of the genocidal acts, and its selective portrayal of Rwandan people, Hotel Rwanda becomes something of what Courtemanche called a "protective

Technicolor cushion" (see quotation above). By focusing exclusively on Paul and the hotel, the film creates a very Western perspective: sheltered, distanced, censored, witnessing only small, un-analytical and un-contextualized glimpses of "an ugly African war," and ventures only schematic, hard-and-fast explanations for it. And, indeed, if, like Paul or the Western spectator, one takes wealth and peace as everyday givens, the killings thus portrayed would look like insanity and "pure" hatred or "elemental" evil.

Behind these representational choices lies a set of tried and true Hollywood rhetorical conventions. The individual as the central causal agent is a classic device in Hollywood films, and the choice of Paul as the main protagonist rests firmly on this tradition. Paul's Westernized lifestyle provides an easy target for identification in the West where most of *Hotel Rwanda*'s audiences are located. This feature can be seen in the context of Hollywood's tendency to tame, familiarize, and appropriate foreign cultures and nonhuman environments and recast them in Westernized molds.

Although another trend can be found in the tactics between the censorship ratings and probable audience sizes, *Hotel Rwanda*'s "tasteful" and restricted portrayal of atrocities can still be interpreted as following Hollywood's habit of sanitization and schematization of war, which excludes the randomness, injustice, and messy ugliness inherent in most wars. Finally, in time-honored fashion, *Hotel Rwanda,* because of its limited and selective depiction of genocide and its perpetrators, produces a clear binary distinction between the altruistic and humane "good" and the inhumanely calculating or plain insane "evil." Through these positions the film adopts a stance according to which genocide is an elemental, inhuman, mad force, incomprehensible and inexplicable; to try to explain it would be to sympathize with the killers or, at the very least, to trivialize the horrors that ordinary people went through.

These audiovisual conventions have an ideological analogy at the wider cultural level of the Western world. Having grown up in a culture of hyper-individualism and conspicuous consumption, we tend to price and privilege the individual and his or her right to do whatever he or she wants and, especially, to consume goods and services without any consideration of the ecological implications this behavior might have. Individuals might be corrupt or even fundamentally evil, but the centrality of her or him for the culture, and her or his self-evident superiority and priority over nature is never in doubt; in fact, it is usually never even addressed. Even Paul, when he realizes the vacuity of the consumerist lifestyle, automatically refers back to humanist concepts of history, memory, and indigenous culture, not to the larger ecological framework of Rwanda. In other words, his rejection of Western culture and his individualistic portrayal as "a real African hero"[9] are laudable within the context of postcolonial critique, but become problematic within a wider ecocritical framework.

First, Paul is not a representative Rwandan. His Western lifestyle, however, displaces the conflict from being a complex ecological problem to one of cultures and opportunistic, "evil" individuals. In 1994 an average Rwandan farmer was likely to be beset by some or all of the following: dwindling arable lands or complete landlessness, chronic unemployment, ruinous economic policies, regular bouts of civil war and hunger, or starvation and withering death by AIDS. Added to these bleak prospects, the ferocious anti-Tutsi propaganda might have just provided a pretext for attaining some advantages, such as land, by killing the neighbor, whether he was a Tutsi or not. Yet again, Courtemanche's prose both illuminates this point and concurs with the ecological and economic arguments made by Diamond, André and Platteau, and other researchers.

> This hill is still today Kawa's family's hill. See how peaceful and fixed in time it is. That is the landscape's lie, telling you that all the ferocity of Nature, every steep slope, has been tamed by man's patient toil, humanity's exemplary conquest of the unconquerable. What delusion! While we were clearing each square centimetre of these precipitous slopes, planting beans and bananas where nothing was growing but stones and brambles, a cousin was hiding behind a rugo hedge, waiting for his cousin so he could kill him and thus prove his own Hutu identity. (199)

The deep ecological matrix behind the calamities listed above is absent from the film and forms the second vital deficiency in its discourse about the conflict. Rwandan geology, exorbitant birth rates, and the resultant population growth nearing a Malthusian disaster are not addressed in *Hotel Rwanda*—perhaps because they are seldom mentioned in the politically correct discourse in the individualistic and anthropocentric West. For example, both for the Left and the Right, the talk of the global population explosion and its consequences to human ecology has become something of a taboo, "the green issue that dare not speak its name" (Nicholson-Lord; see also Rapley). Yet in places like Rwanda, these issues and the repercussions that flow from them form a vital part of understanding the conflict among human groups and between humans and their environment. In a finite area, more people means less land and less sustenance per person, and an increased potential for conflict. Ordinary Rwandans did not and do not have the luxury of shutting out these problems, of blithely disregarding the limits imposed by nature. Paul, at the same time an African hero of a Hollywood film and a reflection of a basic, limited, anthropocentric outlook, can only see halfway through the problem, to the meaninglessness of consumer culture. For the audience, human ecology remains out of sight: the film's main ideological impact focuses on reinforcing familiar thought patterns clustered around individualism and anthropocentrism.

In due fashion, representations of the root problems of the conflict lie tucked away in the margins of Hotel Rwanda, in the fleeting, panoramic shots of the hills around Kigali, in the slums and the marketplaces buzzing with people, in the bloody history of the country revisited briefly in the dialogue, and in the name Mille Collines, or "thousand hills." Together, they form the dot clusters that are left unexplored and unconnected, perhaps because of their uncinematic scale, perhaps because of the uneasy truth they contain: what ecocatastrophe and the resultant extreme poverty can do to the thin crust of civilization. Instead, in accordance with Hollywood conventions and the familiar, self-evident anthropocentric thought patterns idolized and sanctified in the West, Hotel Rwanda constructs the tragedy around the fact that there are murderous maniacs and callous, power-hungry fanatics who can carry out genocides. The real tragedy, however, is that a country can linger under so many devastating but preventable problems for so long that its ordinary people are reduced more or less willingly to carry out acts of genocide.

NOTES

1. Other major fiction films include HBO's TV movie Sometimes in April (2005) and Michael Caton-Jones's Shooting Dogs (2005), both of which have remained marginal in terms of audience when compared with Hotel Rwanda.

2. Epistemologically, this approach rests on a wider notion of critical realism that is founded on the following assumptions: (1) there exists an external reality; (2) this reality is described and often appropriated and distorted by discourses about that reality; yet (3) there still remains the possibility of deciding which of those discourses are less selective, more comprehensive, and more plausible than others (see, for example, Ingram 1–7).

3. See http://www.variety.com/profiles/Film/main/168946/Hotel+Rwanda.html ?dataSet=1&query=Hotel+Rwanda (retrieved 18 November 2009) and http://www.boxofficemojo.com/movies/?id=hotelrwanda.htm (retrieved 18 November 2009).

4. See http://www.unitedartists.com/hotelrwanda/main.html (retrieved 25 November 2009).

5. RottenTomatoes.com rated the film as "92 percent fresh," based on 178 reviews in American media (http://www.rottentomatoes.com/m/hotel_rwanda/, retrieved 25 November 2009). Over 61 percent (352 of 574) of BoxOfficeMojo.com users rated it with an "A" grade (http://www.boxofficemojo.com/movies/?id =hotelrwanda.htm, retrieved 25 November 2009), while MetaCritic.com gave it 79 out of 100, based on 40 reviews across the United States (http://www.metacritic.com/film/titles/hotelrwanda?q=hotel%20rwanda, retrieved 25 November 2009).
6. See http://hdr.undp.org/en/media/hdr_1994_en_indicators2.pdf, p. 175 (retrieved 25 November 2009). See also http://hdr.undp.org/en/statistics/ (retrieved 25 November 2009) and http://hdrstats.undp.org/en/countries/country_fact_sheets/cty_fs_RWA.html (retrieved 25 November 2009).
7. See http://www.unitedartists.com/hotelrwanda/main.html, Section: Story, A Modern Genocide (retrieved 19 November 2009).
8. See http://www.unitedartists.com/hotelrwanda/main.html, Section: Inspiration, Director's Statement (retrieved 19 November 2009).
9. See http://www.unitedartists.com/hotelrwanda/main.html, Section: Inspiration, Director's Statement (retrieved 19 November 2009).

WORKS CITED

André, Catherine, and Jean-Phillippe Platteau. "Land Relations under Unbearable Stress: Rwanda Caught in the Malthusian Trap." *Journal of Economic Behaviour and Organisation* 34 (1998): 1–47.

Ansen, David. "*Hotel Rwanda.*" *Newsweek* 20 December 2004. http://www.newsweek.com/id/56150. Retrieved 26 November 2009.

Burr, Ty. "*Hotel Rwanda.*" *Boston Globe* 7 January 2005. http://www.boston.com/movies/display?display=movie&id=7112. Retrieved 26 November 2009.

Courtemanche, Gil. *A Sunday at the Pool in Kigali.* Edinburgh: Canongate, 2004.

Denby, David. "High Rollers." *New Yorker* 20 December 2004. http://www.newyorker.com/archive/2004/12/20/041220crci_cinema. Retrieved 26 November 2009.

Diamond, Jared. *Collapse: How Societies Choose to Fail or Survive.* London: Allen Lane, 2005.

Ebert, Roger. "*Hotel Rwanda.*" *Chicago Sun-Times* 22 December 2004. http://rogerebert.suntimes.com/apps/pbcs.dll/article?AID=/20041221/REVIEWS/41213001. Retrieved 26 November 2009.

Joli, Dan. "*Hotel Rwanda.*" *Empire.* http://www.empireonline.com/reviews/reviewcomplete.asp?DVDID=10703. Retrieved 25 November 2009.

Gourevitch, Philip. *We Wish to Inform You That Tomorrow We Will Be Killed with Our Families: Stories from Rwanda.* London: Picador, 1999.

Hornaday, Ann. "*Hotel Rwanda* Heralds the Triumph of One Man's Decency." *Washington Post* 7 January 2005. http://www.washingtonpost.com/wp-dyn/articles/A55029-2005Jan6.html. Retrieved 26 November 2009.

Hotel Rwanda. Dir. Terry George. United Artists, 2004.

Human Rights Watch. *Leave None to Tell the Story: Genocide in Rwanda*. New York: Human Rights Watch, 1999.

Ingram, David. *Green Screen: Environmentalism and Hollywood Cinema*. Exeter: Univ. of Exeter Press, 2002.

LaSalle, Mick. "Amid a Massacre, an Ordinary Man Stands Tall to Protect Others." *San Francisco Chronicle* 7 January 2005. http://www.sfgate.com/cgi-bin/article.cgi?f=/c/a/2005/01/07/DDGIBALKFH1.DTL&type=movies. Retrieved 26 November 2009.

Mamdani, Mahmood. "From Conquest to Consent as the Basis of State Formation: Reflections of Rwanda." *New Left Review* 216 (April 1995): 3–36.

Mironko, Charles K. "Ibitero: Means and Motives in the Rwandan Genocide." *Genocide in Cambodia and Rwanda: New Perspectives*. Ed. Susan E. Cook. New Brunswick, NJ: Transaction Publishers, 2006. 163–89.

Nicholson-Lord, David. "The Green Issue That Dare Not Speak Its Name." *People & the Planet* 4 July 2005. http://www.peopleandplanet.net/doc.php?id=2497. Retrieved 19 November 2009.

Oppenheimer, Jean. "Blade Runners. Hotel Rwanda Finds Hope amid the Horrors of Tribal Genocide." *Dallas Observer* 6 January 2005. http://www.dallasobserver.com/2005-01-06/film/blade-runners. Retrieved 26 November 2009.

Puig, Claudia. "Haunting *Hotel Rwanda*." *USA Today* 21 December 2004. http://www.usatoday.com/life/movies/reviews/2004-12-21-hotel-rwanda_x.htm. Retrieved 26 November 2009.

Rapley, Chris. "Earth Is Too Crowded for Utopia." *People & the Planet* 17 January 2006. http://www.peopleandplanet.net/doc.php?id=2640. Retrieved 19 November 2009.

Salgado, Sebastião. *Migrations: Humanity in Transition*. New York: Aperture, 2000.

Shake Hands with the Devil: The Journey of Romeo Dallaire. Dir. Peter Raymont. White Pine Pictures, Canadian Broadcasting Corporation (CBC), Société Radio-Canada, 2004.

United Nations Development Programme (UNDP).http://hdrstats.undp.org/en/countries/data_sheets/cty_ds_RWA.html. Retrieved 18 November 2009.

FAST, FURIOUS, AND OUT OF CONTROL

THE ERASURE OF NATURAL LANDSCAPES IN CAR CULTURE FILMS

. . . .

ROBIN L. MURRAY AND JOSEPH K. HEUMANN

*As a kid growing up in Vietnam and meeting the
(American) military personnel, we all grew up wanting an
American car—and the Mustang was it. . . . The Mustang
really stood for everything that's about America. It's big and
bold and powerful and it's accessible. It's available to everyone.*
—Tang Thai, "The Mustang Was It"

Rob Cohen's *The Fast and the Furious* (2001), John Singleton's *2 Fast 2 Furious* (2003), Justin Lin's *The Fast and the Furious: Tokyo Drift* (2006) and *Fast and Furious* (2009), like the 1955 John Ireland and Edward Sampson film, *The Fast and the Furious*, which inspired them, illustrate the devotion to souped-up high-speed cars and the stylish culture they represent. These films also take environmental degradation to hyperbolic levels, going beyond merely highlighting the car as an American icon and valorizing a concrete highway built for racing. In spite of the more liberal class and race politics in the later films that seem to critique human exploitation, all these "fast and furious" films advocate the abuse of nature and ecosystems. They reinforce patterns of thought and action that contribute to environmental degradation, and rest on the environmental impact that is inherently a part of car culture. Most important for us, they exalt transformed natural and man-made environments.

Few would dispute the impact the car has had on the environment, especially in the United States; according to Ralph Vartabedian, "More than 21 million households in the nation have more than two cars, according to a 2005 survey by the U.S. Census Bureau. Twenty-five percent of families that own their own home have more than two cars. Almost 2 million families have five or more cars." Vartabedian asserts, "The effect of more cars on the road is significant on a societal scale, increasing traffic in established neighborhoods that once had adequate surface roads. It obviously affects air quality, helping keep the United States as the world's leading producer of greenhouse gases." By the mid-1990s, Americans owned 34 percent of the world's motor vehicles (some 201 million) even though Americans comprise less than 5 percent of the world's population. With so many motor vehicles, Americans burn 143 billion gallons of fuel a year. Motor vehicles in the United States cause more than 50 percent of air pollution and produce heaping solid waste (millions of cars and tires) and leaking oil and gasoline (250 million gallons of motor oil and countless gallons of gasoline leaking from at least 500,000 underground tanks).

Cars also account for the paving of a large percentage of natural landscapes. In Los Angeles, for example, two-thirds "of the ground space is reserved for the sole purpose of moving and storing cars" (Goff). Yet as environmentalists from Alexander Wilson to Al Gore now assert, constructing the car as a source and symbol of freedom, pleasure, and identity, while drawing on images of an open road built on our drive to move west toward progress, is counter to any truly progressive ecological vision for the future.

Because they are products of the same cultural context as Wilson and Gore, one would expect the 2001, 2003, 2006, and 2009 *Fast and Furious* films to embody a more enlightened view of the consequences of speeding down a paved and open road, since they respond to contemporary popular culture, a culture now universally aware of the reality of environmental degradation and its causes. In the context of recent documentary films such as *The End of Suburbia: Oil Depletion and the Collapse of the American Dream* (2004), *An Inconvenient Truth* (2006), and *Who Killed the Electric Car?* (2006), these *Fast and Furious* films appear irresponsible and archaic in spite of having updated their social politics by effectively blurring racial boundaries.

In the contemporary *Fast and Furious* films, the situation is the same as it was in 1955: car culture celebrates speed and control as well as the transformation of the natural environment into a man-made landscape that is, in turn, itself transformed without questioning the environmental expense. These films demonstrate that the environmental impact of cars and the car culture in America and elsewhere has been treated as natural and desirable, as a given.

Drivers in all the films appear to rebel against a conformist suburban culture that uses roadways for commuting and garages for parking, instead of racing; however, they also conform to this same culture through their acceptance of environmental degradation in the form of both a transformation of natural and man-made landscapes, and a reliance on nonrenewable fuels that contribute to global warming.

We find, then, that drivers in all five films not only use artificial landscapes built on ecosystems but also further exploit this artificial landscape, transforming its former utility into a roadway for speed, thrills, and status, thus reinforcing the same anti-environmental message behind this rush for acceleration.

The 2001, 2003, 2006, and 2009 films merely mask their attitude toward the landscape by including one inconsequential difference, from an environmental standpoint: an updated race and class politics rooted in post–World War II southern car culture and elements of popular culture such as *The Dukes of Hazzard,* a television series with similar roots. While racial and class hierarchies may have been deconstructed in the later films, exploitation of the environment is not only accepted but also presented as a way to even the class and race stakes.

Even though hierarchies appear to have changed from 1955 to 2009, when it comes to the natural world, environmental degradation is not only a given but also a goal. An ecocritical reading of these films suggests that little has changed between 1955 and 2009, despite changes in attitudes toward the environment—from Rachel Carson's *Silent Spring* and the establishment of the EPA in the 1960s and 1970s, to Al Gore's *An Inconvenient Truth* in 2006 and the Obama administration's efforts to raise EPA standards and infuse the economy with "green" infrastructure projects in 2009. Predominant in all these films is an ideology that worships speed and advocates the conquest of the natural world as a transformative development aligned with progress and democracy.

The thematic and plot parallels between the films crossing more than fifty years are striking. They highlight a car culture that juxtaposes elements of consumption with sex and power—a consumerism that comes in the form of food and fast cars. Linking sex with food is a staple of cinema, since both work together to elicit desire and stimulate our appetites. In these films we are asked to have our appetite for consuming the environment further stimulated, and to think of that consumption as empowering and pleasurable.

All of these films also foreground the alteration of an existing landscape that is already man-made, thus making it easier to forget that it is an already transformed ecosystem. The real natural landscape that serves as the basis of this transformation is not even evoked anymore. In Baudrillard's term, it is all a simulacrum already. The receding natural landscape that is the basis of these films becomes erased by the multiple transformations of the man-made landscape. It is not just the landscape that is transformed but the use that is made of this landscape. The only frontier left is the new use that is made of what is there, following, of course, a similar ideology to the one that informed the transformation in the first place—a particular version of landscape and power.

As the centerpieces of these films, cars, asphalt, and landscape are as important as food, romance, and sex (and male bonding in the latter four films). In the 2001 *The Fast and the Furious* and the 2009 *Fast and Furious,* for example, Japanese compacts are driven on Los Angeles pavement by an assorted group of multiracial young male hellions. With an ethnically ambiguous leader—Vin Diesel's Dominic—and street racers of Asian, African American, and Hispanic descent, the film shows us a globalized car-crazy, hip-hop-driven subculture where urban youth in their twenties invest thousands of dollars to soup up lightweight Toyotas, Mitsubishis, and Hondas for inner-city ultra-speed.

This loud and fast underworld thumbs its nose at the establishment—in this case represented by the FBI and, at first, its undercover agent, Brian (Paul Walker). It even appears to reject the utilitarian reasons behind the construction of the asphalt and concrete landscapes it exploits, even as it reappropriates them for its own use in a semblance of rejecting all that is bourgeois.

THE ORIGINAL THE FAST AND THE
FURIOUS IN ITS CULTURAL CONTEXT

The 1955 *The Fast and the Furious* begins with a truck crash that is juxtaposed with a shot of high-end foreign cars racing down a two-lane road. The film then focuses on Connie (Dorothy Malone) driving into a dinette, the Paddle Creek Lodge, for a sandwich. The low-key scene escalates to a kidnapping and car hijacking when Frank Webster (John Ireland) grabs Connie and escapes the diner in her two-seat Jaguar. Webster had broken out of jail after being wrongly accused of murder—as seen in the film's opening truck crash—and now seeks to prove his innocence and redeem his life. The film's thin plot, though, is meant more to showcase the high-end sports cars at the road rally and race that makes up much of the film—all on a concrete landscape transformed into a race course.

The 1955 film embodies an ideology that erupted after World War II, as returning veterans flocked to the newly developed suburbs where they gained access to home ownership under the Veterans Administration Acts. Eisenhower's goal to build an Interstate Highway system made movement between city jobs and suburban homes not only a possibility but, increasingly, a reality. But since Frederick Jackson Turner's 1890 argument about the significance of the American frontier in the formation of the American character, at a time when the frontier seemed no longer to exist, images of American culture's vision of an open road—a frontier to conquer—have changed. While there are no geographical frontiers left to conquer, the image of an existing frontier remains an important icon in an American consciousness shaped by the mythical frontier ideals of independence, self-reliance, and ingenuity. The automobile creates a symbolic space in which dreams of freedom and conquering frontiers can be kept alive.

For the disenfranchised, those relegated to the inner city rather than the suburbs, the need to create their own illusion of a frontier is played out in parking garages and urban streets. The ethnically diverse films sell the American frontier dream to all cultures. This American dream and American identity depend on the transformation of the landscape, as they always have—whether it is the open space of the West or the closed space of the inner city.

Much has been written about the roots of and reasons behind America's love affair with the automobile. According to Alexander Wilson's *The Culture of Nature,* since 1956 when the Eisenhower administration began constructing the U.S. Interstate Highway System, "the speeding car along the open road has become a metaphor for progress in the U.S. and for the cultural taming of the American wilderness" (34). In *America,* Jean Baudrillard describes a post–World War II America of the "empty, absolute freedom of the freeways . . . the America of desert speed, of motels and mineral surfaces" (5). According to John Urry, these landscapes "stand for modernity and the rejection of the complex histories of European societies. This emptiness is a metaphor of the American dream" (5). But landscapes also stand for the promise of speed. Baudrillard asserts that "speed creates pure objects. . . . Its only rule is to leave no trace behind. . . . Driving like this produces a kind of invisibility, transparency, or transversality in things, simply by emptying them out" (7). The present passed by the vehicle and the past the vehicle leaves behind are seemingly erased, in favor of a future that signifies progress. Wilson argues that in the 1950s "what we saw out the window of a speeding car . . . was the future itself" (34). Concrete and asphalt roadways have come to represent progress, the future sought for in the Old West. As we move over them rapidly in a car, we metaphorically consume the landscape as we race over and past it. Yet we literally consume natural resources and use them to transform natural landscapes so as to create a space for cars and their culture.

In this context the 1950s represent the heyday of car culture and of car culture films. With the beginning of the Interstate System in 1956, cars and their drivers were poised to head out on the ultra-modern four-lane open roads. Car culture films in the 1950s highlight unique class and regional reactions to the automobile. *The Fast and the Furious* is a product of this era. The film illustrates upper-class California car culture and showcases high-end foreign two-seat racers. It revolves around a romance, camaraderie, and mutual respect among car racers, as do the later *Fast and Furious* films, while resting on similar ideas regarding landscape.

In its cross-country race, the first *Fast and Furious* film speaks to issues of freedom and the open road, reflecting the 1950s ethos. Only in one way does the earlier film deviate from visions of individual freedom. Despite similar settings, plot, and thematic elements, the 1955 film does not embrace the progressive class and race values found in the later films.

But these seemingly progressive values are limited and, from an eco-critical standpoint, rely on the same ideology of the '50s highway system, an ideology built on individuals' rights to consume and on freedom of mobility. The film, like the later *Fast and Furious* films, draws on an ideology of progress that burgeoned under a politics of consumption meant to spur the economy and provide a reward for ending a world war. Such an ideology might seem forgivable in this 1955 context, yet it also served as the foundation for a continuing globalized car culture.

CAR CULTURE AS NOSTALGIA

The recent *Fast and Furious* films draw on collective historical memories harking back nostalgically to the 1950s car culture's association with the freedom of the open road, rather than highlighting the real environmental damage this culture promulgates. These films consciously evoke a landscape already transcended by concrete and speeding cars, as when Dominic hijacks a truck from a speeding car with no natural landscape in view in the frame. In a long line of car culture films, the recent *Fast and the Furious* films reinforce the ideology associated with the car culture as they elicit in viewers a longing for the mythical freedom cars provide, especially American "muscle cars." Muscle cars, in particular, are associated with the thrill of speed rather than with utilitarian transportation. From Junior Johnson to Smokey and the Bandit, high horsepower autos are built to race. They draw on strategies found in advertising since companies started selling cars, still using images of Steve McQueen (Bullit) to sell Ford Mustangs.

But the 2001 *The Fast and the Furious* and its sequels, *2 Fast, 2 Furious, Tokyo Drift,* and *Fast and Furious,* go beyond the white American male images presented in both car ads and earlier (white bread) films fore-grounding cars, car racing, and car culture. Unlike the 1955 *The Fast and the Furious,* the recent sequels move cars into a racially progressive era of car racing where men and women of diverse races mingle amicably, and cars represent a new global economy in which utilitarian foreign prod-ucts are far superior to their white American competitors.

Although the recent *Fast and Furious* films present an ideologically progressive portrayal of race and gender politics, they perpetuate a pol-icy of overconsumption and exploitation of environmental resources, displaying cars that run on both gasoline and nitrous oxide. While we are never shown drivers refueling their cars, we do see them switch from gasoline to nitrous oxide almost instantly during races.

The films also exacerbate our acceptance of an already reconstructed landscape in which nature is paved over to accommodate cars, by eras-ing traces of the original natural environment on which these concrete and asphalt roads were built. By further transforming an already trans-formed landscape of inner city roadways and parking garages into race tracks, the films treat pavement as natural, essential, and original.

Although the 1955 *Fast and Furious* film celebrates the transformation of the landscape to accommodate the car and make movement and exploration of the new suburban "frontiers" possible, the remakes as-sume an acceptance of an already altered landscape, with no visible vestiges of what predated the cities. In the later films, the same sense of power and freedom gained from exploring new frontiers is now achieved by reappropriating this manufactured landscape of highways and parking garages. The impetus and motives to transform the land-scape are the same as in the 1955 film.

The return to the inner city appears progressive and challenging of middle-class values represented by the flight to the suburbs, but it is modeled on similar aspirations. These films perpetuate the same atti-tudes toward society and the environment, their visions relying on un-challenged notions of progress and consumption to justify the exploita-tion of the land and natural resources. They exploit the appeal of cars, and of the culture and environment created by them, to draw in audi-ences who like fast cars and thumb their noses at the conformist atti-tudes embraced by middle-class suburbanites—as when the characters challenge the police, shut down sections of cities, and turn them into drag strips and race tracks. Their transformation of the paved landscape also "shuts down" more conventional drivers who rely on the automobile to commute to jobs and who choose reliability, utility, and luxurious rides over speed.

Even though all the *Fast and Furious* films highlight foreign cars, the culture they represent, according to Andrew O'Hehir, supports the view "that freedom and friendship are more important than order," a point particularly clear when Brian protects Dom and his gang from the FBI in the 2001 *Fast and Furious*. This view emphasizes the youth culture underpinning these car culture films as well. O'Hehir argues that one of the film's real issues is that "Americans really believe that driving a kickass machine down an open road, with your past receding in the rearview mirror, will make you live forever." Since colonists first arrived on the shores of North America, the American dream has emphasized eternal youth, new opportunities, and the freedom to pursue progress at any cost, not just opportunities for self-actualization.

On the surface, the *Fast and Furious* films claim to transcend this suburban America ideal, since the freedom offered by the open road must be altered to accommodate urban car racing. Here, the car itself, independently of the landscape through which it moves, represents camaraderie and the American dream of freedom (especially from authority). Authority in this case represents limits to one's actions, limits that should be eliminated to gain the freedom of action an open road promises. Driving cars, even through an urban landscape, promises the exhilaration an open road suggests but ignores the need to address dwindling resources and the environmental consequences of refusing to accept ecological limits.

Placing the emphasis on the car itself, instead of on the open road, also aligns with American car culture ideology. According to Blackburn and Mann, "Driving a car can be a source of intense pleasure: of flexibility, skill, possession and excitement" (quoted in Urry 6). Urry claims, however, that "sociology has regarded cars as a neutral technology, permitting social patterns of life that would have more or less occurred anyway" (3).

Critiques of car culture and its valorization demonstrate the effects cars have had on popular culture and mainstream American society. Sociological studies of car advertising suggest that manufacturers not only construct consumers of automobiles but also stimulate changed perceptions of cars, of commutes from suburbia, and of suburban and urban development built around cars (see Flink). Even while Urry examines environmental resource use and Phillip Goff equates car culture with "the landscape of subtraction," Americans' attitudes toward their cars remain unchanged in light of information about percentages of resources consumed by car manufacturers and pollutants emitted into the air and water. The same can be said for drivers in the *Fast and Furious* films.

In fact, environmentalists studying urban spaces also focus attention on economic development, even if this means bringing industry to the inner city or paving over the landscape, as long as it accommodates the poor. Most Americans embrace development in urban and suburban areas because it symbolizes progress and booming economic markets, that is, jobs and economic security. Environmental writers such as Michael Bennett and Andrew Ross argue against anti-urban white flight to the suburbs, not because it thrives on and encourages further "subtraction" of the landscape through suburban sprawl, but because it parallels "capital flight" (Bennett 176). Andrew Ross asserts that anti-urbanism and back-to-nature movements "can be tied directly to the economic cycles of investment and disinvestment in city centers" (quoted in Bennett 173). Urban environmental movements seek to improve the infrastructure of inner city poor rather than increase green spaces or encourage a more interdependent relationship with the natural world. If the solution to inner city ghettos is jobs and the better support services they might provide, then how can the environmental degradation such development would bring be recognized and curbed?

Ironically, car culture films such as *The Fast and the Furious, 2 Fast 2 Furious, The Fast and the Furious: Tokyo Drift,* and *Fast and Furious* offer the car as a viable solution to the alienation and poverty that seem inevitable in decaying cities such as Los Angeles, Miami, and (to a certain extent) Tokyo—the four films' respective settings. These films endorse the views of contemporary environmentalists, like Bennett and Ross, to call attention to the need of providing inner cities' racially diverse populations with capital and a means of both production and support. The films, like liberal urban environmentalists, support progressive attitudes toward racial diversity and inner city reclamation by native populations. But they perpetuate the implicit and explicit assumptions that the adverse consequences of burning fossil fuel are an inescapable byproduct of class and racial progress.

Looking at the 1955 *The Fast and the Furious* in relation to the 2001 remake and its 2003, 2006, and 2009 sequels demonstrates that the politics of car culture films has progressed in relation to social and urban environmental concerns. But such comparison also illustrates the limits of an urban environmentalism based only on capital and racial and class politics. Even though the later films update race and class politics, they still valorize exploitation of the natural world.

THE LIMITS OF RACE AND CLASS POLITICS

While the *Fast and Furious* films rewrite class and racial politics, condoning multiethnic interactions among inner city (poor) youth, they also embrace the traditionalist values of progress at any cost. They promote exploitation of the natural world and advocate a consumer-driven superficiality that undermines any progress but that represented by speed. The misogyny in the films serves only as another signifier of the goal of the car races: freedom from any limits on actions. These films are much more class-conscious than the 1955 version because they respond to both the 1955 film and to southern car culture and its media offspring.

Southern car culture highlights less affluent drivers driving less expensive cars. It is manifested today in NASCAR races where drivers earning millions of dollars still mingle with the masses (Korth). Tom Wolfe's 1965 *Esquire* article about Junior Johnson, winner of 50 NASCAR Winston Cup Series races, and how stock-car racing earns drivers big bucks, highlights this contradiction (211). While Johnson won $100,000 in 1963, he embodies the working-class image NASCAR still preserves. According to Wolfe's epigraph, Junior Johnson "is a coon hunter, a rich man, an ex-whiskey runner, a good old boy who hard-charges stock cars at 175 mph. Mother dog! He is the lead-footed chicken farmer from Ronda, the true vision of the New South" (211). Southern, working-class, good-old-boy values that make class barriers more than permeable still prevail in the NASCAR circuit. *NASCAR: The Ride of Their Lives* (2008) documents this history, using found footage from the late 1940s and 1950s that illustrates how beaches in Daytona Beach were transformed into a super speedway.

The *Fast and Furious* films embrace the same values exemplified by southern car culture, but with an updated hip-hop multiracial twist. In the cars, drivers are masked and anonymous; in the 2001 film, the cut to characters at a luncheonette reveals a class structure and racial diversity missing in the 1955 *The Fast and the Furious*. The film's protagonist, Brian, is what Hector calls "typical white bread," down to his name, and stands out as the only white blue-eyed blonde in the film. The fight over the "girl" overseeing the luncheonette reveals the racial diversity embraced by urban car culture. Vince—a dark ethnic, perhaps Italian—fights Brian over Dominic's sister, Mia. Even though Dom's and Mia's last name is Toretto, the two have the perfected look of the new "ethnically ambiguous." The drag race Brian enters the evening after the fight highlights this racial difference from earlier car-culture movies with mostly, if not all, white casts. The four drivers in the race exemplify this diversity, with an African American and a Hispanic male, and Dominic and Brian racing for money and group status. Brian's white-bread difference from this racially diverse gang is emphasized by his role as an outsider, an FBI agent investigating this inner city car-racing subculture.

After the 2000 census in which individuals could check more than one race to define themselves, it comes as no surprise that racial lines have become so permeable in film. With the exception of Brian, the characters in Dom's gang look multiracial and remain loyal to a racially diverse gang. Even the FBI includes racially diverse, though middle-aged, detectives and agents. Diversity is celebrated in the film and serves a broad audience well. Only the Asian gang members Brian first suspects as responsible for the truck-jackings look racially "pure."

Brian acts as a link between the two groups, choosing the anti-authority gang and its members over the FBI. Driving fast cars in the spirit of a gang, a loyal family, appeals to Brian so much that he defies his organization, lets Dom escape, and, as we learn in the film's sequel, runs away from the establishment to Miami, where he embraces street racing culture and a new last name. When Brian helps Dom escape, he reinforces the concept that freedom and friendship are more important than order in American (car) culture. Brian, then, blurs boundaries between cultures and classes in the film by choosing the anarchy of inner city car culture over the conformity of the FBI. Within this framework, however, the rebellion Brian embraces maintains similar (conformist) hierarchies, especially those that allow for the degradation of nature. The film takes destruction of nature to hyperbolic levels since it advocates the destruction of resources and landscapes. The race and class politics merely mask the environmentally destructive nature of car culture.

The film's sequels also blur racial barriers while taking a conservative approach toward the establishment. 2 Fast 2 Furious centers on the polyglot car gang subculture of Miami, complete with a Rastafarian, and color codes cars and their drivers to foreground racial diversity and capture an audience obsessed not only with cars but also with video games. In Tokyo Drift, the racial polyglot extends to include international diversity, in the gang culture of Tokyo. The latest Fast and Furious returns to the original stars of the ethnically ambiguous cast of the 2001 The Fast and the Furious.

The races in each film, however, show how extensively car-racing gangs adapt the urban auto-friendly landscape to their racing needs. 2 Fast 2 Furious, for example, brings us a race on a closed city course, altering the concrete landscape for speeding cars. Car gang members block off city streets with orange cones, self-assured that they will keep traffic clear for their race, in inner city Miami. Racers line up four across and run a street course empty of other cars at speeds reaching 160 mph, when nitrous oxide is activated.

Control over a landscape already transformed for the automobile is clearly portrayed near the end of the race, when the race coordinator orders gang members to break into the controls of a drawbridge and open it just wide enough so each side of the bridge is angled like a ramp. Racing cars fly up the ramp and jump across the bridge in an ultimate challenge. Making the jump (and ultimately winning the race) provides both thrills and status for drivers. Running from police in a high-speed chase scene after the race foregrounds these gang members' rejection of the establishment and of the utilitarian reasons behind the construction of the auto-friendly landscape they have transformed. Yet the anti-establishment ethos of the film presupposes an acceptance of the transformation of the landscape by car culture—that is, an acceptance of the establishment values they seem to reject. In this respect the gang culture subscribes to the same set of values as those they defy; they simply appropriate what the culture has already established and defined as desirable.

ENVIRONMENTAL DEGRADATION AS NECESSARY CONSEQUENCE

As progressive as the *Fast and Furious* films purport to be in relation to class and race, the environmental impacts of burning fossil fuel go unquestioned. There are few, if any, explicit mentions of the need for fuel in any of these films. The only acknowledgment that cars need gasoline to race occurs in the 1955 film when Ireland stops at a gas station to fill up a hijacked Jaguar. In the later films, there are no gas stations in sight.

The presence of natural settings is also erased in all the films, including in the scenes shot on highways that have not been altered by the drivers. Even the open highway where Dom and his gang rob trucks in *The Fast and the Furious* (2001) runs through a barren landscape, with no trace of the natural world except when cars crash onto grassy shoulders. In *2 Fast 2 Furious*, Miami's ocean waters and shorelines are viewed only through racing cars or boats. In *Tokyo Drift*, scenes outside the city are filmed only at night. And in *Fast and Furious* (2009), Los Angeles concrete serves again as landscape.

All these films offer tricked-up Japanese cars as a solution to economic and racial injustices, as well as to the alienation caused by the lifeless inner city concrete world in which characters live. They create consumers for car products and accessories, for the films and video games featuring them, and for the products and ads embedded in the films. Most important, they create car-worshiping consumers for whom concrete landscapes, fuel overconsumption, and carbon emissions are not only acceptable but also appropriate signs of progress, of inner city rebuilding, and of an urban environmentalism that purports to overcome ecological racism. As Andrew Ross argues in "The Social Claim on Urban Ecology," city centers suffered at least partially because of anti-urban back-to-nature movements. Bringing capital back to the inner city may help revitalize inner city ghettos. But the development necessary to bolster the economy may also contribute to environmental degradation, making conflicts between environmental justice and environmental racism more difficult to resolve.

This conflict is complicated, because the 2001 *Fast and the Furious* was inspired not only by the 1955 film of the same name but also by an article in *Vibe Magazine* about car-racing gangs, as is documented in numerous reviews and on the Internet Movie Database. The article's description and analysis of car-racing gang life—especially through its portrait of Rafael Estevez—explains much about car culture and the attitude toward the environment and the consumption of resources it encourages. Estevez raced a Nissan 300ZX on streets and parkways in New York, but the "urban polyglot" racing here looks similar to that portrayed in both films' settings—Los Angeles and Miami. Like Dom, Brian, and the other racers in the *Fast and Furious* films, Estevez tricked out his Nissan in three ways—"by stroking the engine, adding a supercharger, and hitting the 'juice' (nitrous oxide: a gaseous liquid once used to boost bomber planes in WWII)" (Li).

Drivers quoted in the article illuminate the psychology behind the race culture presented there and in the films: "It's about power. It's about the control of power," claims one driver. "The excitement of going fast is like nothing else," says another, who also argues that "another group gets excitement from doing drugs or whatever. Speed excites us." Estevez himself asserts, "Drag racing is war. If you bring a knife, and I bring a machine gun, you're dead. That's it." Drag racing, then, provides both thrills and power, especially if a driver wins by conquering his prospective enemy at the wheel. And as Estevez's biggest rival explains, "Half of the race is psychology, [and] mentally [Estevez has] got it." This same sense of power comes from drifting, as defined in the video *Drift Society, Volume 1* (2004), a feeling of power linked with desire and libido—represented by food and sex in the films. Overcoming enemies in cars serves as another sign that drivers have the power to conquer their own frontiers.

The Dukes of Hazzard, Estevez's inspiration for joining the urban car gang culture, calls attention to another key element in urban car culture: defying authority. Like the Dukes, drivers like Estevez skirt the law in cat-and-mouse games that move races from street to street. What sets current street racers apart from their counterparts in films such as Rebel without a Cause (1955) is the racial diversity of car racers and the absence of American muscle cars. Estevez's story echoes that of Junior Johnson, Tom Wolfe's whiskey-running NASCAR champ. Estevez defied the law just like Junior, but now races legally in the East Coast drag race circuit. He quit school to work in garages, where he perfected his skills as a mechanic and earned money to purchase accessories for his own Japanese car. He then earned money by winning illegal races, finally entering legal races—again like Junior—setting records and gaining enough product endorsements to pay for more of his expensive car parts.

Current urban drag racing enthusiasts seek thrills and power through speed and defiance of the law, just as Junior Johnson did in the 1950s and 1960s. Even though contemporary films like The Fast and the Furious, 2 Fast 2 Furious, Tokyo Drift, and Fast and Furious provide a progressive portrait of the ethnically ambiguous urban polyglot, through the windshield of a tricked up Japanese compact or Mustang, the values behind car racing and the culture they represent remain the same as those in car culture films from the beginning of film history. Speed represents power for the radical disenfranchised youth, so consideration of the fuel consumption and paved landscape that make speed possible seems irrelevant, if not ludicrous. These radicals, however, are not as radical and anti-establishment as they think they are, since they are oblivious to the environmental degradation to which they contribute. Instead, these so-called radicals hark back to an illusory time when nature seemed to offer an inexhaustible flow of resources; the myth of the American frontier further fuels the pursuit of freedom and individuality in the name of progress, a powerful mainstream and "establishment" ideology on which to build transformed concrete landscapes.

No one can deny that The Fast and the Furious, 2 Fast 2 Furious, Tokyo Drift, and Fast and Furious highlight a racially diverse cast that appeals to a broader demographic and makes a seemingly progressive point about race and class politics. But more important, they also show what can happen to an urban landscape already altered, paved over to accommodate the car and its driver. These films use the concrete landscape to assert individuality and a refusal to knuckle under to authority. With the exception of Brian and perhaps Roman, these inner city car racers don't want to be reintegrated into society. They race cars to gain status and money, to impress sexy women, and to defy the police, just like Junior Johnson and the Dukes of Hazzard.

But, like the suburbanites they reject, they act as if everything in nature exists to be consumed and exploited. To them, the concrete paved landscapes of inner city Los Angeles, Miami, and Tokyo seem natural. Only their exploitative transformation of them provides them with what they see as a radical edge. These films, then, encourage environmental degradation. When natural and concrete landscapes go unquestioned, so do their transformations.

NOTE

An earlier version of this essay was published in *Ecology and Popular Film: Cinema and the Edge* (Albany: SUNY Press, 2009) and is used here with permission from SUNY Press.

The epigraph is from an article published in the *St. Louis Dispatch,* 7 January 2004: F1.

WORKS CITED

Baudrillard, Jean. *America*. Trans. Chris Turner. London and New York: Verso, 1998.
——. "Simulacra and Simulations." *Selected Writings*. New York: Stanford Univ. Press, 1998.
Bennett, Michael. "Manufacturing the Ghetto: Anti-Urbanism and the Spatialization of Race." *The Nature of Cities: Ecocriticism and Urban Environments*. Ed. Michael Bennett and David W. Teague. Tucson: Univ. of Arizona Press, 1999. 169–88.
Drift Society, Volume 1. Rise Above Entertainment, 2004. http://www.drifting.com.
The Dukes of Hazzard. Dir. Jay Chandrasekhar. Warner Brothers, 2005.
The Dukes of Hazzard. Creator. Gy Waldren. CBS Television, 1979–85.
Fast and Furious. Dir. Justin Lin. Universal Pictures, 2009.
The Fast and the Furious. Dir. John Ireland and Edward Sampson. MGM/Palo Alto, 1955.
The Fast and the Furious. Dir. Rob Cohen. Universal Pictures, 2001.
The Fast and the Furious: Tokyo Drift. Dir. Justin Lin. Universal Pictures, 2006.
Flink, James J. *The Car Culture*. Cambridge: Cambridge Univ. Press, 1975.
Goff, Phillip. "Car Culture and the Landscape of Subtraction." *Monocular Texts* December 2003. http://www.worldcarfree.net/resources/freesources/ CarCult.htm. Retrieved 12 May 2005.
Korth, Joanne. "NASCAR History Awaits." *St. Petersburg Times Sports Online* 4 July 2004. www.sptimes.com/2003/07/04/Sports/NASCAR_history_awaits.shtml. Retrieved 12 May 2005.

Li, Ken. "Racer X." *Vibe Magazine* May 1998. Reprinted in *The Fast and the Furious* (2001 DVD ed.).

NASCAR: The Ride of their Lives. Country Music Television, 2008.

O'Hehir, Andrew. "*The Fast and the Furious:* Fast Cars! Hot Chicks! Pointless Thrills!" *Salon* 22 June 2001. http://www.dir.salon.com/ent/movies/review/2001/06/22fast_furious/index.html. Retrieved 4 December 2003.

Ross, Andrew. *The Chicago Gangster Theory of Life: Nature's Debt to Society.* London: Verso, 1994.

——. "The Social Claim on Urban Ecology." *The Nature of Cities: Ecocriticism in Urban Environments.* Ed. Michael Bennett and David W. Teague. Tucson: Univ. of Arizona Press, 1999. 15–30.

2 Fast 2 Furious. Dir. John Singleton. Universal Pictures, 2003.

Urry, John. "Automobility, Car Culture and Weightless Travel: A Discussion Paper." Department of Sociology, Lancaster University, UK, January 1999. 1–16. www.lancs.ac.uk/fass/sociology/papers/urry-automobility.pdf.

Vartabedian, Ralph. "How Many Cars Do You Own?" *Los Angeles Times* 16 February 2007. http://forums.motortrend.com/70/6334500/the-general-forum/how-many-cars-do-you-own-1-4-households-have-two-o/index.html. Retrieved 20 November 2009.

Wilson, Alexander. *The Culture of Nature.* Toronto: Between the Lines, 1992.

Wolfe, Tom. The Last American Hero Is Junior Johnson, Yes!" *Esquire* March 1965. Reprinted in *Esquire: 40th Anniversary Celebration* (October 1973): 211–22, 436, 438, 442, 446.

THE SCREAMING SILENCE

CONSTRUCTIONS OF NATURE
IN WERNER HERZOG'S
GRIZZLY MAN

ELIZABETH HENRY

A clear, attentive mind
Has no meaning but that
Which sees is truly seen.
—Gary Snyder, "Piute Creek," *Riprap*

In *New German Cinema,* Thomas Elsaesser tells us that German filmmaker Werner Herzog comes to America to explore the possibility of creating a new "cinema of experience." Herzog seeks to generate in the New World, with film, an experience of "pure being and pure seeing" (5). He looks to the camera to capture a vision of the world unencumbered by civilized man's obsessions with industrialized life, car culture, and mass media. In many of Herzog's films, the New World represents a quest of sorts, the opportunity to break out of the norms of civilization. It is, indeed, the norms of civilization that torment many of Herzog's characters. In *Aguirre: The Wrath of God* (1972), Herzog's sixteenth-century antihero wends his way through the thickly blanketed waterscape of the Amazon River in search of El Dorado; but instead of finding gold, he goes mad. In *Fitzcarraldo* (1982), a nineteenth-century-style madman attempts to lumber the weight of civilization, in the form of a 340-ton ship, over a mountain in order to build an opera house in the jungle. As one might imagine, the jungle wins. Even *The Great Ecstasy of the Woodcarver Steiner* (1974), about competitive ski jumping, illuminates the extremes to which humans are prone in their search for an escape from the banal and ordinary.

There is no better example of this Herzogian search for the original man in an original or "New World" than Herzog's 2005 documentary, *Grizzly Man*. The film offers a controversial portrait of a controversial activist by editing together interviews about and original footage shot by the grizzly bear activist Timothy Treadwell. Treadwell was a California beachcomber who moved to a remote area in Alaska for thirteen summers to live with, study, and film grizzly bears at Katmai National Park, until a bear killed him and his girlfriend, Amy Huguenard, in October 2003. The fact of their deaths stops many potential Treadwell sympathizers cold, although it is significant that Treadwell was not killed by a member of the grizzly bear group that had become acquainted with him.

Treadwell's confused self-portrayal in the footage he shot in Alaska, the mutable and often ironic nature of Herzog's interpretive stance toward Treadwell, and the variety of public responses to the Treadwell story, all serve to reveal and exacerbate some of the confusion around—as well as dissent and hostility toward—the term "animal rights advocate" and even, by suggestion, "environmentalist." Defining what Treadwell "was" becomes a challenge for viewers of Treadwell's footage, for viewers of Treadwell as seen through Herzog's sometimes ironic eye, and for viewers of Herzog, as we watch Herzog in *Grizzly Man* watching Treadwell watch the bears. But there are also moments of illumination in this film, when an "ecological" view of nature pours forth through the footage and counters the forces in this film that would have us embrace a skeptical or negative attitude about the natural world. These moments clarify for us what an ecocritical filmmaking might look like, and what a truly environmentalist and ecocentric approach to our experience of the natural world might consist of.

An ecocritical approach to the film allows for a different story to emerge, a new way of re-envisioning our relationship with the natural world. Rather than carrying our old stories with us and imposing them onto the landscape with our imaginations, we might instead allow the landscape itself to form our imaginations; thus, we might more intentionally approach what Emerson called an "occult relation between man and vegetable," one in which humans and nature are both subjects and participants in a relationship, "a harmony" of both (Emerson 11). Perhaps this is what Herzog is hoping for when he calls for a new sense of cinematic vision: "If we do not find adequate images and an adequate language for our civilization with which to express them, we will die out like the dinosaurs. . . . We have already recognized that problems like the energy shortage or the overpopulation of the world are great dangers for our society and for our kind of civilization, but I think that it has not been understood widely enough that we absolutely need new images" (quoted in Corrigan 143).

In this essay, I mean to examine Herzog's and Treadwell's often anthropocentric modes of relating to the nonhuman world, and thereby fend off critics who use this film as another example of a misguided "love" for nature that simply is not realistic. The problem with Treadwell's and Herzog's approach to nature is not that they embrace a Thoreauvian vision of nature, but rather that they, perhaps unintentionally, insist on their separation from nature. In an attempt to scrape away the trappings of civilization, both Treadwell and Herzog often reveal how influenced and tightly bound they are to the societies from which they came; perhaps inevitably, they both have trouble avoiding Western cultural constructions of nature and human/nature relations. Treadwell, for example, inherits his ideas of what it means to be in touch with nature from long-standing American cultural traditions. The land and our interactions with the land have long been essential to the American identity. As Roderick Nash says in his survey of American attitudes toward the landscape, *Wilderness and the American Mind*, "Wilderness was the basic ingredient of American civilization. From the raw materials of the physical wilderness Americans built a civilization; with the idea or symbol of wilderness they sought to give that civilization identity and meaning" (xi). In this film, through Treadwell's attempted definitions of himself as well as Herzog's definitions of Treadwell, the bears, and the landscape, we see reflections of American culture's own historical relationship with the wilderness since the Puritans landed on Plymouth Rock.

The roles, or personas, that Treadwell tries on, all of his "masks," are ways we have imagined ourselves in the New World. And while his exaggerated method of acting caricaturizes our own attitudes and roles, nevertheless, his stories, embarrassingly enough, are also our stories. Although Herzog reveals (and revels in) his own ironic interpretations of the American stories Treadwell attempts to embody, Herzog himself cannot resist providing us with some theories of his own about wilderness and our place in it. In this way *Grizzly Man* becomes the story of America's relationship to the New World: our shifting, conflicting, and sometimes delusional attempts to define ourselves in relationship to this land. Herzog and Treadwell both offer us insightful perspectives on the American psyche: struggling in relationship to the land; continually telling old stories of ourselves in the woods or in wide-open spaces; hoping that these old stories still apply; and perhaps, when they do not, feeling disillusioned with the possibility of any kind of relationship with nature at all.

In the opening shot of the film, Treadwell stares directly at the camera and addresses us, claiming for himself a variety of recognizable identities, in the space of just few minutes: "Most times I'm a kind warrior out here, most times I am gentle, I am like a flower, I am like a fly on the wall observing, non-committal, non-invasive in any way; occasionally, the kind warrior must must must become a Samurai, must become so formidable, so fearless of death, so strong, that he will win." While Treadwell declares himself to be master of the bears, in the background of the shot is a huge bear more than twice his size, with paws larger than his head, chewing and sniffing around. Significantly, Treadwell is positioned at the right edge of the frame. This is a position typically used to suggest that the subject is on his/her way out of the frame, and out of the situation. It is an unstable position, announcing movement and pending disappearance. The grizzly bear, positioned in the more dominant and powerful left half of the frame, will eventually push Treadwell completely out of the shot. Is this framing a foreshadowing on Treadwell's part of his own future "disappearance"? Treadwell would have looked much more dominant, much more the "master" of the shot, had he positioned himself on the left and the bear on the right. Is he consciously or unconsciously implying that, contrary to what he says, the bear will eventually be the master?

Treadwell gazes at the camera with a self-congratulatory, pleased, and yet pinched look about his lips. He cocks his head, tilting his forehead toward us, preparing himself for the show. We get a sense of Treadwell's self-consciousness here, a heightened awareness that he is "on camera" and in front of an audience, even while alone filming himself in the wilderness. Since Treadwell is using a wide-angle lens, which creates the illusion of greater depth in the shot, we intuitively know that the bears are closer than they appear to be. As he nervously looks over his shoulder several times during the shot, making sure the bear is keeping its distance, his bodily caution contradicts his use of language. That language comes from fairy tales and fables—stories of brave samurai, fragile flowers, and masters of nature.

At other times Treadwell reasserts his dominance in the frame. While the shot is carefully framed so that Treadwell has to kneel, appearing submissive to landscape and animals while speaking quietly, he does not remain humble for long and is not very convincingly humble at that. When he points his finger at the camera, his words imply that one should not show weakness in the wild, and his body and gestures dominate the frame. But even as his presence dominates the foreground, the depth and beauty of the background are so overwhelming that to the viewer there is really no doubt about what is really dominant and in control—it is both the mountain and the bears. Thus, from the start of the film, Herzog presents an ironic stance toward Treadwell with an opening shot that suggests we will be watching not so much a bear-dweller as a confused illusionist—or one suffering from his own ego-centric delusions.

There are contradictions in what Treadwell says, how he positions himself on the frame, and how he acts. And there are contradictions, or tensions, in the fables he presents as well: kind/warrior, samurai/flower/fly, observing not invading. By selecting this as an opening shot, Herzog lays heavy emphasis on Treadwell's contradictory character. From these opening shots, one wonders also if Treadwell is only "observing" and "not invading." While borrowing a term from the cinema verité tradition of documentary to describe his own presence in the wilderness, Treadwell is in reality anything but a "fly on the wall." In cinema verité's "fly on the wall" approach, the camera records according to a philosophy of filmmaking that attempts to keep the filmmaking devices as far out of the story as possible. This approach means to make the filmmaking apparatus invisible: no camera, no evidence of crew, no artificiality, and no voice-over narration. Treadwell is usually the antithesis of this kind of filmmaker. He is almost always present, always talking, and with Herzog's editorial help, always revealing the artificiality of his identity and his filmmaking. At the end of this scene, he adopts a head-down posture of humility, looking at the ground, a spiritual poser and performer. But then, he looks up at us with a knowing smile so that we know that he is lying. He knows that we know. He understands that we know he is a poser.

Last, this opening scene reveals Treadwell's announcement, really, of his own death, as he tells us how to interpret his death—as that of a master, not a martyr. Herzog's editing choices here let us know right away that our "hero" will die. The male bears start fighting among themselves as the musical soundtrack begins. While Herzog is talking about Treadwell's mission to protect these animals, they lumber toward the camera, powerful and threatening, with the haunting tones of the musical score intimating some folkloric-style tragedy to come. Herzog draws our attention to Treadwell's hubris in this opening, his foolhardy egoism in the face of these powerful animals, and contrasts Treadwell's rather naïve heroic stance with the stance he works to evoke in us as viewers—a sense of the threat of the bears and thereby the foolhardiness of Treadwell's proximity to them.

The next Treadwell persona to whom Herzog introduces us is that of the "animal advocate." Treadwell is not only a samurai, a flower, and a master; hereafter, we will see Treadwell in many shots making claims about the necessity and heroism of his own decision to come live in

Alaska for several months each year. In one scene, we see Treadwell gently curled around a wild fox, Timmy, petting the animal tenderly while reciting his manifesto: "Only Timmy is the boss of all foxes and all bears. Thanks for being my friend . . . does that feel good? The bond has developed between this very wild animal and this very fairly wild person; and you see he has this gorgeous fur and people are trying to kill him for it. We want this to end; stop killing and hurting these foxes and torturing them. If they knew how beautiful he was they would never hurt him." Here, his voice gains intensity and reaches higher emotional ranges in both diction and tonality. His pursed lips, self-contented demeanor, use of language, and highly emotional pitch communicate the rather self-righteous nature with which he asserts his animal advocate identity.

The childlike animal lover is, of course, a persona that is alive and well in popular culture. Walt Disney films evoke this stance in all of us; but "nature" documentaries, and fictional films that portray animals in the image of humans in order to emphasize their emotional attractiveness, also work to elicit a kind of childlike emotional sympathy in their viewers. In Treadwell's case, however, this sympathetic and childlike persona simply is not palatable. Rather than pique our own sentimental impulses, as *March of the Penguins* (2005) and *Happy Feet* (2006) do so effectively, Treadwell's rhapsodizing about the fox comes across as merely silly.

Perhaps it is the emotional exaggeration of the role of animal advocate that turns us off from the idea entirely. Where Treadwell is earnest, we find ourselves scoffing. Where he is too emotional, we are indifferent, complacent, or proudly judgmental toward him and what he represents. Here, Treadwell is not our hero, not even someone we are comfortable identifying with. Perhaps it is Treadwell's bending of gender and age boundaries that makes us uncomfortable. As a somewhat effeminate male and childlike adult, he challenges our own fragile gendered grown-up identities. Such challenges bring out the defensive scoffer in many of us. Because Treadwell's childlike demeanor contrasts with our cultural constructions of adult males as powerful and masculine, we are likely to see his caring for the life of a fox as a "sissy's game." Effectively, we are encouraged in this scene to write off the "animal protector."

Additionally, Treadwell's professed concern for the animals appears as a thinly disguised form of narcissism; his concern is a performance. His relationship with nature has a sickly codependency flavor; he is not really loving these animals so much as using them to enhance or reflect his own self-importance and heroics. "Thanks for being my friend," he says to Timmy the fox (named after himself). This line betrays his sense of inferiority and neediness. Treadwell is desperate for friendship and cloying in his attempts to "persuade" Timmy to stick around. The focus is on Treadwell and his needs, not the animals. Once again, typical prejudices and stereotypes about animal rights activists and, probably, environmentalists are reaffirmed in this scene: these types are disingenuous, self-centered, and view the natural world as a fairyland. Treadwell comes across as only interested in molding nature into his own image so that, ultimately, his entire adventure in the wild will be about himself. Treadwell's performance is, in a sense, political correctness at its worst. It is done for show.

The performative nature of Treadwell's identity becomes more explicit and more laughable as the film progresses. As Herzog points out, Treadwell's apparent intention in filming himself over these one hundred hours of footage was "to craft his own movie," or at the very least, a television series along the lines of Steve Irwin's *Crocodile Hunter*. "With himself as the central character," Herzog narrates, "he began to craft something way beyond a wildlife film." It soon becomes apparent that Herzog, too, is crafting Treadwell's identity. By selecting fragments from Treadwell's footage (from the one hundred hours to which he had access) that emphasize his bravado and self-consciousness, his obsessions with the camera and looking good, Herzog implies that this "animal rights protector" is really only in it for himself. It is hard not to extrapolate, thereby, from Treadwell to eco-activists generally—be they environmental or animal rights activists. Is such activism also self-promoting, self-conscious, self-serving? Are Treadwell's personas the face of a movement? And are Herzog's choices to show us all of Treadwell's foibles actually harming and degrading an ecological or eco-centric approach to human-natural relations? Both Treadwell's self-presentation and the use Herzog makes of Treadwell may, once again, harm the cause rather than help it.

In one scene Herzog selected for inclusion, for example, Treadwell is re-shooting a take, with a well-rehearsed line of dialogue intact in each take, while trying on different colored bandanas. In these "wild Timmy jungle scenes," Treadwell says, "I'll do it with the bandana on, with the bandana off, maybe two different colored bandanas, some without a bandana, some with the camera being held; this stuff could be cut into a show later on, but who knows what look I had, whether I had the black bandana or no bandana, very rarely the camo one, but I like the camo look." Treadwell's concern is not for the grizzly bears in this scene. Herzog's inclusion of this scene emphasizes Treadwell's narcissism and serves to discredit Treadwell as an activist, or, more potently, to imply that animal rights activists are childlike, self-absorbed, and concerned with banalities. The insignificance of the bandanas contrasts with Treadwell's apparent excitement over that insignificance. We are encouraged to keep our distance from Treadwell, to look at him objectively, if not critically; to see him as a fool for his insistence on getting the shot right, the performance right, and the bandana right.

The enthusiasm with which Treadwell runs up to the camera for an extreme close-up echoes much of the excited enthusiasm displayed by hosts of television nature documentaries. Steve Irwin, for instance, would often dash up to the camera from out of the woods, excited by what he had seen, breathless over what he was about to tell us. In Treadwell's case, what he is breathless over is his bandana. So it is the breathless excitement that becomes Herzog's ironic comment here. Herzog seems to be pointing out not only that Treadwell is crafting his own movie, "with himself as the central character," but also that he is something of a fool in doing so. Running up to the camera also ensures that Treadwell is always moving toward a dominant position in the frame, always from long shot to close-up. He is clearly not concerned with giving nature the last word by pulling back out to a long shot at the end of the scene. One expects this is what he would do if he were truly interested in letting nature be the *subject* of this film, in being merely a "fly on the wall" of this wilderness.

Among the other personas with which Treadwell experiments are a variety of religious postures. He becomes a penitent and supplicant when he begs for God's blessing and shares, or confesses, his innermost self. He convinces himself that his work with grizzlies is God's work. He performs this work with missionary zeal, tentatively soliciting God's favor: "If there's a God, God would be very pleased with me. It's good work. I feel good about it . . . but . . . be warned . . . I will die for these animals, I will die for these animals, I will die for these animals. Thank you so much for letting me do this. Thank you so much for these animals. For giving me a life." Treadwell's missionary persona reflects another American tradition, that of the Puritans who came to the New World to forge an errand into the Wilderness. Dangerous but essential missionary work, the missionary zeal to enter the wild was built upon a conception of the New World that sprang from the Old Testament. As Nash points out, "The Puritans, especially, understood the Christian conception of wilderness, since they conceived of themselves as the latest in a long line of dissenting groups who had braved the wild in order to advance God's cause" (34). The Puritan's errand, according to Nash, was analogous to the Old Testament exodus. William Bradford looked for his "Pisgah," just as Moses did. Edward Johnson saw his Puritan tribe entering a new Canaan toward a new mission.

Treadwell also sees himself as an intercessor of sorts, a savior of the areas he has come to protect. In an intensely funny and visually evocative scene of Treadwell in his tent—begging the gods for rain, screaming at them for a downpour—we find echoes of the Old Testament concept of man as earth's steward, as protector of creation. Treadwell's expansive emotions in this scene contrast with the claustrophobia of the tight framing and the highly filtered density of color and light inside the tent. But the prayers apparently work. Soon the drought is lifted, the rain pours, the river fills, the salmon run, and the bears have something to eat—all because of Treadwell's prayer.

At the opening of the scene in the tent, Treadwell declares that "it's September twentieth, the year 2000, expedition 2000." It's not just September twentieth, it's "Expedition 2000." Treadwell commands the calendar. He commands and controls other aspects of this scene as well. There are a lot of jump cuts in this sequence of prayers. Seemingly unnecessary, the jump cuts emphasize Treadwell's (or Herzog's) control over the scene. By illuminating the many takes, showing Treadwell putting the lens cap on and taking the lens cap off repeatedly, this footage reminds us of the overly rehearsed and controlled nature of Treadwell's performance. By leaving all of Treadwell's false starts intact in the sequence, Herzog emphasizes how scripted and performative the scene is, how much Treadwell considers his place before the camera. Treadwell constantly adjusts and repositions the camera, wipes the lens as if to demonstrate his control over the situation. He is central in the frame and commands it completely. The light is filtered through the blue tent like a Chinese lantern, but the black lines of the tent pole create shapes of filtered light more suggestive of a stained glass window. It is, after all, his "church," his "Expedition 2000," his pulpit. He demands rain while he has sanctuary from it. And after the rainfall, he quotes himself verbatim from the previous shot by referring again to the "Hindu floaty things" and being Allah's "go-fer boy." It can only mean that Treadwell watches his own footage immediately after filming it, and writes ensuing scenes based on his previous performance. This is footage that is rehearsed, constructed, and highly artificial.

Treadwell's hypervigilant holiness, or the appearance of it, does not last for long. Soon after the piety in the tent, Treadwell lets loose with a barrage of obscenities and gestures that establish him as anything but a peaceful, loving "nature boy." By following religion with rebellion, Herzog deconstructs any chance for us to sympathize with Treadwell as a man trying to do the right thing, reminding us instead that it is Treadwell's ego and rage that dominate this preservation project. Is Herzog making a broader statement about human nature, or at least about the American character: that not far beneath the surface of pious attitudes is an egomaniacal and angry soul? Is this another example of Herzog constructing Treadwell to ensure we have no sympathy for Treadwell or his cause?

In this most vehement and "angry young man" scene, Treadwell visits his rage upon the organization that, for thirteen years, had mostly served him well—the National Park Service. What he says in this scene is quite vulgar, and Treadwell's gestures, words, and attitude are all recognizable to those who ever felt disillusioned with modernity, highway traffic, or societal norms of all kinds. Treadwell's gestures and posturing seem so familiar in these shots that they appear to be imitations of actions he has seen before, rather than Treadwell authentically expressing himself. He, and the scene he sets up, feel like a product of the media. Treadwell adopts an urban rap persona. He is a rapster in the wilderness, marketing himself with a deliberately chosen, color-coordinated wardrobe, sunglasses strategically placed on his head. The background of the mountains behind him is also an image mediated by the lake that serves as a reflective mirror, a kind of movie or television screen reflecting and mediating our view of the mountains. Treadwell's body language betrays the fact that he is aware of having to move back for the long shot and then forward for the medium shot, while he delivers the recognizable *Terminator* line, "I'll be back."

When he begins to swear, it is obvious that this footage is no longer suitable material for grade school or high school students, the ostensible audience for whom he has been filming himself and the bears all these years. For whose benefit is Treadwell performing here? Is he imagining nature as his audience, which sits back behind him, implacable and, in comparison, reflecting back to us the ridiculousness of Treadwell's oversized ego in the face of such mountainous grandeur? Or is he filming himself merely for the benefit of his own narcissism? Herzog's inclusion of Treadwell's outbursts ensures our distance from him—from an emotional connection to him and possibly to nature itself. Treadwell may appear slightly mad here, but even his madness has an unoriginal feel. The exaggerated and performative nature of his rebellion may well serve to repress the same impulses in us. If protecting the wild looks like this kind of madness, it is quite unattractive to any would-be activists watching this film. Treadwell's over-the-top construction of "environmentalist" performance does not reflect well on environmentalism generally.

In this mode Treadwell embodies the "angry young man," the rebel figure who has long been popular in American media culture. When Marlon Brando's character in *The Wild One* (1953) is asked what he is rebelling against, he blankly responds, "Whaddya got?" In other words, the act of rebellion is more important than the reason for it. And although rebellion in American counterculture has typically been against rules, regulations, standards, governments, bureaucracies, or tradition, Treadwell shows us that the target of his rebellion does not really matter. He is rebelling here against the Park Service, one of his benefactors. Hence, it's clear that rebellion itself is the goal.

Nash points out that the American counterculture has typically aligned the concept of wilderness, of the "wild," with notions of "freedom, authenticity, or spontaneity" (252). "Given its general orientation, the counterculture inevitably found value in wilderness which was, after all, diametrically opposed to a civilization many had come to distrust and resent" (Nash 251). Yet even when a romanticized "back to nature" mythology is embraced as one's own, the separation between humans and nature can actually be reinforced rather than dispelled. Treadwell's version of the rebel is built on an "us versus them" approach to the natural world. In such a dualism, culture and nature remain separate and antithetical. As Nash puts it, "Thus is established a dualistic aesthetic and mindset of civilization versus wilderness" (240).

If Treadwell is to be called a "romantic," his romanticism is both naïve and cynical. It is naïve in that he refuses to explore the artificiality of his return to nature, the easy separation he assumes between the society he shuns and the natural world he hopes will enable him to leave behind all that has educated, domesticated, trained, and raised him. Treadwell's romanticism is cynical in the sense that his "return to nature" affirms his egomaniacal approach to the world. Nature does not so much exist for its own sake, as it is an opportunity for Treadwell's anger and ego to expand. Rather than humbling himself before the awesome face of the wild, he makes himself larger upon it. He territorializes Kodiak Island and makes it his canvas. His ego grows with his "colonization" of the land. The fox becomes *his* fox; the grizzly maze becomes *his* maze; the grizzlies become *his* grizzlies. He has named all the bears. The natural environment Treadwell inhabits becomes a mirror of himself—a mirror upon which his image can grow larger than his physical boundaries. This is why viewers are burdened by the overwhelming sense of self-consciousness in this "nature" documentary. Searching for lost inno-cence, Treadwell is distracted by his own image in the video camera. And in that silent lens, Treadwell sees only what the media projections before his have created and encouraged.

In writing about Herzog's films, film scholar Ingo Petzke says that "another important feature of Herzog's work, and closely related to his use of myth and imagery, is landscape. . . . The landscape's subtle depic-tion . . . sets the mood of a film. But gradually landscape becomes a kind of mindscape of the lead character who almost always is an obsessed lunatic, a pathological outsider, a loser on a grand scale—a mythological loser" (2). As we trace Treadwell's personas throughout the film, we see that in all his attempts to return to the wild and find an authentic self, his preconceived notions of behavior and identity get in the way. He tries too hard to be master and flower, Prince Valiant, protector and mission-ary of the wild, rebel and martyr ("I will die for them"). As viewers, we begin to suspect the motivation for his animal activism is an egotistical stance. That camera-conscious ego, those misguided personas, cast doubt on the apparent motivations of those who would protect the natu-ral world. The animal activists who die by the animals they mean to protect are just getting what they deserve. Sam Egli, in an interview for the film, makes this point: "To me he was acting like he was work-ing with people wearing bear costumes instead of wild animals. Those bears are big and ferocious and they come equipped to kill you and eat you, and that's just what Treadwell was asking for. He got what he was asking for. He got what he deserved in my opinion."

One gets the feeling that Herzog agrees with Egli. Herzog's own phi-losophy about nature is made quite clear throughout the film: that there is a great divide between humans and nature. To Herzog, nature is dan-gerous. The great divide between nature and culture is cold and broad and dangerous to cross. Herzog's filmic choices—his voice-over nar-ration, mysterious and morbidly atmospheric musical score, heavy-handed editing style—tell us at least as much about Herzog as about Treadwell. Herzog seems convinced of the ultimate horror and cold in-difference of nature, insisting that the great imaginary divide between nature and culture is to be crossed at our peril. As he asserts, "In all the faces of all the bears, I discover no kinship, no understanding, no mercy. I see only the overwhelming indifference of nature. To me there is no such thing as a secret world of the bears, and this blank stare speaks only of a half-bored interest in food."

While we explore Treadwell's personalities, Herzog explores various ways of interpreting them. That is, our experience of Treadwell's personas is highly mediated, controlled by Herzog's own intercutting and narration, in the same way that Treadwell's experience of himself as a savior/activist is mediated by social constructions of nature, by other representations of the wild and humans in it, and by Treadwell's own interpretations of them. Herzog's editing style is quite heavy-handed in this way. A shot of Treadwell talking about how much he loves the animals is immediately followed by a shot of Treadwell's coroner explaining what a bear did to his body during the attack. In another shot, Treadwell's rhapsodizing about his dominance and mastery over the bears is juxtaposed with a shot showing the bears themselves stomping toward the camera, or fighting, clawing, and biting one another. Through these juxtapositions, Herzog makes the point that these huge, ferocious, formidable, and dangerous animals are decidedly not the teddy-bear creatures Treadwell names "Mr. Chocolate" or "Grinch" or "Downy." Herzog presents a view of nature as cold, remote, even cruel, which thereby permits us to respond to nature with coldness, remoteness, and cruelty. There is not a ten-minute period in the film when the gruesome, powerful, or horrible side of nature is not alluded to or shown, usually in juxtaposition with something more florid from Treadwell. The didacticism of Herzog's editing choices makes it impossible to escape his morbid perceptions of nature and animals. Herzog may make fun of Treadwell's ego and delusions, but the director's own position regarding human/nature relations and humanity's place in the web of life is projected onto the landscape, and onto the grizzly bears. Just as Treadwell's "return to nature" becomes something of a parody of television nature shows and childhood fables, so Herzog's desire to "get back to the nature of film" succumbs to the equally simplistic views of nature as cruel and terrible, violent and indifferent.

Herzog includes footage of his own to support this point. He interviews a biologist who asserts that Treadwell was mistakenly trying to insert himself in a very "harsh world," and a Native American who feels that Treadwell had crossed a line of separation between humans and bears. He also inserts remarkable footage of "wild primordial nature" in the cold blue glacier canyons, deep and foreboding, impassable. Linking this landscape to Treadwell's troubled "soul," Herzog states, "This gigantic complexity of tumbling ice and abysses separated Treadwell from the world out there; this landscape in turmoil is a metaphor of his soul." Oddly enough, this steady and solid glacial landscape does not appear to be in turmoil at all, unless Herzog is making a veiled reference to global warming. It seems solid, implacable, more than peaceful. Herzog heavy-handedly interprets nature as a violent "other" to be fought or avoided.

In this way Herzog is presenting us with a socially constructed view of humans' relationship to their environment—a determinist's approach that posits nature as the enemy against which humans struggle and ultimately will always lose.

Whether we focus on Treadwell's self-presentation or on Herzog's construction of Treadwell as an animal rights activist, the film offers us a portrait that relies on narrow stereotypes and, thus, that misses the mark in terms of accurately defining an ecological and ecocentric point of view. Unfortunately, it serves to replicate and amplify stereotypes already promoted and agreed upon in pop culture iterations of what it means to protect the wild and the animals within it. A more accurate portrayal of an environmentalist orientation would have to include the contributions of science to our understanding of ecosystems and human/nature relations. Science provides us with evidence of the impact of human action on ecosystems, and evidence, therefore, of the ecological interconnectedness of all planetary life. These impacts are real, not imagined projections of a narcissistic ego, represented here by Treadwell.

Neither Treadwell nor Herzog appeals to scientific evidence in support of his position regarding nature and human/nature relations. Ecological thinking points to the interdependence of all life and represents an important step toward a biocentric, rather than anthropocentric, understanding of the relations between beings and environments. An ecological approach to human/nature relations and an ecocritical engagement with artistic expressions of these relations would foster sustainability and survival for all species. What Michael Branch notes in regards to the field of literary ecocriticism applies equally to approaching films ecocritically: "Implicit (and often explicit) in much of this new criticism is a call for cultural change. Ecocriticism is not just a means of analyzing nature in literature; it implies a move toward a more biocentric worldview, an extension of ethics, a broadening of humans' conception of global community to include nonhuman life forms and the physical environment" (Branch et al. xiii).

By this definition, self-centeredness and human-centeredness must loosen their grip on us if we are to be "ecocritical" in our worldview. Ralph Waldo Emerson insisted that the ego must be quieted in order for an original experience of nature to arise. In a climactic moment in his essay "Nature" (1836), Emerson himself is able to let go of his ego and his preconceived ideas in order to receive nature in a different way: "Standing on the bare ground—my head bathed by the blithe air and uplifted into infinite space—all mean egotism vanishes. I become a transparent eyeball; I am nothing! I see all; the currents of the Universal Being circulate through me; I am part or parcel of God" (11). That is a tall order for a man (or woman) with a movie camera. But there are moments in *Grizzly Man* when Herzog allows Treadwell's camera-work to speak for itself, or rather, nature to speak for itself through the presence of the camera. In these rare moments, the camera lens, like Emerson's eyeball, becomes more transparent, allowing Nature's presence to be communicated more directly, unfettered by filters of ego, personas, or socially constructed ideas about nature. In these moments the frame opens up and we obtain a window into a human awareness that seems more at one with, or at least at peace with, the waving, windy quiet of the wilderness sanctuary, and the magnificent and powerful presence of the grizzly bears.

Remarkably enough, Herzog notices these moments, allows them to be, and points them out. At the end of a scene in which Treadwell makes a speech on behalf of the bear he names "Mr. Chocolate," a baby fox unexpectedly comes into the frame and trots across the screen, creating its own silent commentary about the spontaneity of life, even the joy of living. Herzog's voice-over commentary calls attention to the sense of surprise and spontaneity afforded by moments like these: "The scene seems to be over but as a filmmaker sometimes things fall into your lap, an inexplicable magic of cinema." Herzog acknowledges that while filming in the wild, filmmakers sometimes "capture[d] such glorious improvised moments that studio directors with union crews can never dream of." What Herzog is suggesting, both by showing us this footage and by commenting on it, is a more ecological, rather than egotistical or anthropocentric, approach to filmmaking. Treadwell stops talking, as does Herzog, in these frames. The foxes bounce into the frame from unexpected corners; they move through the frame with their own quiet joy of being. At the same time, we as viewers experience a sense of connection with the natural world, rather than a sense of distance induced by Treadwell's desperate attempts to define himself in relation to the nature he aspires to "save."

There are other rare but provocative moments during which, for a few seconds, nothing is "happening" except grass blowing in the wind. The experience of watching these moments is much closer to the experience of taking a walk in a meadow; they are experiential rather than spectacular. Herzog points to this difference. "In his action movie mode, Treadwell probably did not realize that seemingly empty moments had a strange secret beauty. Sometimes images themselves develop their own life."

In Herzog's *Kasper Hauser*, about a man kept prisoner since childhood in a barren room with little exposure to the outside world, the character of Kasper Hauser emerges into nature and culture simultaneously when he acquires the use of writing; he plants seeds in the ground in the shape of his own name. When the flowers sprout and bloom, writing his name in the earth, Kasper Hauser lays himself down amid the blooms. As the camera pulls away from this inscription of self upon nature and moves up to reveal an open field on the hillside behind the character, the long grasses we see, blown by the wind like strands of hair, encourage our own psyche to be silent, to cease defining and naming, for just a moment, in order to experience the land, relatively unfettered by cultural mediations. This, I would argue, is an ecological moment in filmmaking, as is the one described above from *Grizzly Man*. In these shots of blowing grass, the ego and the territorialization of space are quieted down, and we are allowed to experience for ourselves what ecologists are telling us: that we are interconnected. Such moments in film are akin to what Emerson called our "original relation to the universe" (7), or what Timothy Corrigan has referred to as Herzog's search for "the unblemished eye" (122). Herzog and Treadwell achieve this in *Grizzly Man* when they cease trying to achieve anything. As Corrigan puts it, "For here the vision originates in an unchanneled encounter with a world in which human sight is not its center but a participant dissolved in its energies" (127). Herzog and Treadwell include shots of a world "whose meaning lies not in any significance attained from the human order but in their own self-conspicuous vitality" (128).

In the final moments of the film, following the coroner's detailed interpretation of Treadwell's and Amy Huguenard's terror and violent death, Herzog concludes with a shot of grizzly bears running along a beach, literally kicking up their heels as a broad stretch of water laps against them. Here, we are encouraged to see not our terror of bears, not our imagined representations of cold indifference and violent death, not our vanity or foolishness in attempting to get close to them, but simply the bears, magnificent creatures in their own right. Herzog himself submits to the openness, to the spontaneity of nature when he declares, "Treadwell is gone; the argument how wrong or how right he was disappears into a distance and a fog. What remains is his footage . . . the animals in their joys of being, in their grace and ferociousness."

According to Timothy Corrigan, Herzog's contradictory approach to nature in many of his films "struggles to efface a homocentric perspective" (133). There are moments in Herzog's films, asserts Corrigan, when he means to "engage the spectator's eye not in the titillating fashion of Hollywood cinema where voyeuristic distance maintains the spectacle but as an exploration and hypnotic participation in the energies of space" (139). So, too, in the rare ecological moments in Grizzly Man, Herzog's own didacticism is subverted as hypnotic space gazes out at us, as we, too, gaze into the "luminous presence of nature" (Corrigan 141). Nature, in this mode, is neither consciously malevolent, nor a blank screen upon which we can project our mediated personas, nor a teddy bear from our childhood. Powerful, it looks back at us. We can sense ourselves being sensed. Perception, even filmed, becomes a kind of participation.

WORKS CITED

Aguirre, the Wrath of God (Aguirre, der Zorn Gottes). Dir. Werner Herzog. Hessischer Rundfunk, 1972.

Branch, Michael, Rochelle Johnson, Daniel Patterson, and Scott Slovic. Reading the Earth: New Directions in the Study of Literature and the Environment. Boise: Univ. of Idaho Press, 1999.

Corrigan, Timothy. New German Film: The Displaced Image. Austin: Univ. of Texas Press, 1983.

Elsaesser, Thomas. New German Cinema: A History. New Brunswick, NJ: Rutgers Univ. Press, 1989.

Emerson, Ralph Waldo. The Portable Emerson. Ed. Carl Bode. New York: Penguin, 1981.

Fitzcarraldo. Dir. Werner Herzog. Filmverlag der Autoren, 1982.

The Great Ecstasy of the Woodcarver Steiner (Die Grosse Ekstase des Bildschnitzers Steiner). Dir. Werner Herzog. Suddeutscher Rundfunk, 1974.

Grizzly Man. Dir. Werner Herzog. Discovery Docs, 2005.

The Mystery of Kaspar Hauser (Jeder fur sich und Gott gegen alle). Dir. Werner Herzog. Filmverlag der Autoren, 1974.

Nash, Roderick. Wilderness and the American Mind. New Haven, CT: Yale Univ. Press, 1967.

Petzke, Ingo. "Aguirre, Wrath of God." Senses of Cinema February 2002. http://www.archive.sensesofcinema.com/contents/cteq/01/19/aguirre.html. Retrieved 5 January 2007.

BAMBI AND FINDING NEMO
A SENSE OF WONDER IN THE
WONDERFUL WORLD OF DISNEY?

. . . .

LYNNE DICKSON BRUCKNER

Writing in the 1950s, Rachel Carson noted that "if a child is to keep alive his inborn sense of wonder . . . he needs the companionship of at least one adult who can share it, rediscovering with him the joy, excitement and mystery of the world we live in" (45). In this cultural moment, however, children are less likely to receive knowledge about the nonhuman world from an interested adult than from the media and popular culture, especially animated films. Framed by an ecological perspective, this essay looks at the potential impacts of *Bambi* (1942) and *Finding Nemo* (2003) on children's knowledge of and sense of wonder for the nonhuman world.[1]

When re-released in March 2005, *Bambi* "eclipsed all same day DVD/VHS competition with first day sales reaching one million units on DVD and video in North America."[2] Similarly, as of February 2005, the Disney/Pixar venture *Finding Nemo* had grossed nearly $1.5 billion.[3] The impact of such financially successful films on children's perception of and relationship to the nonhuman world cannot be underestimated. For Henry Giroux, for example, "Animated films operate on many registers, but one of the most persuasive is the role they play as the new 'teaching machines.'" Not only do Disney films have "as much cultural authority and legitimacy for teaching roles, values, and ideals as more traditional sites of learning" (84), but the corporation also participates in the school system through sponsoring teacher of the year awards and providing scholarships, financial aid, and other learning opportunities—all of which work to create the Disney "image as a public service industry" (87). The environmental information and extras that are packaged with *Bambi* and *Finding Nemo* show how the corporation uses the mantle of pedagogy to veil the very commodification of nature that Disney products promote. While *Bambi* and *Finding Nemo* encourage ecological sensitivity, they do so in qualified terms. The marketplace effect of the Disney brand, its approach to the representation of animals and ecology, and its appeal to a well-intentioned but underinformed public converge to produce results that are, at best, contradictory.

Released six decades apart, *Bambi* and *Finding Nemo* share important common elements. They depict anthropomorphized animals inhabiting animated versions of their natural environments; and they feature animals, rather than humans, toys, or mermaids, as the central characters. Both use the newest technologies available to them to represent natural habitats with remarkable realism and care. In both, the primary threat to the animal characters is "man."[4] The hunters and the forest fire they cause in *Bambi*, and the Dentist, Darla, and military debris on the ocean floor in *Finding Nemo*, underscore the destructive impact humans have on the natural world. The DVDs for the re-released *Bambi* and for *Finding Nemo* include extra features dispensing ecological knowledge, and their Web sites offer "lite" green environmental information and activities.

When viewed in isolation from other cultural factors, *Finding Nemo* appears to be more ecologically sound than *Bambi*; it distributes environmental responsibility more widely than the earlier film, which places all blame on hunters alone. Yet both films have generated a "syndrome" or "effect," pointing to their cultural impact. The "Bambi effect" is its wholesale indictment of hunting and its sentimental adoration of woodland creatures. The "Nemo syndrome" refers to its promotion of naïve solutions, such as releasing captive nature into the "wild," in this case by flushing the fish down the drain and into the ocean. *Bambi* has a long history of encouraging affection for nature while also shaping public opinion on the merits of hunting and forest fires. *Finding Nemo* has generated faulty human behavior, ranging from a rash of purchases of clown fish and anemones to children flushing their pet fish in an effort to free them. Nonetheless, *Finding Nemo*'s end result may well be greater public education about the tropical fish trade and the global threat to coral reefs.

Despite their overt ecological dimensions, these films present us with problematic representations of nature. While both work to achieve accuracy in their representation of animals and ecosystems, their depiction of animals relies on caricature and are often inaccurate, or overly sentimentalized and "cuddly."[5] A central ecocritical concern elicited by these films is their anthropomorphizing of animal characters. Anthropomorphism necessarily sees the natural world through an anthropocentric lens that establishes humanity as the barometer for normative values and affirms the centrality of human life. Because anthropocentrism views the world in terms of human needs and desires, rather than whole ecosystems, a number of environmental ethicists make the case that "anthropocentric views are antithetical to the agenda of environmentalists" (McKenna 122). Yet others argue that anthropocentricism can potentially militate against seeing nature as inert matter and as endlessly exploitable. Jonathan Bate, for example, refuses to discount anthropomorphic texts as devoid of environmental value. Speaking about anthropomorphically themed ecopoetry, he argues that the "values of home, community and loyalty are thus invested in an animal. Whether or not this investment is regarded as pure human projection, its function is to break down the distinction between human and animal being" (178). While anthropomorphism needs to be balanced with knowledge of animal behavior, when it incites a generation to see nature as a living system of which we are only a part, then it has the potential to undermine the very anthropocentric perspective it necessarily entails.

Studying nature films from an ecocritical perspective also entails taking into account when the spectatorial mode enacts a separation of viewer from ecosystems through framing and fetishizing nature.[6] Disney's *True Life Adventure* series (initially inspired by footage taken for *Bambi*) features vivid and true-life plant and animal photography. However, as Kenneth Kidd avers, "realistic" nature footage is often a matter of "entertainment and spectacle" (267). Some footage is shaped during the shooting process before it hits the editing room. After waiting weeks to get a shot of a beaver gnawing a tree, for example, one Disney filmmaker was enraged to discover his camera was not loaded at the crucial moment. To get the shot he wanted, he ran out of his blind, grabbed the felled sapling, and jabbed it into the ground. Minutes later, the beaver he was trying to photograph was "obligingly sawing away at the tree" (Schickel 287). Animated representations can be less problematic than live action as they call attention to, rather than hide, their own staging and artificiality. Unlike spectacularized illusions of nature untouched, animated films foreground their manipulation of the nonhuman world, pointing up rather than obviating how nature is framed and produced for human visual consumption.

Nevertheless, the Disney marketing machine has overtly linked *Bambi* and *Finding Nemo* to "real" nature and ecological issues. While David Whitley argues persuasively that *Bambi* reflects the conservationist ethos of the 1940s (3, 67), the film was initially marketed as a love story. By the 55th Anniversary Edition (1997), however, Disney recognized the burgeoning appeal of eco-friendly films. The 1994 documentary accompanying this release stresses that "*Bambi* stands out as one of the first environmentally conscious films ever made" ("Magic"), and notes Walt's affection for nature. The bonus features accompanying the 2005 release affirm Disney's intention to capitalize on changing trends in market preferences. The DVD set includes "DisneyPedia: Bambi's Forest Friends," a four-minute film of "fun and interesting facts." Viewers learn not only that deer and rabbits are herbivores while skunks are omnivores but also that owls can turn their heads 270 degrees, and "not all the way around like some people say!" On the Web site for the DVD, children are invited to create their own virtual forest; they are challenged to "see how healthy your forest is. Do you have enough water? Do you have too many animals?" The child can "go back to Create Your Forest to make changes."[7] Treading problematically on the fine line between stewardship and domination, this activity confers ownership to humans by repeatedly telling the player that this is "your" forest. Also, the ease with which natural imbalances can be repaired (here, with a click of the mouse) creates the illusion that ecological problems are readily solved.

Where *Bambi* succeeds ecologically is in the centrality it assigns to nature and the nonhuman world; as one of the earliest reviewers wrote, "Nature [i]s the chief character,"[8] and the Audubon Society "compared its consciousness-raising power to *Uncle Tom's Cabin*" (Cohen). The 69-minute film opens with a remarkably long shot of the forest, depicted with the depth and beauty of Disney's then new multiplane animation. Music plays, accompanied by a human voice singing in wordless vocalization; there are no lyrics. The camera pans through the forest, showing lower deciduous growth, rocks, earth, and evergreens in various stages of the life cycle. Craggy trees and close-ups of bark give way to a waterfall and sunlit water; birdsong is layered on to the musical score, gradually replacing the human voice. Conveying age, beauty, and mystery, the forest is the central interest in much of the film. After 1 minute 24 seconds, the old owl flies across the screen, yawns, and begins snoring in time with nature. Dialogue is still withheld.

The forest becomes increasingly populated and active with anthropomorphized but recognizable animals—the chipmunk, the squirrel, baby birds, a mouse washing its face in droplets of water. Bluebirds fly across the top of the screen, rousing the forest community to gather. Three minutes and 33 seconds into the film, Thumper speaks the first words: "Wake up! Wake up! Wake up, Friend Owl!" While some of the animals border on cloying, the sustained and dialogue-free focus on the nonhuman world lends significance to nature as a whole, not just to animals as surrogate humans. Bate has argued that language potentially separates us from the very nonhuman world we seek to understand (37); filmic representation also serves as a sort of barrier, yet the absence of dialogue highlights the focus on the forest.

The young viewer may develop curiosity about the forest as he or she follows Bambi's development. After finding out that rabbits "thump" (though not knowing why), Bambi goes off on his first romp with Thumper and his siblings. As Bambi discovers that butterflies are neither birds nor flowers and that skunks hibernate, the excitement of learning about nature is richly conveyed. Throughout this scene, specific plants and elements of the forest are depicted with care. Nature in such moments is beautiful not because it offers grand or sublime vistas, but rather because the particular plants and flowers, old wood, and rocks are drawn with detail and interest—almost free of caricature.

Nevertheless, the natural world is also distorted in multiple ways. David Payne argues that the forest community mimics the structures of patriarchy, and *Bambi* is inflected by an overriding mode of patriarchal adulation. As the scene develops, forest animals, grouped in families, assemble to greet and admire the new prince. The scene of Bambi's birth closes with the camera panning up to an outcropping of rocks, where Bambi's father, a massive stag viewed from a low angle, presides over the forest. This image of paternal order and security returns at the end of the film when Bambi assumes the role of grand patriarch.

Problematically, the forest is created as a predation-free community in which owls and chipmunks coexist harmoniously. For Lutts, *Bambi* portrays a "distorted image of woodland ecology, one in which all animals live at peace" (167).[9] The representation of the woodland creatures owes more to popular belief than to observed animal behavior. In one scene a mother opossum hangs upside down next to her young. While opossums do have prehensile tails, they can only hang briefly and do not sleep upside down, as the film implies.

Disney did aim for authenticity—or, more precisely, for a simulacrum of authenticity—in its depiction of nature. One of Walt's goals was to capture the "hidden textures of the forest environment," and he sent Maurice Day to Maine "to photograph thousands of feet of forests, snowfall, rainstorms, spider webs, changes of light and seasons" (Thomas 155). Artists watched this footage, made field trips to the Los Angeles Zoo, heard lectures from experts, and studied the movements of two fawns that were donated to the studio.[10] Eventually, "rabbits, ducks, skunks, owls and other species were added until the studio resembled a small zoo" (Thomas 155).

The production team's efforts to achieve verisimilitude comes through. In the "April Showers" segment, the viewer sees carefully drawn Jack-in-the-Pulpits, ferns, and grasses. Even "the splash of the rain is accurate" (Lutts 13). In winter, we see deer on their hind legs straining to strip bark off trees. The spring renewal after Mother dies includes dogwood blossoms and Queen Anne's lace. Bambi, now an adolescent buck, rubs the velvet off his antlers (though out of season). Throughout the film, dialogue is relatively sparse, and the long shots of seasonal change feature a level of visual specificity that makes nature a central presence. Images of the forest tend toward the pastoral, idealized, lovely, and endlessly renewable, even annoyingly perky; yet storms, snow, and the possibility of starvation are also given a place in this story.

Such threats, however, are minimal compared to the danger presented by "man." Man's destructive force appears in the first meadow scene. Mother cautions Bambi, "Out there we're unprotected . . . so we have to be very careful." After six minutes featuring the delights of the meadow, danger is signaled by threatening music and the cawing of crows. Led by the Great Prince, Bambi and his mother flee to safety as the first gunshot erupts into the film. This time, it misses. When Bambi asks, "What happened, Mother? Why did we all run?," she somberly responds, "Man was in the forest." From this point on the film underscores man's destruction of nature, a theme amplified by the film's erasure of predation and its tempered depiction of nature's hardships.

Consider the famous and traumatic center of the film. Eating spring's first shoots of green, Mother senses danger: "Bambi, quick, the thicket." A shot rings out, and Mother urges Bambi to run. Bambi races toward cover, and we hear the second and fatal shot. After his initial joy ("We made it!"), Bambi shrinks and cries, alone amid silhouettes of bleak columnar trees. In keeping with the film's patriarchal reverence, the Great Prince appears and leads him away, stating, "Come, my son." As bucks don't tend to the care of their young, the film distorts nature to produce the image of father as protector.

While the traumatic death of the doe suggests that patriarchy can supplant the absent mother, it also equates the primal fear of the loss of the mother with the death of an animal. The anthropocentrism in the film cuts both ways: terrifying the viewer with the death of the mother (from a human orientation), but also associating such immense loss with a nonhuman death (that of a doe). In this sense the conventional binary of human/nonhuman is productively disrupted. Yet with the film's ending, which simultaneously enacts a return of the mother (embodied in Bambi's mate, Faline) and the restoration of mother nature, the film disturbingly hints that mothers and forests are easily (endlessly?) renewable.

Man, who is never actually depicted, is again referenced after the "twitter-pated" scene in which Bambi, Flower, and Thumper all find mates. As Faline sleeps, Bambi wakes to see smoke rising from a campsite. His father intones, "It is man; he is here again. There are many this time." The terror that ensues is sustained for eight full minutes. In field brush, petrified pheasants attempt to calm each other—"Don't fly, don't fly"—yet one "can't stand it any longer." She flies. She is shot. Additional birds fly; they too are shot. What follows is a frenzy of shootings, in the sky at birds, on the ground at rabbits and squirrels; rampant shots make potholes in the dirt. Man's violence is constructed as random and relentless.

Pursued by immense and bloodthirsty dogs (oddly implying that predation between animals is man-made), Faline enters the frame. The devastation brought on by man only accelerates from this point. As Faline flees, Bambi fights off the dogs (embodied jaws), only to be grazed as he leaps across a cavern. Bambi collapses. Highlighting the hunters' destructive presence, the film turns to the campfire, which ignites and travels with uncontrollable speed. As the forest is violently consumed, Bambi remains fallen and lifeless. He is only saved by his father, who forces Bambi to get up; the two race through perilous fire-torn woods. Viewers' identification with the animals and the attendant demonization of the hunters is made complete as the film shifts to the forest animals crawling to safety on an island. Bedraggled and exhausted forest mothers bring their young to safety, nestling them with maternal concern. Joyful music recommences as Bambi finally approaches Faline; they nuzzle while the forest continues to burn behind them.

Bambi closes by skipping ahead to the following spring. At first, the natural world appears a bit damaged, charred by the forest fire and somewhat barren; but in a matter of 57 seconds, nature is restored and flourishing. Whitley finds that such restoration potentially reflects an understanding of how fire has long been a part of natural ecological systems.[11] While Whitley's argument has merit, the scene functions less as a comment on whether natural or prescribed burning is elemental to healthy ecosystems than an offering of the "happily ever after" resolution that a Disney film requires. Such endings are made possible by film's ability to accelerate time, to collapse years of recovery into a few seconds, creating a false understanding of how natural processes work.

At the film's closing, the forest is rich in flowers and greenery; the environment's renewing power quickly overrides the massive and enduring damage the viewer witnessed in the previous scenes. The message in this final scene is problematic: regardless of man's destruction, nature can eternally renew itself. Nature's abundance and magically restorative capabilities are amplified as we learn that Faline has given birth to not one but two fawns. In the film's final images, the forest problematically appears as a resource that not only survives but also flourishes in the face of human carelessness and damage. Equally disturbing is the way *Bambi* absolves viewers from examining their role in environmental degradation. Rather than locating ecological destruction as a problem for which we all bear a measure of responsibility, blame is assigned exclusively to the hunters. As such, the film allows us to locate the environmental problem "over there," rather than "here," in the aggregate practices of all human beings.

Over time, *Bambi* has contributed to the polarization of two issues that demand more complex ecological responses: hunting and forest fires. The film has been criticized for contributing to the notion that forest fires are unequivocally destructive (Schullery 691). While views on natural fires and controlled burning have shifted over the years, *Bambi* continues to influence public sentiment on this issue. Replaced by Smokey Bear in 1944, *Bambi* was initially tied to the anti–forest fire campaign, and was again linked to the campaign in 1979 as well as 2004 and 2005.[12] Problematically, the images in the film in concert with this campaign create a unilateral view of forest fires as destructive, without educating the public on their role in renewing woodland ecology.

Another dominant response that has continued to follow *Bambi* is the strong anti-hunting sentiment that it fosters. Ralph Lutts finds that *Bambi* "has become perhaps the single most successful and enduring statement in American popular culture against hunting" (160), and asserts that its "antihunting message was conveyed on a completely emotional level through sympathy with its characters" (162). Waller Hastings complicates this view, asserting that Disney softens considerably the treatment of hunters in Felix Salten's original story, *Bambi: A Life in the Woods* (1926). Nonetheless, Hastings concedes that the film scripts viewers into the "place of the hunted" (54) and that the death of Bambi's mother is the most perennially remembered scene (55).

The ecopolitics of hunting are outside the purview of this essay; however, any responsible discussion of hunting and environmental issues would have to take into account the stress on and damage to ecosystems that are overpopulated by deer—damage that threatens the survival of other smaller species whose cover and food deer consume. While deer overpopulation stems from our intrusion on natural habitats and the reduction of natural predators, the solution can only be a complex one. Interestingly, Aldo Leopold's 1943 deer reduction plan was halted by public sentiment after the initial release of *Bambi*. While *Bambi* makes nature central to the narrative and may inspire in viewers an interest in and appreciation for ecology, the 1942 film does not sufficiently promote well-informed human responses to ecosystem imbalances. Even the educational features on the 2005 DVD and Web site do little to truly educate viewers or urge them to take responsibility for their part in environmental degradation.

While Bambi's overt framing of ecological issues was added retroactively with the re-release of the film on DVD, the Finding Nemo DVD set comes packaged with a "Fish Encyclopedia," so children can "Learn about the Real Fish behind the Characters." It also includes a short film: Exploring the Reef with Jean-Michel Cousteau. In Mr. Ray's Encyclopedia, viewers learn that royal blue tangs are vegetarians; mother turtles crawl up on the beach to lay their eggs; sharks are warm-blooded; royal gramma lorettos can swim upside down; and fish don't have eyelids. More humorously, Mr. Ray explains that "clown fish can live among the anemones' stinging tentacles because their bodies are coated with protective mucus. Mucus, yuck!" While the snippets of humor in this segment may militate against seeing the content as significant, they may also serve to sustain interest and imprint the information for the young viewer.

In Exploring the Reef, viewers are informed that the reef is "a complex world full of color, life, and wonder . . . a timeless thing of beauty for all to enjoy, and yet mankind's actions have destroyed over one-fourth of the world's reefs." Comedic interjections (largely from Dory) are peppered throughout Cousteau's comments, yet the short film treats the issue quite poignantly in the end. Nemo asks, "Dad, why is that coral white?" Evoking pathos, Marlin explains that the coral is sick and pale, not unlike Nemo when he is feeling ill. As they speak, the camera pans across acres of dead white coral. When Nemo asks, "Will it be okay?" Cousteau replies, "Well, Nemo, it won't be easy. People must learn to live in better balance with nature—conserving energy, recycling, reducing pollution. But if we do all this, the ocean's temperature may lower, allowing the coral to flourish." The answer is far more complex and responsible than the inexplicable renewal of nature in Bambi, and it is cast in terms that children can understand. Under "5 Things You Should Know" on the Web site for the DVD, the reef is given a first-person voice, thus offering an alternative, albeit anthropomorphic, perspective to the dominion implied by "your forest" on the Bambi site: "My temperature is rising and I am getting sick because of global warming." Children can click on a link to Jean-Michel Cousteau's Ocean Futures Society for information on reefs and how to help protect them.

While it is good to see Disney partnering with a nonprofit, "nongovernment, marine conservation and education organization," we cannot neglect its strong ties to other less environmentally minded multinational corporations: AT&T, General Motors, General Electric, Kraft Foods, Kodak, and United Technologies all sponsor various pavilions at the EPCOT Center (Fjellman 14). Moreover, while Disney has cloaked its products in increasingly green wrapping, it simultaneously commodifies both animals and ecology in disturbing ways.[13] One of the Disney imagineers (imagination engineers) explains that Animal Kingdom creates "a Disney realism, sort of utopian in nature . . . where we carefully program out all the negative, unwanted elements and program in all the positive elements" (quoted in M. Smith 268). The negative elements, however, are far from programmed out for the living animals. As Susan Willis observes, visitors "watch the tigers animated . . . by carefully contrived 'enrichment' devices that ensure the animal actors will always be on stage. Scents, sometimes of food, often of urine, are the lures. . . . Moreover, the offstage tunnel that connects the two areas of the tiger exhibit is perversely cooled in winter and warmed in summer so the cats will not linger there but will use it only for traveling back and forth" (58). Such manipulation of live animals undercuts the environmental ethos Disney claims for films like *Bambi* and *Finding Nemo*.

Unlike *Bambi*, *Finding Nemo* does not begin with footage emphasizing the natural world. Rather, it opens with Marlin asking his wife, Coral, for reassurance regarding the home he has procured for their budding family. Admiring the neighborhood, the quality of the schools, and the view, the couple's suburban values are so exaggerated that one wonders if the filmmakers are mocking their own anthropocentricism. Nonetheless, like the animators for *Bambi*, those who worked on this Disney/Pixar CG animated film recognized that authenticity and accuracy are crucial to good caricature. The executive producer, John Lasseter, encouraged those working on the film to get certified in scuba, so each could personally experience the underwater world of the reef (Vaz 14). Dr. Adam Summers, technical advisor for the film, arranged lectures on "everything from the behavior of light in water to the movement of waves" (Lynch 2).[14] Artists studied the preserved sharks at the Steinhart Aquarium warehouse, while the animation shaders analyzed light and contour, using dead fish from fish stores. As the shading director states, "Tropical fish die a lot, unfortunately. So we always had a good supply at fish stores of dead fish" (*Nemo* "Documentary"). The correlation between the death toll of real tropical fish and the film's anti-tank message cannot have been lost on its illustrators.

Like the *Bambi* animators who viewed reels of footage of the Maine woods, those working on *Finding Nemo* watched hours of underwater footage. The animators were aiming for some of the same "real-life" qualities of the 1942 film. Writer-director Andrew Stanton notes, "We kept coming back to *Bambi* because of the way the filmmakers adhered to the real nature of how these animals moved and what their motor skills were. They used that as the basis for getting as much expression, activity and appeal. We wanted our characters to work in the same way. We thought of it as *Bambi* underwater" (Writing Studio).

Pixar filmmakers seem attuned to the layering of accuracy and artifice that animation involves. Lasseter explains that the goal at Pixar is "to make something believable in a make-believe, fantasy way" (Vaz 15). Research and accuracy are viewed as crucial, but *Finding Nemo* also announces itself as representation. Such make-believe realism perhaps qualifies the problematic portrayal of the Edenic state of the reef in the film. While *Bambi* includes fallen trees and elements of the woods in decay, *Finding Nemo*'s coral reef is idyllically rendered in saturated colors and without any indication of nature in process. As Kirsty Best notes, rather than showing that one-quarter of the earth's coral has been killed, "Films like *Finding Nemo* paint vivid tableaux of natural landscapes ... [,] omitting pollution and the depredation of global coral reefs" (66). Moreover, the film's vibrant imagery potentially renders real natural environments dull in comparison, inciting an anthropocentric expectation for nature to meet our aesthetic preferences.

More than *Bambi*, however, the film promotes specific knowledge of habitat and species. Viewers learn that sea turtles live for 150 years, baleen whales eat krill not fish, and the East Australia Current (EAC) is a migration track for ocean life. Clown fish lay roughly 400 eggs and brush against their host anemone's tentacles to further their inoculation against its sting. The film's investment in ecological education is most pronounced in Mr. Ray's school, which correlates with one of the longest and most glorious shots of the reef (approximately 50 seconds). Arriving to pick up his students, he sings, "Ohhhhh, Let's name the zones, the zones, the zones, / Let's name the zones of the open sea! / Epipelagic, Mesopelagic, Bathyl, Abyssopelagic / All the rest are too deep for you and me to see."

To become one of Mr. Ray's explorers, Nemo "must answer a science question": "You live in what kind of home?" (Various mispronunciations of "anemone" ensue.) Mr. Ray uses scientifically accurate and highly specialized language with deep enthusiasm, but in combination with words and terms the viewer can understand. As he wings through the water, Mr. Ray sings a variety of songs that celebrate an intimate knowledge of the natural world: "O knowledge exploring is oh so lyrical when you think thoughts that are empirical," or "Seaweed is good. Seaweed is fun. It makes its food from the rays of the sun!" Seeing a small organism —a "stromalitic cyanobacteria"—he calls to his students with wonder to admire "an entire ecosystem contained in one infinitesimal speck!"

The film's many ecological features have been noted with interest by scientists: University of Technology (Sydney) biologist David Booth states, "A lot of marine biologists were quite excited to watch the Nemo film actually. Obviously someone has done their homework. They'd talked about the movement of tropical fishes into temperate waters which is something we're looking at" (R. Smith). Of course, not all scientists are comfortable with the film's treatment of ecology. Objecting to the anthropomorphism of *Finding Nemo*, Melanie Stiassny reminds us that after the death of Nemo's mother, Marlin "would have become a she and Nemo would have had his mom back"; also, "clownfishes are protandrous hermaphrodites. . . . They start life as males, but under certain circumstances become females" (8). The very fact that various experts are commenting on the accuracies and inaccuracies of the film speaks to the ecological interest *Finding Nemo* sparks and to its educational potential. NationalGeographic.com featured a story about which elements of the film are "fact, and which parts just don't float." Kids learn, among other things, that a barracuda would not have a taste for fish eggs, but would eat small fish; that a great white shark would not be a vegetarian, but a basking shark "eats only plankton"; and that Baleen whales have "strainer-like plates . . . instead of teeth," so Marlin could survive the whale's mouth (Kiffel). Due to its combination of accuracies and distortions, *Finding Nemo* has already served as the foundation for multiple lesson plans in American schools (see, for example, Evely).

While still highly tempered, predation is more fully depicted in *Finding Nemo* than in *Bambi*. Though the primary threat to Nemo is man, his mother (again supplanted by the father, though a more fallible one) is killed in the first moments of the film by a barracuda. The twelve-stepping sharks largely defy natural predation (despite Bruce's lapse in his "fish are friends" policy), yet the film does not neglect the predators and dangers that Marlin and Dory face on their journey, as the hungry seagulls make clear. Most terrifying is the Angler Fish, which entrances its prey with a small "antennae with a bio-luminescent fluid that glows in the dark and attracts other fish" (*Nemo* "Commentary").

Cast in opposition to the film's remarkable underworld environment is man. The image of man as intruder is graphically presented when, immense behind the tiny Nemo, a massive, masked human head fills the screen. The diver easily scoops the small fish into his net. Reiterating this terror, a second diver rises up to take photos of the reef. Camera flashes disorient Marlin, who bangs and bounces off reef elements, suggesting that even low-impact human activities can distress underwater species.

If gunfire and fire itself are the images of man's pervasive violence in *Bambi*, technology is the signifier for human interference with nature in *Finding Nemo*. Emblematized in the spinning boat propeller that Marlin chases in pursuit of Nemo, technology is threatening and dangerous for undersea life. Such imagery recurs when Nemo later attempts to jam the aquarium filter. When the pebble slips, he is pulled toward a similarly spinning mechanism waiting to shred him. The shark scene underscores the intrusion of human. Bruce (the great white), Marlin, and Dory swim through an underwater minefield as they approach the submarine. During the meeting, the camera pans multiple times toward a box marked "knives"—again gesturing toward the destructive potential of humans. Human violence is underscored when a missile, again with a propeller on the end, detonates, igniting a series of underwater explosions. Snippets of dialogue shortly before the explosions connect such destruction to anthropocentrism. Learning that Marlin is searching for his son captured by a diver, Chum (the mako) comments, "Humans think they own everything"; and even though the scuba-diving Dentist turns out to be Australian, the hammerhead, Anchor, cynically adds, "Probably American."

Alternately tracking Nemo and Marlin's stories, the film cuts to Nemo as he is first immersed in the aquarium where he meets the tank gang. The film highlights that an aquarium may not be the ideal environment for wild fish when Nemo, attempting to swim, rams multiple times into its glass walls. As Gill (a Moorish idol fish) plainly states, "Fish aren't meant to be in a box, kid." The tank gang shows multiple (anthropomorphic) signs of the pressures of living in a box: Bubbles is obsessed with Bubbles; Gurgle is germaphobic; and Flo/Deb believes her identical sister (her reflection) lives in the tank with her.

Even so, *Finding Nemo* creates an aquarium environment that is highly enticing to the human viewer, though Pixar did succeed in making the tank look artificial against the film's make-believe realism of the ocean environment. The plants in the tank, for example, are static when compared to the life forms on the reef. Deliberately or not, such imagery suggests that all attempts at understanding and representing nature (including those of the film itself) are to some degree manufactured.

Finding Nemo distributes environmental responsibility far more justly and widely than *Bambi*. While *Bambi* encouraged its viewers to demonize hunters, locating them as the sole perpetrators of environmental destruction, *Finding Nemo* makes the subtle point that sometimes efforts to "save" or "help" nature actually damage living systems. Explaining how he came to have Nemo in his fish tank, the Dentist comments, "Cute, isn't he? I found that guy struggling for life out on the reef and I saved him." Some viewers may miss the film's critique of the Dentist's good intentions, yet all are sure to understand that Darla is a "fish killer." Nemo is told to "say hello to your new mommy" as he is shown a photograph of Darla grasping a baggie containing a dead fish. Through Darla, the film critiques behavior not uncommon in children or even adults: she taps loudly on the fish tank and repeatedly shakes the bag holding the injured Nemo, with whom the viewer identifies. In contrast to *Bambi*, *Finding Nemo* promotes environmental sensitivity in all of its viewers— though, as the aftermath of the film has shown, this message has largely been overridden by market desires and misguided "good" deeds.

The film's closing scenes fulfill all the promises a Disney film makes: Nemo triumphantly escapes down the drain to reunite with his father. Such happiness is compounded by the liberation of both the tank gang and a huge catch of grouper. This final twist is based on a real event. Years before *Finding Nemo* went into production, Stanton read a brief news piece about a catch of fish capsizing a trawler; he always planned to end the film with this story (*Nemo* "Commentary").[15] While the grouper scene is based in reality, Gill's promise that all drains lead to the sea is far less accurate, resulting in serious consequences for real fish. After news of children "flushing Nemo," the JWC Environmental Company issued the following press statement: "Drain pipes do lead to the ocean, eventually, but first the fluid goes through powerful machines that 'shred solids into tiny particles.'"[16] Multiple sources reported on the "Nemo Syndrome" as distressed parents called plumbers "asking if there is any way to retrieve their pets" (Nestruck). Sadly, a central ecological lesson in this film—that even those who seek to assist nature can cause harm— resulted in mistaken efforts to free fish from captivity. Though perhaps not a direct result of the film, some pet owners have "returned" tropical fish to the wrong ocean. These released pets—such as the hearty platys or aggressive lionfish—disrupt ecosystems, threatening the food supply and well-being of indigenous species (see Arthur and Dart).

While both the Humane Society of the United States and PETA (People for the Ethical Treatment of Animals) praised the film "for its message of freedom and respect for animals," *Finding Nemo* boosted business in pet stores (Walton). Reminiscent of the sale of overbred Dalmatians that quickly found their way to dog shelters after 101 *Dalmatians*, sales in "clownfish, blue tangs, and aquarium accessories" skyrocketed. Too often buyers understood neither the complexity nor the expense of maintaining a saltwater environment (Walton). Moreover, the Dentist's tank in the film is so visually appealing that people are replicating it in their homes and offices. One writer on Yahoo asks how to "make my fish tank look like the ocean. I want my fish tank to look like the one in 'Finding Nemo.' "[17] A fifteen-year-old on the FishGeeks site notes that all the fish in his saltwater tank are from *Finding Nemo*. In the FishGeeks' album of tank setups, one member has posted a tank (image 75) modeled on the one in the film.[18]

The film—or perhaps its immediate impact—has had some positive results. It has led to news stories on the grimmer realities of the tropical fish trade.[19] At least some of the public has learned that 95 percent of tropical fish are captured in the wild (Barton 1), which means that 20 million of the 1,471 species of reef fish are harvested annually (UNEP 2). Some must have learned that unethical harvesters use sodium cyanide to stun fish, thus damaging the reef. The film has also contributed to policy discussions. A report, *From Ocean to Aquarium: The Global Trade in Marine Ornamentals*, was part of the 2003 United Nations Environment Programme (UNEP). Citing the influence of *Finding Nemo*, the report "scrutinizes the industry following concerns over destructive fishing, over-harvesting, lack of scientific information on collected species, high mortality due to inadequate handling and transportation, as well as the threat of extinction" (UNEP 3). It closes by advocating "long-term conservation and sustainable use of coral reefs in regions where other options for generating revenue are limited" (4). The problem, it hints, lies more with northern/western demand and purchasing habits, than with the harvesters who are often struggling economically.

Certain groups are using the interest generated by the film to promote environmental awareness. Like the Ocean Futures Society, the Marine Aquarium Council (in conjunction with the release of *Finding Nemo*) promoted "the first-ever marine-life certification system. . . . MAC Certification enables consumers to select retailers who sell organisms that comply with internationally approved environmental and quality standards from reef to retail."[20] Moreover, the Australian Broadcasting Company reported that the Great Barrier Reef Marine Park Authority (GBRMPA) and commercial anglers "agreed to a ban on collecting clownfish and the anemone they live on" (Glanville). There is other good news. Aquarium attendance is up, and while people may come to see Nemo (as many aquariums have created exhibits around the film), many will learn something about ocean habitats while they are there (Zoltak).

While social awareness has probably increased, Disney consumers have long been trained to buy the vast array of products that accompany its films. From "Bambi perfume"—"A Kid's Fragrance That Is a Fun Blend of Citrus and Floral Notes"—to the "Personalized Nemo Loungeable Floor Pillow," the purchasing habits (and illusions) of Disney viewers extend beyond the official product line. As discussed above, children who have grown up under Disney's tutelage far too often want their animated animal characters brought to life and are disappointed by the real animal.

Disney films can produce a limited environmental sensitivity that is only a starting place for the necessary ecological discussions to be had with children. We can make use of the green aspects of films such as *Bambi* and *Finding Nemo* by discussing with our children the values, accuracies, and inaccuracies represented in the films. Such discussions can be enhanced by making use of the green packaging that Disney now provides. It may not be difficult to explain to a five-year-old why a stuffed Nemo might just be a better option than buying a live one, especially given post–*Finding Nemo* exposés on the tropical fish trade. Disney will certainly remain happy if we choose to purchase the *Finding Nemo* 16-inch Nemo Plush, the *Finding Nemo* 14-inch Dory Plush, the *Finding Nemo* 16-inch Crush Plush Doll, and any other member of the animal cast of the film. But then, we will also have to consider what the plush dolls are made of, the labor conditions under which they are produced, and whether they can be recycled. Either way, the tension between our own consumerist and environmentalist drives will continue. The challenge will be to find the balance that keeps our sense of wonder for the natural world alive.

NOTES

I would like to thank Paula Willoquet-Maricondi for her editorial advice. Thanks are also due to William E. Lenz and Allie Reznik.

1. Scholars have amply noted the gendered and racialized bias of animated films; recent criticism attends to the ecological sensibility promoted or derailed by popular Disney films. See Lutts, Hastings, and Jhappan and Stasiulis. See also Whitley.
2. *Business Wire* 2 March 2005.
3. *New York Post* 11 February 2005: 39. The figure includes U.S., worldwide, and DVD sales.
4. My choice to use "man" rather than "humanity" encapsulates ambiguously

both male and female genders, while also signaling the role of patriarchy in environmental degradation.

5. Orr critiques *Bambi*'s "sweet little critters" (93).
6. As Best writes, "Visual capture, like all representation, selects what it includes and excludes to set before its audience" (66).
7. See http://www.disney.go.com/disneyvideos/animatedfilms/bambi/home.html.
8. E.H.F. "Bambi." *New York Times* 7 December 1942: SM16.
9. An exception is Bambi's fight with another buck (Ronno), part of the film's love story.
10. See http://www.disney/go.com/vault/archives/movies/bambi.html.
11. Whitley argues that *Bambi* presents the seared forest with double vision, both "devastated and regenerating" (73).
12. For ads or information on ads, see http://www.youtube.com/watch?v=wiyvX9 pnTOs&NR=1 (retrieved 30 November 2009); http://www.smokeybear.com/vault/trails.asp?id=2000 (retrieved 30 November 2009); and http://www.adco uncil.org/newsDetail.aspx?id=41 (retrieved 30 November 2009).
13. For Scott Hermanson, Animal Kingdom's eco-adventure ride "exemplifies how Disney co-opts environmentalism toward its entertainment ends" (209).
14. Summers is an assistant professor of ecology and evolutionary biology at the University of California, Irvine.
15. The story appeared in *Lloyd's List International* 8 January 1998.
16. See http://www.opinionjournal.com/best/?id=110003607 (retrieved 30 November 2009).
17. See http://www.answers.yahoo.com/questions/index?qid+2006121810535 AAph (retrieved 12 December 2006).
18. See http://www.aquaria.info/modules/gallery/tank_setups/ (retrieved 12 December 2006) or http://flickr.com/photos/grizab3lla/422623111/ (retrieved 30 November 2009).
19. "*Nemo* Craze Threatens Sea Life," *USA Today* 2 July 2003: 9A.
20. http://www.unepwcmc.org/information_services/publications/oceanaquar ium/Aquarium_NR (retrieved 30 November 2009).

WORKS CITED

Arthur, Charles. "*Finding Nemo* Pets Harm Ocean Ecology." 1 July 2004. http://www.lists.envirolink.org/pipermail/ar-news/Week-of-Mon-20040628/026 607.html. Retrieved 28 July 2008.

Bambi 55th Anniversary Edition. 1942. Dir. David W. Hand. Walt Disney Home Video, 1994.

Bambi Platinum Edition. 1942. Dir. David W. Hand. Disney DVD, 2005.

Barton, Jill. "Clown Fish Farms Create Thousands of *Nemos* Away from Coral Reefs." *Associated Press Worldstream* 19 July 2003.

Bate, Jonathan. *The Song of the Earth.* Cambridge, MA: Harvard Univ. Press, 2000.

Best, Kirsty. "Interfacing the Environment: Networked Screens and the Ethics of Visual Consumption." *Ethics and the Environment* 9.2 (2004): 65–85.

Carson, Rachel. *The Sense of Wonder.* New York: Harper and Row, 1956.

Cohen, Patricia. "Animated Bambi Debate Arouses Pastoral Passions." *New York Times* 23 April 2008: E1.

Dart, Jonathan. "Finding Nemesis: Pet Fish Threat." *Sidney Morning Herald* 18 April 2008: 1.

Evely, Christine. "*Finding Nemo:* A Study Guide." *Screen Education* 40 (2005): 70–78.

Fjellman, Stephen M. *Vinyl Leaves: Walt Disney World and America.* Boulder, CO: Westview Press, 1992.

Finding Nemo (Two-Disc Collector's Edition). Dir. Andrew Stanton. Disney/Pixar, 2003.

Giroux, Henry A. *The Mouse That Roared: Disney and the End of Innocence.* New York: Rowman and Littlefield, 1999.

Glanville, Brigid. "Marine Authorities Agree to Ban on Catching *Nemo.*" *ABC Transcripts* (Australia) 20 December 2007. http://www.abc.net.au/pm/content/2007/s2124553.htm. Retrieved 6 August 2008.

Hastings, A. Waller. "Bambi and the Hunting Ethos." *Journal of Popular Film and Television* 24 (1996): 53–59.

Hermanson, Scott. "Truer Than Life: Disney's Animated Kingdom." *Rethinking Disney: Private Control, Public Dimensions.* Ed. Mike Budd and Max H. Kirsch. Middleton, CT: Wesleyan Univ. Press, 2005. 199–27.

Jhappan, Radha, and Daiva Stasiulis. "Anglophilia and the Discreet Charm of the English Voice in Disney's Pocahontas Films." *Rethinking Disney: Private Control, Public Dimensions.* Ed. Mike Budd and Max Kirsch. Middletown, CT: Wesleyan Univ. Press, 2005. 151–77.

Kidd, Kenneth B. "Disney of Orlando's Animal Kingdom." *Wild Things: Children's Culture and Ecocriticism.* Ed. Sidney Dobrin. Detroit: Wayne State Univ. Press, 2004. 267–88.

Kiffel, Jamie. "*Finding Nemo:* The Truth behind the Movie." 17 December 2006. http://www.nationalgeographic.com/ngkids/0305/scene2.html. Retrieved 6 August 2008.

Lutts, Ralph H. "The Trouble with Bambi: Walt Disney's Bambi and the American Vision of Nature." *Forest and Conservation History* 36 (1992): 160–71.

Lynch, Stephen. "*Nemo,* No Fish Story Thanks to UCI Adviser." *Orange County Register* 4 June 2003. http://biomechanics.bio.uci.edu/_media/media%20coverage/'Nemo'%20no%20fish%20story%20thanks%20to%20UCI%20adviser.htm. Retrieved 20 November 2009.

"The Magic behind the Masterpiece." *Bambi: 55th Anniversary Edition.* Walt Disney Home Video. Produced and written by Harry Arends and Savenick, 1994.

McKenna, Erin, and Andrew Light, eds. *Animal Pragmatism: Rethinking Nonhuman Relationships.* Bloomington: Indiana Univ. Press, 2004.

Nestruck, Kelly. "Way to Go, Disney, Way to Go." *National Post* (Canada) 27 June 2003: PM4.

Orr, David. *Ecological Literacy: Education and the Transition to a Postmodern World*. Albany: SUNY Press, 1992.

Payne, David. *"Bambi." From Mouse to Mermaid: The Politics of Film, Gender, and Culture*. Ed. Elizabeth Bell, Lynda Haas, and Lauren Sells. Bloomington: Indiana Univ. Press, 1995. 137–47.

Schickel, Richard. *The Disney Version: The Life, Times, Art and Commerce of Walt Disney*. 3rd ed. Chicago: Ivan R. Dee, 1997.

Schullery, Paul. "The Fires and Fire Policy." *Bioscience* 39.10 (1989): 686–94.

Smith, Matthew Wilson. "Bayreuth, Disneyland, and the Return to Nature." *Land/Scape/Theatre* 12 (2002): 252–79.

Smith, Richard. "Looking for Nemo." 3 June 2004. http://www.abc.net.au/catalyst/stories/s1123880.htm. Retrieved 12 December 2006.

Stiassny, Melanie L. J. "Saving Nemo." *Natural History Magazine* March 2004. http://www.naturalhistorymag.com/0304/0304_feature.html. Retrieved 31 October 2006.

Thomas, Bob. *Walt Disney: An American Original*. New York: Simon and Schuster, 1976.

United Nations Environment Programme (UNEP). *From Ocean to Aquarium: The Global Trade in Marine Ornamentals*. 7 October 2003. http://www.unep-wcmc.org/latenews/aquarium.htm. Retrieved 28 July 2008.

Vaz, Mark Cotta. *The Art of Finding Nemo*. San Francisco: Chronicle Books, 2003.

Walton, Marsha. "Nemo Fans Net Fish Warning." 30 June 2003. http://www.cnn.com/2003/TECH/science/06/30/coolsc.nemo.fish Retrieved 28 July 2008.

Whitley, David. *The Idea of Nature in Disney Animation*. Burlington and Hampshire: Ashgate, 2008.

Willis, Susan. "Disney's Bestiary." *Rethinking Disney: Private Control, Public Dimensions*. Ed. Mike Budd and Max Kirsch. Middleton: Wesleyan Univ. Press, 2005. 53–71.

Writing Studio. "The Art of Writing and Making Films." Animation: *Finding Nemo*. 17 December 2006. http://www.writingstudio.co.za/page397.html. Retrieved 28 July 2008.

Zoltak, James. "Aquariums Finding: *Nemo* Is Good For Biz." *Amusement Business*, 26 January 2004.

PART IV
ART CINEMA
ECO-AUTEURS

THE RULES OF THE WORLD
JAPANESE ECOCINEMA
AND KIYOSHI KUROSAWA

TIM PALMER

Crucial to Japanese cinema's global identity is how it represents the Japanese environment, the physical entity of Japan itself. To take a representative recent example, Kiyoshi Kurosawa's *Charisma* (1999) provides a poignant set of ecological anxieties. Heavily allegorical, the film opens as a burnt-out policeman, Yabuike (Koji Yakusho), negotiates with a gunman holding a hostage in an isolated office. The man wordlessly hands him a note stating simply, "Restore the Rules of the World." Before the message is relayed, however, the police intervene disastrously and both gunman and hostage are killed, traumatizing Yabuike, who flees the city to a remote forest wilderness. There, though, he is drawn into more hostilities, this time among rival groups of scientists and ecoterrorists clashing over a rare, fragile tree, nicknamed Charisma. One faction demands Charisma's protection as a unique part of nature; another declares the tree a pollutant and seeks its destruction; another wants to profit from its value to collectors as a commodity. The film ends as Charisma is symbolically burned but apparently not quite killed, and an alienated Yabuike heads home. But in the film's strangely abrupt closing sequence, an extreme long shot reveals the city consumed by flames and devastation, in the throes of an unknown apocalypse.

With such forceful, provocative ecological analyses, *Charisma* embodies not only Kurosawa's body of work but also a major discourse of Japanese film, both past and present. At stake is the cinematic self-portrait designed by Japan for international consumption. The main issues coalesce around the portentous yet cryptic note that Kurosawa's protagonist, Yabuike, struggles to understand. What, in Japanese terms, are the rules of the world, and how have they been broken? Or, more specifically, how are the ecological conditions of Japan depicted and exported by its cinema? In a modern framework, Kurosawa pursues this agenda through a peculiar fusion of familiar, popular genres—typically the police procedural thriller and/or horror—and the more exacting features of international art cinema. In effect, the tastes of local and global au-diences are simultaneously targeted, an approach shared by Kurosawa's highest-profile contemporaries, notably Takashi Shimizu (creator of the *Ju-on/The Grudge* series, begun in 2000 and recently reincarnated with a 2009 video game installment) and Hideo Nakata (director of the *Ringu/The Ring* franchise, spanning a decade of films, radio, manga, and tele-vision series from 1998 to date). Based upon this trio's work,[1] and their regular producer Taka Ichise, recent Japanese film has gained inter-national attention by reinventing mainstream materials with challeng-ing, sometimes radical elements: open-endings, ambiguous narratives, complex intertextuality, opaque protagonists, and, most glaringly, sinis-ter social diagnoses. From this formal hybridity emerges a major motif of contemporary Japanese cinema: inexorable catastrophe manifesting on-screen through curses, virulent plagues, natural or supernatural contaminants, urban degeneration, and violent social breakdown.

Of course, Japan has not always been projected this way; its on-screen environmentalism has altered drastically over time. To study the ne-glected phenomenon of Japanese ecocinema, this essay will explore the environmental perspectives conveyed by Japanese film in its two most widely traveled historical moments: initially, during the emergence of its classical cinema, as was belatedly celebrated by the West during the 1950s and 1960s; and then again during the contemporary renaissance unfolding in the late twentieth and early twenty-first centuries. In the first phase of its international recognition, I will argue, Japanese film's reputation hinged upon its treatment of Japan as a lush garden paradise, in which the (screened) landscape was used as an idyllic mise-en-scène for the narrative formulae of the *jidei-geki*, or historical-set melodrama. The natural primacy of this classical Japanese cinema, as we will see, arose from a combination of careful studio policies tailored to foreign film audiences, a skilful use of location shooting, and the bravura tech-niques of directors such as Akira Kurosawa and Kenji Mizoguchi. In my second section, I use the case study of Kiyoshi Kurosawa to contrast this classical blueprint with modern Japanese film, which has once again emerged on the global stage—through international festivals, Hollywood studio remakes, and foreign distribution—as a dynamic commercial cin-ema, but one linked now to more experimental features and a dystopian representation of Japan. Whereas it was once disseminated on-screen as an unspoiled, verdant natural preserve, Japan is now presented through an eco-horror model, as a badlands in crisis, a megalopolis poised on the brink of environmental disaster. The rules of the world, like the methods of Japanese cinema, have fundamentally changed.

FROM WILDERNESS TO WASTELAND:
CLASSICAL AND CONTEMPORARY JAPANESE CINEMAS

The arrival of classical Japanese cinema on the international circuit can be traced to a series of unusually specific historical events. While Japan had long since established its own robust, vertically integrated studio system—Nikkatsu was founded in 1912; Shochiku followed in 1920; a boom of theatrical and production expansion was in effect by the late 1930s (Standish 34–35)—its products were virtually unknown abroad. It was only in the early 1950s that Japanese films started to circulate globally, with phenomenal success. The decisive moment was Akira Kurosawa's *Rashomon* (1950) winning the top prize, the Golden Lion, at the Venice International Film Festival in September 1951. Although Daiei, *Rashomon*'s studio, and Masaichi Nagata, its president, notoriously expressed bewilderment at such an oddity achieving this distinction (Nogami 91–93), a vogue for Japanese cinema of this type nonetheless began. Subsequent to *Rashomon,* Kurosawa's senior contemporary Kenji Mizoguchi was awarded Venice's secondary honor, the Silver Lion, over three successive years for *The Life of Oharu* (1952), *Ugetsu* (1953), and *Sansho the Bailiff* (1954). As Mark Le Fanu puts it, based upon these formative encounters, "Japanese cinema was first decisively put on the map of Western consciousness" (49).

With Venice as the cultural epicenter, Western acclaim for Japanese film intensified. Teinosuke Kinugasa's *Gate of Hell* (1953) won the Grand Prize at the 1954 Cannes Film Festival, then received the 1955 Best Foreign Film Academy Award; Yasujiro Ozu's *Tokyo Story* (1953) got a special award from the British Film Institute in 1958; and by the 1960s full-scale retrospectives of Japanese masterworks, usually by the classical triumvirate of Kurosawa, Mizoguchi, and Ozu, became increasingly common at ciné-clubs and festivals across Europe and North America. (Many contemporary historians now make the case for Mikio Naruse as being equal in stature to this trio.) Monographs appeared in various languages, most keen to pinpoint the Japaneseness of the cinema's aesthetic and spiritual principles. In 1959 Joseph Anderson and Donald Richie's *The Japanese Film* became the first English-language book on Japanese cinema, outlining a mode of production and industrial history. More influential theoretically, however, was Paul Schrader's 1972 *Transcendental Style in Film,* which characterized Ozu and Japanese philosophy through a logic of Zen abstraction from the vicissitudes of human strife, and Donald Richie's 1974 *Ozu,* which charted the decline of the traditional, male-dominated Japanese family unit within a modernizing social order.

More pressing from an ecological perspective is the "Japan" that was popularized globally by this wave of Japanese classical cinema. One defining context to the national self-portrait was the historical epic, or *jidei-geki*, which set the films in Japan's turbulent feudal past, in the isolationist centuries prior to the 1868 Meiji reformation. Characteristic films, such as *Rashomon, Ugetsu,* and *The Life of Oharu,* also reflected a calculated, effective policy developed by studio heads such as Nagata, at Daiei, and Shiro Kido, at Shochiku. The group strategy was to export en masse premodern Japanese historical subjects to carve out a particular cultural niche within the flow of 1950s world cinema. These were narratives about relentless and sometimes heroic clan warfare, battling samurai bound to strict codes of loyalty, and the struggles of the Japanese peasant class, shown keenly through the sufferings of women. The films were also strongly pictorialist, highlighting their stylistic flourishes to the receptive viewer as much as, if not more so, the travails of their characters and their pessimistic plots. Mizoguchi's films for Daiei, for example, were marked by an extravagantly florid design, showing sweeping long takes, elegant vistas of deep space, and precise modulations of staging and mise-en-scène (Palmer, "*Ugetsu*" 1–6). As David Bordwell observes, such products could be dismissed as "kitschy exoticism catering to the growing festival circuit" (133). In retrospect, however, this projection of Japanese national identity certainly "cashed in on an international hunger for delicious illusions [but was also] a shorthand stylization of things Japanese for Western consumption" (Davis 220).

An overlooked perspective in this historical emergence of classical Japanese cinema is an explicitly ecological analysis. In fact, a defining motif among these seminal works is their systematic creation of a garden aesthetic, representing Japan as a source of natural abundance, beautiful and untarnished wilderness, a limitless milieu of diverse organic splendor. Consider the opening of *Rashomon.* Under a gigantic ruined gate (a ninety-eight-foot construction on the Daiei studio back lot in Kyoto), a priest (Minoru Chiaki), a woodcutter (Takashi Shimura), and a commoner (Kichijiro Ueda) converge to escape the driving monsoon rain. The woodcutter, pressed by his companions, recounts the story of a recent criminal case in which, allegedly, Tajomaru (Toshiro Mifune), a bandit, killed a nobleman (Masayuki Mori) and raped his wife (Machiko Kyo). Cut to a flashback from the woodcutter's point of view, as he recalls finding the husband's corpse. Famously, the film then provides alternative, conflicting testimonies about what actually happened that day, such as from the bandit's, wife's, and husband's perspectives. But a major element of *Rashomon*'s impact—a key to its enduring legacy—is its use of natural settings as dramatic background to the events so diversely told.

As the flashbacks begin, we shift to what are clearly authentic landscape shots taken on location (a more common practice in Japan than in Hollywood during this time period). Kurosawa, in fact, based his production around the hilly forestlands on the outskirts of Nara, a medium-sized town one hour's drive to the east of Osaka, built in 710 AD as the ancient Japanese capital. For the pivotal scenes of confrontation between the bandit, the husband, and the wife, Kurosawa chose the more intimate space of an enclosed woodland behind the Komyo-ji temple, near the Katsura Detached Palace in Kyoto (Nogami 79–81). To foreground these natural resources and incorporate them cinematically into his piecemeal narrative, Kurosawa and his cinematographer, Kazuo Miyagawa, contrived a series of highly suggestive stylistic devices. The initial flashback, set up from the woodcutter's perspective as he first enters the woodlands, is characteristically assertive. The entire sequence, first of all, unfolds for nearly four minutes without any dialogue at all, emphasizing music (Fumio Hayasaka's variation of Ravel's "Boléro") and a montage of natural imagery. Fragmentary details of the lush environment, framed by a camera constantly in motion, are edited into vivid collisions. There are low-angle tracking shots taken directly into the sun (a daring technique at the time); downward tilts over wizened, ancient tree trunks; chiaroscuro compositions of dappled sunlight and dark pools of shade; 180-degree pans over fallen branches and glittering fronds of leaves; longer takes of drifting clouds and jutting greenery. *Rashomon*'s design here is arrestingly poetic, far outrunning the customary needs of classical establishing shots. Instead, the four-minute sequence, an ode to the wild, creates a sensory collage of organic texture and fertility, images Richie calls "rhapsodic . . . pure cinematic impressionism" (*Films* 77).

Elsewhere in the film, however, similarly composed segments of wilderness imagery create specific narrative associations. The bandit first glimpses the wife, he claims in self-defense, when a chance gust of wind blows her veil aside and reveals her beautiful face to him—nature as fate. At the film's conclusion, the sudden end of the torrential rainstorm offers a positive response to what the woodcutter despairs is humanity's total cynicism—nature as morality. Time and again, Kurosawa cuts from close-ups of arguments or violent struggles to extreme long shots of the unaffected, tranquil surrounding environment—nature as (belittling) thematic context. In these terms *Rashomon*'s dense virgin terrain enters forcefully into the text, as evocative idyll and natural counterpoint, offering ironic commentary on the brutish behavior of the characters. Nature exists as boundless paradise, while humanity registers, barely, as a blot on the landscape.

An equally expressive use of the landscape configures Mizoguchi's *Ugetsu*, like *Rashomon* a textual ambassador for Japanese classicism and its garden aesthetic. *Ugetsu*'s plot, typically for Mizoguchi, connects the decline of women to the capricious urges of errant men (Palmer, "Exotic Aesthetics" 78–80). Set again in medieval Japan, the film concerns Genjuro (Masayuki Mori), a humble village potter, whose craving for fortune matches that of his would-be samurai brother-in-law Tobei (Sakae Ozawa). The two men's whims progressively destroy the women alongside them. Genjuro is seduced by the forlorn phantom Lady Wakasa (Machiko Kyo) and abandons his wife, Miyagi (Kinuyo Tanaka), who is casually murdered; when Tobei, by blind luck, succeeds in becoming a samurai, his wife, Ohama (Mitsuko Mito), is forced into prostitution and disgrace. Narrative notwithstanding, *Ugetsu* derives its extraordinary effects from artful locations—selected, like *Rashomon*, from open or unclaimed lands surrounding the rural towns outside Kyoto—dynamically rendered on-screen. Tadao Sato, in this vein, characterizes Mizoguchi's style through traditional Japanese art practices. Sato observes how Mizoguchi stages pivotal sequences next to rivers, sites traditionally linked to deep introspection and Buddhist notions of transience; he uses long takes that mimic the unfolding, sequential form of *emaki* scroll paintings; and frames his human subjects as tiny details, in deep-staged extreme long shots, amid vistas that adopt the perspectively kinetic compositions of *ukiyo-e* woodblock prints (170–79).

Certainly, Mizoguchi's style juxtaposes petty human strife with natural beauty. *Ugetsu*'s opening, a meticulous set piece like the woodcutter's walk through the woods in *Rashomon*, not only establishes time and place—early spring in sixteenth-century Japan, near Lake Biwa in Omi province—but goes on, more broadly, to evoke a powerful wilderness sensibility. Fade-in comes as two crane shots track the camera gracefully from right to left (the conventional direction for scanning Japanese texts), setting the viewer's vantage point high above rolling flatlands and scrub, a far-off tree line of densely growing birch and pines, and, further distant, a range of rugged foothill peaks. Dazzling sunshine bathes wheatfields, while in the foreground toiling peasants till their pastures. From here we dissolve, still moving left, to human habitation, and Genjuro and Miyagi loading a cart with pottery for sale. It is only when, suddenly, two off-screen gunshots echo down the valley that Mizoguchi finally cuts to a tighter view, a medium close-up, that privileges the actors who speak for the first time. And the arrival of human concerns catalyzes inevitable disaster: here, the onset of civil war, which Genjuro and Miyagi correctly predict will sabotage their labors.

Throughout *Ugetsu,* this paradigm persists, a logic of long shots of natural harmony, the film's dramatic backdrop, intruded upon by arbitrary human hostilities. The spectacle of the Japanese landscape, in beautiful stasis, situates, ironically, the violent compulsions of Mizoguchi's (male) characters. A key moment in this regard comes when Miyagi, in extreme long shot, walks through a valley of grasslands and is set upon by three starving *ronin* samurai. Begging for food, one stabs her with his spear; the trio retreats into an abandoned crop-field while Miyagi struggles on in the foreground, leaning heavily on her staff before collapsing to the ground. Robin Wood suggests how such one-take scenes reveal "the director's sense of the precariousness of things [as well as] the sense of a world beyond the frame, the compositions never final, subject to continual variation and modification. . . . The violence [is] . . . placed in a context of stillness and serenity" (230). Such was the appeal of this first wave of classical Japanese cinema, so eagerly appreciated by international audiences. As the pitiless plots of *Rashomon, Ugetsu,* and their classical counterparts unfold, the landscape itself, this richly composed garden aesthetic, offers larger context to the human dramas in progress. Like a perfectly sculpted set of environmental product placements, the rolling canvas of Japanese nature is used to off set or deflate the failures of pre-urban society. Within the unspoiled expanses of this mythic on-screen Japan, humanity's flaws are made to seem small, fleeting, tragically incidental by comparison.

BARREN ILLUSIONS:
KIYOSHI KUROSAWA AND NEW JAPANESE ECO-HORROR

Little remains of the high prestige and ecological idealism of classical Japanese cinema, as was celebrated abroad during the 1950s and 1960s. Shifting our focus to a representative modern case study, the work of Kiyoshi Kurosawa, it is clear how in the late twentieth and early twenty-first century, Japanese cinema's dialogue with international film culture has evolved drastically, as has its rendition of the Japanese environment. Rather than the once-prized purity of natural wilderness, Kurosawa's films, like many of his contemporaries, reveal a country in environmental crisis, confronted by looming catastrophes perceived to be unstoppable and, more troubling still, largely unheeded. So our opening question yields surprising new answers: What, today, are the cinematic rules of the world for Japan, both off- and on-screen?

Unlike those icons supported by the classical studio infrastructure in its heyday, international celebrity—or visibility of any kind—among modern Japanese filmmakers is a rare, prized asset. In this light, Kurosawa is both symptomatic and a fortunate exception. With the advent of television, rising overheads, heightened competition from Hollywood, and decreasingly receptive local audiences, Japanese cinema underwent a series of far-reaching retrenchments from the 1970s through the 1990s. Budgets were slashed, movie theaters closed, debilitatingly conservative generic output (and soft-core pornography) abounded, and the distribution of indigenous product receded in the wake of rising foreign imports. Few Japanese-produced films were distributed or seen abroad.[2] Among studios and independent outfits, Japanese production halved in a matter of decades: from a historical high point, when 537 Japanese films were made in 1960, to just 282 films being released in 2000 (Richie, *Hundred Years* 177). But with collapse came opportunity, and Kurosawa's career embodies equally the tribulations and the possibilities that today await the Japanese filmmaking apprentice.

Survival in an unreliable marketplace is nowadays a defining imperative in Japanese cinema. Unlike the creative mentoring and distributional support given by the classical studio system, most Japanese directors today enjoy few technical means and fewer professional securities. Kurosawa's fraught early career, its recourse to grungy production design, trendy genres, and impromptu experimentation, is highly instructive in this vein. As Kurosawa has put it in one interview, "I belong to the generation that came of age after the end of the studio system as we used to know it" (Desjardins 217). While studying sociology at Rikkyo University in Tokyo, Kurosawa found inspiration in the lectures of Shigehiko Hasumi, a noted Japanese film theorist, to shoot his own amateur projects, a series of 8 mm shorts. Kurosawa won an award for one effort, *Vertigo College,* at the 1980 PIA Film Festival, a prestigious event for emerging independents. But unlike his namesake Akira, Kurosawa's prize facilitated a career of only very modest industrial potential. After three years crewing independent projects, Kurosawa was hired by Nikkatsu, one of Japan's three remaining majors, and assigned to direct soft-core pornography. His short-lived career as an erotic filmmaker-for-hire culminated in *The Excitement of the Do-Re-Mi-Fa Girl* (1985), which was so stylistically obscure, verging on a Godardian consumerist satire, that

Nikkatsu refused to release it and, to make things worse, blacklisted Kurosawa within the industry.[3]

Kurosawa next made ends meet by giving paid campus lectures, while working independently on hastily produced, low-budget horror and crime films shot for video (an underground Japanese sub-industry known as v-cinema) and television, before belatedly working in the studio complex again (Mes and Sharp 92–95). Gradually attaining more control, Kurosawa continued to work, rapidly, in genre-bound, micro-budget situations on slasher films like *The Guard from Underground* (1992) and the six-film gangster franchise *Suit Yourself or Shoot Yourself* (two films in 1995; four in 1996). But like his classical predecessors, Kurosawa only began to attract critical notice, and more concerted studio resources, once his films were chosen to play at foreign film festivals. Breakout success came with *Charisma,* selected for the 1999 Cannes Film Festival, which led to international distribution for many of his more recent, mature films: the serial killer parable *Cure* (1997); the techno-horror *Pulse* (2001); his characteristically unclassifiable tale of urban paranoia, *Bright Future* (2003); supernatural thrillers *Loft* (2005) and *Retribution* (2006); and the 2008 Cannes prize-winner, *Tokyo Sonata* (2008). Belatedly recognized on the festival circuit and through foreign DVD releases, Kurosawa's body of work increasingly subverts the conventions of popular genres, assimilating mainstream content through the devices of high art cinema. Equally consistent as a textual motif is Kurosawa's use of the faltering Japanese ecosystem as a dramatic backdrop, dwelling on its precarious capacity to withstand human interference.

This hard-fought international emergence of Kurosawa, his status as a still underrated contemporary Japanese eco-auteur, coincides with a new surge of global interest in the ecology of Japan. The intensity of this reception—equal to *Rashomon* and its wake in the 1950s—is motivated, however, by a severely changed perception of the Japanese landmass. Rather than the classical garden aesthetic, purveying the image of Japan as utopia, textual debate rages now about the country's despoilment, its poisoned passivity. A spate of revisionist histories and ecological analyses, in particular, dwell on the ravaged, toxified Japanese landscape. Alex Kerr's seminal *Lost Japan* (1996) and *Dogs and Demons: Tales from the Dark Side of Japan* (2001), for example, indict issues that have increasingly become environmental refrains: the growing concretization of the Japanese coastline in misplaced efforts to prevent erosion; the maniacal (and unnecessary) state-funded roadworks that now crisscross pristine woodlands; the mass outbreaks of arsenic, asbestos, and dioxin pollutions in recent decades; and the apathy of the Japanese Environmental Agency in response to contaminated air, water, and soil. As Kerr argues, industry advocates now dictate government policy, leaving uninformed citizens to "grieve at the steady disappearance of all that was once so beautiful in their environment" (73). Writing from the same critical position, David Suzuki and Keibo Oiwa echo Kerr's ecological manifesto, targeting Japan's mass deforestations, unchecked industrialization, and brazen depletion of natural resources, most obviously through short-term practices like drift net fishing. In Suzuki and Oiwa's account, indeed, contemporary Japan stands utterly alienated from the Shinto nature worship of the pre–World War II generation (209–64). Pradyumna Karan, another Western eco-historian, nuances these concerns by noting the contemporary *acceleration* of Japan's industrial pollution, its generation of hazardous waste, and wholesale urbanization—which comes, ironically, despite the limited but growing impact of grassroots opposition (359–74). A steady course to disaster has been set, and continues.

Besides these activist histories, a compelling group of Japan's recent cultural exports also fixates on the nation's socio-ecological failings. In print, specialist translator-publishers, such as New York City–based Vertical Books, today base their catalog of releases around this textual rendition of Japanese dystopia. Randy Taguchi's *Outlet* (published in North America in 2003), Taichi Yamada's *Strangers* (2003), Ami Sakurai's *Innocent World* (2005), Hitomi Kanehara's *Snakes and Earrings* (2005), and Koji Suzuki's compendium *Dark Water* (2006) are leading cases of this tendency; many were also best sellers in Japan. Their narrative templates, obsessively reworked for Western audiences, feature young, socially marginalized, often nihilistic protagonists who are deadened to the world, going through the motions of listless, amoral routines in a sterile modern Japan.[4] *Innocent World*, perhaps the starkest yet in both title and approach, is a quasi-autobiographical account of Ami, a teenage prostitute and rape victim whose only release is an incestuous relationship with her mentally ill brother. Numbed by the futile hedonism of Tokyo and its oppressive urban density, Ami leaves the city but cannot escape her own self-destructive urges. The book was a cited influence on Kurosawa himself, one of its highest-profile supporters in Japan.

Much of this new Japanese fiction, moreover, returns repeatedly to the environment, a symbolically lethal backdrop for the empty labors of depressed outsiders. One seminal text, Haruki Murakami's *A Wild Sheep Chase* (1989), offers, as context to its unnamed protagonist's brooding, an especially sharp lament for Japan's brutalized, once-resplendent landscape: "Holding my breath in the darkness, I let images of the town melt and ooze all around me. The houses rotted away, the rails rusted and were gone, weeds overwhelmed the farmland. The town came to the end of its short hundred-year history and sank into the earth. Time regressed like a film running backward. Once again Ainu deer, black bears, and wolves came to live on the plain, thick swarms of locusts filled the sky, an ocean of bamboo grass swayed in the autumn wind, and the luxurious evergreen forests hid the sun" (265).

Murakami's sad evocation of the lost garden aesthetic, using specifically filmic imagery, relates closely to Kurosawa and new Japanese eco-cinema. Today, this is Japan's highest-profile cultural export, and arguably its most powerful account of environmental pessimism.

But how are such materials conveyed cinematically, versus the classical paradigm? At the level of narrative design, the eco-horror of Kurosawa and his contemporaries relies on a relentless, pared-down diegetic logic. Once events are set in motion, devastation occurs inevitably, with little or no human agency capable of intervening. In Shimizu's *Ju-on,* a vengeful family of ghosts murders anyone connected to its decaying Tokyo home; the film wanders wildly in its chronology, but every appearance of Kayako (Takako Fuji), the phantom matriarch, manifests with the same rising clicking noise, like a Geiger counter, as if alerting her victims to deadly supernatural radiation.[5] *Ju-on* ends with Kayako awakening alone in a deserted Tokyo wasteland, her grudge against the living having seemingly emptied the mainland completely. (Overpopulated Japan is often left disturbingly vacant in these films.) Here and elsewhere in contemporary Japanese eco-horror is this narrative arc of inexorable ruin and exponential slaughter—one death after another, after another, with open-endings that merely confirm the terminal spread of pestilence. In Nakata's *Ringu* (adapted from Suzuki's 1991 novel), it is a contaminated videotape that curses its viewers and spreads fatalities across Japan and beyond; in Ochiai's *Infection,* an unexplained plague sweeps Tokyo's Central Hospital, and apparently the world outside it, with no one likely to survive. The onset of pandemic, indeed, is subtextually vital to new Japanese eco-horror, perhaps reflecting, or else prescient about, the recent Asian outbreaks of communicable, pathogenic diseases, notably SARS (traced to Guangdong, China, in late 2002) and Asian bird flu (causing widespread deaths in Hong Kong, Thailand, Vietnam, and farther afield).

While Kurosawa's films report the same view of imminent mass destruction, they offset its approach with a meticulously evasive design. This is, by result, a startlingly deadpan and unsentimental process, detailing an almost incidental apocalypse. Japanese film has long been associated with ellipsis and understatement (Richie "Notes"); Kurosawa takes the tendency to bizarre extremes. Returning to our opening case study, *Charisma*, the final disclosure of the city's annihilation is framed as a concluding aside, confirming the director's preference for abrupt narrative tangents. The conflict over Charisma (a surprisingly tiny specimen) concluded, Yabuike begins to wander through the forestland. Night falls. Yabuike is then shown atop a hillside; he calls his police boss on his cell phone, cutting off his superior's indignant questions with a line drained of emotion: "I'm returning home." The next shot, the film's last, cuts across the axis of action to reveal in a long take that Yabuike has already seen, yet does not discernibly react to, the chaos of the city far away beneath him. Moonlight illuminates cloud patterns rushing toward him at unnatural speed; distant gunfire and police sirens reverberate over the flatlands; fires rage in the metropolis below, resembling a seismic disturbance or volcanic eruption. Three riot helicopters pass overhead, training their searchlights on an unseen rioting mob. So open-ended is this (non-)payoff that Kurosawa simply rolls the end credits as the shot continues, uninterrupted, as if indifferent to the very notion of closure.

Systematically indeed, Kurosawa's techniques, again infusing generic materials with auteurist idiosyncrasy, make his environmental critiques all the more unsettling for their precise, ordered ambivalence. While his films unflinchingly prepare us for impending cataclysm, they avoid any trite or didactic appeals: no resolutions, no ready solutions, no hasty or emotive calls to action. Kurosawa simply positions his—usually passive and impassive—protagonists at the margins of larger-scale disasters, then lets both continue unabated and unchecked.[6] Pockets of dead time, in addition, during which little or nothing tangible occurs, coexist disconcertingly with sudden, terrible revelations.

Pulse reiterates this pattern on a global scale. Nominally a horror film, it concerns a group of young Tokyoites, all of whom work with computers and modern technologies. A spate of inexplicable suicides, growing in number every day, is traced to ghostly phenomena emerging from the Internet. Society just quietly collapses—another Kurosawian aside shows a flaming plane crashing, unremarked-upon, far off in the city— as one of the group, Kawashima (Haruhiko Kato), himself now a phantom, abandons the metropolis with a female acquaintance, Harue (Koyuki). The two escape into the Pacific on a boat, heading for an unknown destination as the end of the world looms large. Here, in another measured reversal of the garden aesthetic, Kurosawa favors extreme long shots of natural vistas—the forestland valley that concludes *Charisma;* a final overhead shot of the ocean-bound ship in *Pulse*—only at a point of termination, when his films confirm that all prospects of saving the world, its potential to withstand humanity, have gone. Nature in Kurosawa's contemporary Japanese cinema is clearly no match for the unthinking machinations of mankind.

This ecological critique is developed on a more intimate scale through what can only be described as an entropy aesthetic. Shot by shot, in stark contrast with Kurosawa's classical antecedents, his films depict both natural and urbanized Japan in a state of terminal decay, with incriminating motifs of setting, staging, lighting, and composition. Most evocative, perhaps, is Kurosawa's device of shooting interior scenes in buildings that have been condemned and abandoned. During preproduction he and his crews scour Tokyo to find its most rundown, dilapidated, even dangerous constructions. Kurosawa is apparently most satisfied if the spaces he captures on-screen have been razed by the time his film is released. These destitute locales, like the long-evacuated elementary school in *Doppelganger* (2003) and *Charisma*'s ancient spa, are stripped of life and order, with windows smashed, furniture shattered, and unsafe walls caked with dirt and moisture. The entropy aesthetic, then, emerges from a mise-en-scène of encroaching ruin, highlighted by Kurosawa's customary long shot/long takes of little tangible visual interest except for these memorably disused, crumbling backgrounds.

In its entropic design, *Retribution* is arguably Kurosawa's most fully realized test case. The film concerns a detective, Yoshioka (played again by the weather-beaten Koji Yakusho), whose investigation of serial murders is hampered by a series of earthquakes and, worse still, clues that first implicate himself as the killer, then suggest a mysterious (and never fully explained) vendetta by the phantom of a woman left to rot in a old shut-down government mental institution. *Retribution* takes place in the noxious industrial spaces, unappealing dumping grounds, and sodden reclaimed Eastern margins of Tokyo, on the banks of Tokyo Bay, where 90 percent of the old wetlands and once-bustling lakefront have been buried under fill (Karan 46–48). As the seismic and supernatural disturbances continue, the filthy bay water advances up the coastline, threatening, perhaps mercifully, the hulks of buildings we see in drastic decline at the city's periphery. But even when apart from deteriorating natural conditions, Kurosawa's settings are presented like disaster areas waiting to happen: the vast, corroding warehouse that houses the police's base of operations; Yoshioka's dank and impersonal apartment

whose walls he dreams are cracking apart before his eyes; the appall-
ingly preserved skeleton of the closed sanitarium from which ghostly
apparitions emanate. Instead of the bustling, exponentially booming
Tokyo of cultural and cinematic cliché, Kurosawa's metropolis is a ravaged, obsolete, deeply compromised junkyard.

On-screen, in fact, Kurosawa grounds the whole failing Japanese ecosystem in banal images of the everyday, with pervasive images of nature
corrupted, technologically dominated, organically tainted or circum-
vented. Signs of entropy, again, are everywhere. Throughout *Pulse,* Kurosawa stages his characters huddling atop skyscrapers (where the only
green space is a hothouse biology experiment), shuffling around within
decrepit architecture and high-rises that dominate the concretized Tokyo skyline. *Bright Future,* shot on deliberately grimy, low-resolution digital video, goes further, eliminating almost all traces of nature; besides
humans, there are only crowds of toxic jellyfish, biologically altered to
withstand freshwater, swarming through Tokyo's polluted waterways,
massing again like a gathering plague. Kurosawa, moreover, is a filmmaker grimly obsessed with inhospitable meteorology and climate: he
shoots on days with little or no sunlight, favoring pallid, jaundiced lighting that barely penetrates the murky gloom of day. His films exist in
heavy autumnal or wet wintry settings, in which greenery and leaves
barely feature. The wind hardly ever blows; the air itself is stale and
stultified. Japan's infamously turbulent weather, its dynamic natural elements, are worryingly stilled in Kurosawa's cinema.

As we have seen, unlike the classical Japanese garden aesthetic—in
which the scale of Japan's abundant landmass overwhelmed the tribulations of humanity—in Kurosawa's contemporary cinema, the environment is deadened, its organic spontaneity contained. While both phases
of Japanese cinema's international circulation, classical and contemporary, relied so much on the landscape of Japan, distilling it so artfully on-
screen, the trajectory emerges as one of mounting ecological alienation,
confident pride turning to a disillusioned sense of loss. In terms of gaug-
ing the impact of environmentalism itself, its cultural resonance, the
Japanese cinema offers one incisive instance of how ecocriticism has
permeated the mainstream. The cinematic presentation of Japan, once
the land of the rising sun, today on-screen an archipelago of pollution
and blight, can be seen to represent the marketability of environmental
concerns, their pressing relevance to depictions of Japaneseness itself.
Fitting, too, that this barometer of environmental concerns manifests in
the work of Japan's very greatest filmmakers, both past and present.

NOTES

1. Kurosawa, Nakata, and Shimizu are the most widely distributed contemporary Japanese filmmakers, but their approach is echoed in other, lesser-known films. See, for example, Joji Iida's *Rasen* (1998), Higuchinsky's *Uzumaki* (2000), Masayuki Ochiai's *Infection* (2004), Norio Tsurata's many horror films, including *Ring 0: Birthday* (2000) and *Premonition* (2004), and the horror anthology *Dark Tales of Japan* (2004).

2. Notable but unusual exceptions include Kinji Fukasaku's *Battles without Honor or Humanity* cycle (1973–74), Juzo Itami's *Tampopo* (1985), and Takeshi Kitano's *Sonatine* (1993).

3. Kurosawa's troubled relationship with Nikkatsu, historically a demanding employer when its filmmakers deviated from generic mandates, is often paralleled with the abortive career of *yakuza* (gangster) filmmaker Seijun Suzuki. Suzuki, infamously, was fired by Nikkatsu president Hori Kyusaku in 1968 after his films *Tokyo Drifter* (1966) and *Branded to Kill* (1967) were declared to be incomprehensible to audiences. Nowadays both films are revered as masterpieces, and Suzuki is considered a major Japanese auteur.

4. The same format and approach have even been used by non-Japanese writers who set their fiction in a contemporary Japan, usually Tokyo, which is characterized as a barren, modern-day purgatory. Carl Shuker's massively inventive debut novel, *The Method Actors* (2005), is one particularly brilliant example.

5. *Ju-on*, in this context, might seem a contemporary echo of the atom bomb fallout/monster films of Japan in the 1950s, most famously *Gojira* (1954), which appeared, drastically recut, in limited urban release in North America during the 1960s.

6. Kurosawa himself has noted the perplexing inactivity of his protagonists, their unconventional screen behavior. After bringing his *Charisma* script to the Sundance Film Festival Workshop in 1992, Kurosawa reflected that "my understanding of American cinema is that the protagonist must be taking actions towards a clearly defined goal. In my screenplay, there are many moments where my protagonist has no goal. He is just existing. Many of the Americans there kept bothering me, kept saying, 'What's going on with this character now? What's his intent? What's his motive?' And I would have to say, 'He doesn't have any intent. He's just being.' They found that very strange and odd" (Shapiro). It is worth noting in this context that unlike his contemporaries Nakata and Shimizu, Kurosawa has refused all offers to work for a Hollywood company.

WORKS CITED

Anderson, Joseph and Donald Richie. *The Japanese Film: Art and Industry*. Rutland, VT: Tuttle, 1959.

Bordwell, David. *Figures Traced in Light: On Cinematic Staging*. Berkeley and Los Angeles: Univ. of California Press, 2005.

Davis, Darrell William. *Picturing Japaneseness: Monumental Style, National Identity, Japanese Film*. New York: Columbia Univ. Press, 1996.

Desjardins, Chris. *Outlaw Masters of Japanese Film*. New York: I. B. Tauris, 2005.

Karan, Pradyumna P. *Japan in the 21st Century: Environment, Economy, and Society*. Lexington: Univ. of Kentucky Press, 2005.

Kerr, Alex. *Dogs and Demons: Tales from the Dark Side of Japan*. New York: Hill and Wang, 2001.

Le Fanu, Mark. *Mizoguchi and Japan*. London: BFI, 2005.

Mes, Tom and Jasper Sharp. *The Midnight Eye Guide to New Japanese Film*. Berkeley: Stone Bridge Press, 2005.

Murakami, Haruki. *A Wild Sheep Chase*. New York: Vintage, 1989.

Nogami, Teruyo. *Waiting on the Weather: Making Movies with Kurosawa*. Trans. Juliet Winters Carpenter. Berkeley: Stone Bridge Press, 2006.

Palmer, Tim. "Exotic Aesthetics: Long Take Style and Staging in the Films of Mizoguchi and von Sternberg." *Filmhäftet* 123 (2002): 1–6.

———. "*Ugetsu*." *Film International* 19 (2006): 78–81.

Richie, Donald. "Notes for a Definition of the Japanese Film." *Performance* 1.2 (Spring 1972): 20–30.

———. *Ozu*. Berkeley and Los Angeles: Univ. of California Press, 1974.

———. *The Films of Akira Kurosawa*. Rev ed. Berkeley and Los Angeles: Univ. of California Press, 1996.

———. *A Hundred Years of Japanese Film*. New York: Kodansha International, 2001.

Satô, Tadao. "Japanese Cinema and the Traditional Arts: Imagery, Technique, and Cultural Context." Trans. Ann Sherif. *Cinematic Landscapes: Observations on the Visual Arts and Cinema of China and Japan*. Ed. Linda Ehrlich and David Desser. Austin: Univ. of Texas Press, 2000. 165–87.

Schrader, Paul. *Transcendental Style in Film: Ozu, Bresson, Dreyer*. New York: Da Capo Press, 1988. Originally published in 1972 by Univ. of California Press.

Shapiro, James Emanuel. Trans. Linda Hoaglund. "Emerging Cinema Master: Kiyoshi Kurosawa." http://www.dvdtalk.com/interviews/004275.html. Retrieved 28 May 2008.

Standish, Isolde. *A New History of Japanese Cinema: A Century of Narrative Film*. New York: Continuum, 2005.

Suzuki, David, and Keino Oiwa. *The Japan We Never Knew*. Toronto: Stoddart, 1996.

Wood, Robin. *Personal Views: Explorations in Film*. London: Gordon Fraser, 1976.

BEYOND THE FRAME
THE SPIRIT OF PLACE IN
PETER GREENAWAY'S THE
DRAUGHTSMAN'S CONTRACT

. . . .

PAULA WILLOQUET-MARICONDI

Art is a way of seeing, and what we see in art helps to
define what we understand by the word "reality."
—Jamake Highwater, *The Primal Mind*

Peter Greenaway's films are informed by an impulse to investigate the politics of linguistic and visual representation. A painter by training, a writer and self-taught filmmaker, the British director has devoted particular attention to exploring the power of words and images to reflect and shape our perceptions of reality. These perceptions, Greenaway shows, in turn inform our actions in relation to both the human and nonhuman worlds. Greenaway would agree, I believe, with W. J. T. Mitchell's contention that visual culture has reached a power quotient that is "too palpable, too deeply embedded in technologies of desire, domination, and violence, too saturated with reminders of neofascism and global corporate culture to be ignored" (24). Greenaway's investigation of modes of perception intimates that our relationship to representations is increasingly taking precedence over our relationship to a reality that preexists its representation. In *The End of Nature*, Bill McKibben suggests that "an idea, a relationship, can go extinct, just like an animal or a plant" (41). In today's highly mediated culture, the idea, indeed, the very experience, of an unmediated, given, "natural" reality may be going extinct as this reality is being replaced by its simulacrum. What then, we might ask, is the effect of this turn of events on planetary health and on our relationship to one another and to the nonhuman world?

Having authored all of his film scripts, Greenaway is deeply attuned to the power of the word not only to influence but also to shape and create realities.[1] This power is most vividly rendered in *Prospero's Books* (1991), Greenaway's adaptation of Shakespeare's *The Tempest*, and in *The Pillow Book* (1996), a film inspired by the classic tenth-century Japanese text *The Pillow Book*, by Sei Shonagon. In Greenaway's rendition of *The*

225

Tempest, Prospero's absolute power over the island to which he is exiled is derived from his many books, including the one he is writing, called *The Tempest.* He uses the knowledge contained in these books to rewrite, that is, to redefine, reconstruct, reshape, re-create, and control what has become "his" environment. Through the power of the word, Prospero exerts control over the island's physical geography, history, and inhabitants. In this tale of colonial rule and expansion, the island's ecosystem becomes a product of Prospero's masterful use of language. In *The Pillow Book,* it is the physical body of the male protagonist, Jerome, that undergoes a process of transformation analogous to the one imposed on the island by Prospero. His body is first written upon with calligraphy as if it were a blank page waiting to be authored. After his death, his skin is removed and used as parchment in the making of a book.

While these two films are Greenaway's most explicit and graphic investigation of the power of linguistic representation to take the place of a "given" organic reality, Greenaway's first feature film, *The Draughtsman's Contract* (1982), is his earliest exploration of the power of images to define, shape, and re-place a given reality. This essay offers an ecocritically informed analysis of the politics of representation in *The Draughtsman's Contract* and its impact on human and nonhuman subjects. *The Draughtsman's Contract* is uniquely situated for a green reading because it stages the tension between two kinds of contracts: the explicit *human* or social contract between the characters in the film and between these characters and the natural environment; and the *natural* contract that Greenaway implicitly draws between an enigmatic character, the Green Man, and the film's audience. Through the figure of the Green Man, Greenaway positions nature *as character,* rather than as a mere prop or backdrop to human action.[2] While critics have often noted the enigmatic nature of this figure's presence in the film, they have given it little importance beyond noting its role as an anti-naturalistic device in the film, as an emblem of stylistic excess, or as irrelevant. Taken allegorically, however, the Green Man offers viewers the means to reflect on the history of humanity's relationship to the rest of nature, and on the state of our current perceptions and representations of nature, and thus of our relations to the natural world.

Like many of Greenaway's films, *The Draughtsman's Contract* traces the power quotient of visual culture to its early roots in the seventeenth century. As Greenaway once put it, "The 17th century has created the modern world. Here begins, especially in a British perspective, the institution of monarchy, democracy, the collapse of religion, the beginnings of empirical thought and the scientific revolution" (Purdon). It is during the seventeenth century that what we call "nature" begins fully to be explored as a distinct and separable "object" of human study and control, rather than as a subject in an intricate web of organic and dynamic relationships that includes human and nonhuman nature. This is also when the sense of vision starts to take precedence over the other senses, becoming the dominant metaphor for knowing and engaging with the world. The seventeenth century welcomes an array of representational technologies, ranging from the telescope and microscope to perspective painting, maps, and grids, technologies that became the principle tools for knowledge acquisition. The "frame," so ubiquitous today as to have become invisible to our consciousness, is established as a dominant reality-structuring device, determining and defining our very relationship to the world around us.

In this and other films, Greenaway insistently draws the viewer's attention to the frame as a powerful ideological device shaping our perceptions and representations of reality, and reducing the natural world to a representation. Greenaway treats the frame as a system of ordering and containment, as a plotting device and aid to a conspiracy, and as a human construct that has become the dominant mode of engaging with and accessing reality. By "holding" the world's living entities within its borders, the frame becomes the means and the medium through which we see and understand natural processes; the frame thus re-presents the world back to us as primarily a human artifact and an object of vision.

One of the film's thematic threads is that the construction of meaning, whether through words or images, is always motivated; those in control of the narrative means are also the holders of power. Thus, framing and plotting, metaphorically and literally, are central tropes in this and many of Greenaway's films.[3] The grid, the map, and more generally the frame are among Greenaway's most often used plotting, or structuring, devices. They are systems of containment through which one orders—both organizes and summons—and takes possession of a previously "free" or unclaimed reality and space. It is through mapping and plotting, for instance, that a place previously shared by all types of creatures becomes the *property* of one human individual or community. As the eighteenth-century French philosopher Jean Jacques Rousseau suggested, the establishment of property might be considered an act of transgression and thievery. The assignment of a property deed, a *contract*, would then constitute the legitimization of an illicit action.[4] Given that both explicit and implicit contracts are central to the plot of *The Draughtsman's Contract,* a sensitivity to how contracts structure relationships and define reality becomes crucial to appreciating their power.

The Green Man of *The Draughtsman's Contract* is an actual and symbolic character that functions as a party to the implicit contract that Greenaway establishes with his audience, while also standing in for nature and all natural processes. He is one of many archetypal figures within Greenaway's allegorical cinema. His importance in this film must therefore be understood allegorically and symbolically, as a fictional trickster designed to help us perceive, experience, and reconnect to the natural world around us from a sensibility other than that of the "instrumental rationality" represented by the human characters in the film (Elliott and Purdy 19). As Anthony Purdy and Bridget Elliott argue in their study of Greenaway's deployment of allegory in his films:

> When Greenaway insists that his cinema is based on allegory, artifice, and self-reflexivity, rather than on the conventions of Hollywood realism, he is drawing our attention to the value of allegory as a device of defamilarisation. . . . Meaning is neither natural nor spontaneous, says allegory, but depends on conventions that mediate our knowledge both of the world and of ourselves. . . . Allegorical structures hence require more interpretive ingenuity and a sensitive and knowledgeable audience that is willing and able to take pleasure in the active elaboration of discursive meanings from more or less enigmatic fragments. (19)

The Green Man is one of these "enigmatic fragments" and the film itself is a complex visual essay that not only accommodates but also encourages multiple and conflicting readings.

THE PLACE OF NATURE IN GREENAWAY'S CINEMA

To many viewers, Greenaway's films may seem rather unlikely candidates for an ecocritical reading that takes as its focus of investigation the fate of nature and the relationship between nature and culture. While there is no denying that natural elements (such as trees, landscape gardens, oceans, as well as an abundance of rotting organic life forms) feature prominently in Greenaway's films, in general nature is neither the principal visual backdrop nor the setting for human action. With few exceptions, Greenaway's films are mostly set indoors in human-made and deliberately artificial environments, do not showcase spectacular landscape views, and do not primarily revolve around simplistic culture versus nature plot lines. However, what may seem like a lack, a visual absence of dazzling vistas and breathtaking landscapes, only serves to direct our attention to the underlying thematic presence of the natural world in Greenaway's cinema.[5]

While there has been no systematic exploration of environmental themes in Greenaway's work, scholars nonetheless agree that his films tend to be about the failure of our ordering systems and, in particular, the failure of our attempts to order and control natural processes. Vernon Gras, for instance, writes that at the end of Greenaway's films, "Nature usually renews herself while the artist dies" (126). David Pascoe sees in Greenaway's films a reminder that "the natural world can never be affected by artifice" (8–9). Amy Lawrence points out that in Greenaway's early short experimental films, nature already "exists outside any attempt to impose order through storytelling" (12). Greenaway's early short films, with titles such as *Tree* (1966), *Erosion* (1971), *Water* (1975), *The Coastline* (1983), and *The Sea in Their Blood* (1983), betray the artist's personal connection to nature and concern for its ever-increasing domestication and species extinction. In 1979, after seeing a screening of all his early films, Greenaway admitted to having experienced an amazement at the "overpowering presence of nature" in them (Andrews 94).

The Green Man of *The Draughtsman's Contract* might be read as an embodiment of this "overpowering presence of nature," also palpable in the manicured but nonetheless verdant grounds of the estate in which the film is set. This mysterious figure draws our attention to and challenges the ideologies that have helped shape and define our conception of humanity as "masters and possessors" of a nature we regard as separate from us and inanimate. As Matthew Fox succinctly puts it in a recent discussion of the Green Man as an archetype of the "sacred masculine," "The Green Man is decidedly *not* about mastering nature. Rather, the Green Man is about *relating to nature,* about finding the essence of nature within our own nature—indeed, he is about our generative nature. . . . The Green Man is about wisdom holding sway over mere knowledge" (19).

This conception of humanity as master of nature is embodied in the film by the draughtsman, Mr. Neville, and the European aristocracy who commissioned him to draw the estate. To the late-seventeenth-century landowners who inhabit the estate, the gardens surrounding the property are emblematic of their social position and of their " 'right' to possession" (Watney 187). As Simon Watney points out in his reading of the film, with the advent of modernity, capitalism, and scientific instrumental reason, nature would no longer be valued as an end in itself, as sacred and as spirited. To this set of characters, Greenaway juxtaposes the

Green Man. Like the figure of Caliban in *Prospero's Books,* the Green Man represents an alternative to the modern, scientific, industrial, and now postindustrial modes of cognition that have defined the natural world as mere "resource"—as, in effect, an artifact and an abstraction.[6]

The self-reflexive aspects of *The Draughtsman's Contract* also reflect Greenaway's exploration of his own role as an artist who, like the draughtsman he portrays, is an agent of representation of both the social and the natural worlds. This self-reflexivity is put in evidence in *The Draughtsman's Contract* by means of the foregrounding of the frame and of framing devices that serve to comment on the process of representation itself. Greenaway explains that the structure of the film draws the viewer's awareness to the comparison being made between "the real landscape, Mr. Neville's image of it and, ultimately, us as viewers seeing those ideas represented on film" (Brown 35). As Mary Alemany-Galway elucidates in her study of the film, Greenaway

> implicates the audience and the cinematographic apparatus itself in the bourgeois ideology that sets up a relationship of objectification/ownership with nature. The implied contradiction is that art both celebrates nature and exploits it. The other contradiction that occurs is that the draughtsman's drawings, while intended to show off the wealth of the property-owning class, also reveal their crimes, both by inadvertently showing evidence of Mr. Herbert's murder and by pointing to the crimes of a capitalist/rationalist society. The square view-finder that [the draughtsman] uses, with its emphasis on measuring and squaring-off the view, is an apt metaphor for the ways in which the bourgeoisie sees nature as an object that can be measured, quantified, and owned. (123)

Greenaway's treatment of nature, from landscapes and particular fruits to its symbolic embodiment in the Green Man, offers an alternative and a challenge to the long-held Western tradition of relegating the natural environment to the status of backdrop to human action. The Green Man stands as an alternative to the mode of being-in-the-world represented by Mr. Neville. In fact, Mr. Neville's attempts to control the landscape for the purpose of representing it are often sabotaged by this archetypal figure.

By virtue of his profession, Mr. Neville engages with the world as a representation rather than as a living and changing organism. While Mr. Neville makes his living manufacturing framed images—that is, *perceptions* of the world for public consumption—his demise at the end of the film is, ironically, due to a *misperception*: both of the world he was hired to represent and of the estate owners who have commissioned his work. Like the world he re-presents, Mr. Neville is the victim of a conspiracy, a *plotting* scheme devised by his patrons to kill him. Mr. Neville is the victim of a conspiracy because of his inability to properly perceive his employers; at the same time, he himself enacts a conspiracy of sorts against the landscape he draws and systematically misperceives, in spite of his claim to try "very hard never to distort or to dissemble." This figurative framing of Mr. Neville is another link Greenaway establishes between the character and the film's thematic treatment of the artistic "frame" and of the act of "framing." Both reflect and perpetuate a particular ideology of fragmentation and alienation of culture from nature.

THE FRAME, THE FRAMER, AND THE FRAMED

The many ways in which the word "frame" figures in the English language is suggestive of its ideological import and of its ubiquity, particularly today as we conduct our transactions and experience many of our pleasures by means of screens. A quick perusal of the *Oxford English Dictionary* reveals that the term is or has been used in areas as diverse as navigation, printing, weaving, horticulture, mining, religion, art, and literature. As a verb, "to frame" can refer to fashioning, ordering, circumscribing, confining, formulating, setting up, or falsely accusing. As a noun it can mean skeleton, constitution, scheme, system, formula, type of reasoning, molding, plot, mental state, or emotional disposition. Expressions containing the word "frame" include to frame up; to be framed; to frame an issue; the frame of the body; the frame of society; the frame of words; a time-frame; a frame of mind; a frame-saw; a mainframe; a door-frame; a window-frame; and the frame of a story, of a painting, or of a screen. We look at or through frames when we look out the window; watch television; go to the movies; stroll in a museum; search the Internet; ride in automobiles, buses, planes, or trains; take snapshots; look through binoculars; read books, postcards, maps, or menus; and even when we go to the theater—the proscenium arch being a kind of frame. What we see in these situations—words on a page, images on a screen, or a natural landscape—we see through a frame or framing device.

The ubiquity of the frame points to the central role vision plays in our experience of and interactions with the world around us. As theorists of vision have often noted, vision is the most paradoxical of the senses: while it establishes a potentially reciprocal relationship between the seer and the seen, it also emphasizes the gap between them. The framing by vision and the experience of seeing as-if-through-a-frame have the effects of defining what we see as a representation and of reducing reality to what can be represented, fitted within the parameters of the frame, and enjoyed from a fixed vantage point that lies outside the represented world.[7] As W. J. T. Mitchell contends, our "technologies of representation" have accelerated and given exponential growth to the fabrication of realities already made possible by writing, print, engraving, and mechanical reproduction (41).

Greenaway calls the frame a "visual straightjacket" that we use to "restrict and confine, crop, cut, shear, prune, chop, manacle, bind, imprison, and jail the chaos of visual realities."[8] He also notes that the frame is a human construct that "has dominated our pictorial world ever since the Renaissance" (Spieler 117). It is against this domination by the frame that Greenaway's use of the film frame is often directed: he experiments with multiple framings and image-layering to challenge the fixity of the frame and to suggest that reality is always in flux, that "objects" are neither fixed nor constant in space and time.

Unlike Greenaway, Mr. Neville seems incapable of, or unwilling to accept the fluidity of the landscape he endeavors to re-present. For example, he demands that all living moving organisms be kept off the grounds during the designated hours of drawing. Mr. Talmann, one of the characters, comments on Mr. Neville's "god-like power of emptying the landscape." He *orders* the removal of what he *perceives* to be intrusive life forms from the premises, so that he may *order* the reality he seeks to represent. Before the artist even begins to produce representations of nature in the form of drawings, he must represent this nature to himself *as a landscape,* in his own mind's eye. This is easily done, since the landscape that the artist is about to draw is already a product of representation on two levels: it is a *landscaped* garden and it is conceived in imitation of popular landscape paintings. Furthermore, as Amy Lawrence notes, seventeenth-century estate gardens, such as the one in *The Draughtsman's Contract,* were meant to be seen from the house, through windows that framed them (64). The outdoors was part of the overall architectural design of the estate, and the gardens were meant to be experienced from within the house as representations. The landscape as scenic property is literalized by the landscape garden, which itself becomes the model for nature. Simon Watney notes that by the eighteenth century this process was nearly complete and the English landscape garden was an "idealized space which drew its appearance ultimately from the work of such painters as Poussin and Claude Lorrain" (190). Rebecca Solnit concurs that the British aristocracy had began modeling their landscape gardens on the landscape paintings they collected. The gardens were "translations" of works by artists such as Claude Lorrain, "to make their paint and canvas into dirt, water, trees, lawn, and architecture" (252). Moreover, she writes, "The aristocracy had trained itself to appreciate in the landscape gardens elements of painting that became more and more evident in the rest of the world, until they suddenly realized that such experiences always had been available in the world at large. . . . They had gone from looking at Claude's paintings to looking at gardens to looking at the larger world, and they had learned to look at it as an aesthetic phenomenon. This was the dawn of scenic tourism" (255).[9]

From this point on, travelers would look at nature in a mediated way, having developed the mental "habit" of experiencing nature by analogy to landscape paintings. They could also refine their aesthetic understanding and appreciation of natural scenery by consulting landscape appreciation manuals that would teach them how to classify landscapes and critique their composition. As Paul Shepard puts it, "Having learned the clues to scenery from looking at pictures, they were prepared to look for picturesque wherever they found it" (124). It could be said, then, that already in the seventeenth century, representations preceded viewers' perceptions and experiences of reality. They were becoming models for reality, now relegated to the status of copy. This ideological habit finds its full expression today in our mediatic world of virtually real computer-generated and reproduced images. Thus, the potential for the world to be modeled on or to be the product of representation came into existence the moment the world became the object of a certain representational style.

This perspectivist representational style was aided by Claude Lorrain's invention of the Claude glass, a concave portable hand mirror designed to transform the landscape into *scenery*, into a representation, before it was painted. As Shepard reminds us, scenery, from the Greek word for "stage," is the staging of the organic world into an abstraction: "The observer of scenery has a disinterested attitude which would be inconceivable if he believed the surroundings to be haunted by spirits and art to be a form of magic. Scenery comes with science and with museum art, a product of analytical and detached vision" (119).

Not surprisingly, the use of the Claude glass required that the artist turn his back to the landscape so as to admire its *reflection* on the glass before reproducing it. It is the reflection of the landscape, not the landscape itself, that the artist paints. The Claude glass, like the draughtsman's viewfinder, defines the artist's view of the natural world as already a two-dimensional, decontextualized, and abstracted object of vision whose "purpose" is purely aesthetic and commercial.

An artist of his time, Mr. Neville carries with him an internalized mental image of paintings through which he looks at the external world. Not only are the landscaped gardens Mr. Neville draws already the product of representation, but Mr. Neville himself is trained to look at outer reality as if it were a representation. This is an ideological habit Mr. Neville shares with the aristocracy he serves. According to Simon Watney, having developed the mental habit of experiencing nature as an "idealised space" by analogy to landscape paintings, this aristocracy (and the bourgeoisie who imitate it) learned to refine their aesthetic understanding of natural scenery by consulting landscape appreciation manuals designed to teach them how to classify landscapes and critique their composition (Watney 190).

Mr. Neville's relationship to the world he *captures* in his drawing is epitomized by his use of the viewfinder. Much like the camera, the window, and the Claude glass, the viewfinder structures the landscape, mathematizing, mapping, and plotting it out onto a grid by means of vertical and horizontal lines. The perspectivist, static, and frontal use of framing represented by Mr. Neville's viewfinder is mirrored by the composition of the shots in the film. Greenaway often positions his camera so as to capture the image as if through Mr. Neville's viewfinder, thus self-reflexively creating a series of frames within frames that work to implicate both the filmmaker and the audience in the kind of vision represented by Mr. Neville.

This self-conscious use of framing is one means by which *The Draughtsman's Contract* never ceases to remind the viewer that the nature being represented is always under human dominion: its artistic and biological reproduction are under human control. This is the case for the gardens that are landscaped, but also for the many horticultural products that appear in the film: prunes, oranges, raspberries, figs, limes, and particularly pomegranates and pineapples.

Commentators have often noted that fruit symbolism is very important to the film, and its significance allegorical. The orange, for example, references the political situation at the time the film is set, 1694. It serves as a reminder of William of Orange's victory at the battle of Boyne in 1689 and of the new political order, as well as being a reference to colonization and imperialism (Garcias 37). Other fruits reference well-known legends. The three pomegranates that Mr. Neville brings as a gift to Mrs. Herbert evoke the myth of Persephone and explicitly raise the theme of

fertility. By their association with the story of Persephone's yearly return from the underworld to usher in the new growing season, they
represent birth and renewal and are thus linked to the natural cycles of
death and rebirth. Through their link to death, they are also associated
with infertility.

The allegorical significance of the pomegranates is therefore complex. They stand for the natural cycles of fertility and infertility, but also
for artificiality. Mrs. Herbert compares the red juice of the fruit to both
the blood of the newborn and the blood of murder. Grown in the artificial
conditions of the hothouse, the pomegranates are the fruits of our attempts to confine nature to a controlled environment, within frames,
and to monitor its growth. The hothouse is described in the film as a
framing device of sorts: Mr. Neville refers to it as a human enclosure
made up of "one hundred panes of glass and half a year's supply of
artificial heat." The hothouse embodies the hope that the vicissitudes of
nature will be kept in check, and that the production of pomegranates
will be monitored, managed, and enhanced by artificially restricting its
growth to a controlled environment. The result is a fruit that is "seldom
fertile," as one of the characters in the film points out.

The pineapple that Mrs. Herbert offers Mr. Neville in return for his gift
of pomegranates is yet another artificially grown exotic delicacy that
proves to be sour to the palate. At the end of the film, the unsavory fruit
that was to represent hospitality is shown cut in half, a knife stuck in its
heart. When the Green Man takes a bite of the pineapple in the closing
scene, he promptly spits it out.[10] The viewer is then left with a gesture
that expresses rejection and disgust as the film's final image. That the
last action performed in the film is an act of rejection of the pineapple—a
fruit representing hospitality and its betrayal, as well as artificiality and
death—and that this gesture is executed by the Green Man warrants
attention. The privileging of the figure of the Green Man in the final shot
of the film points to Greenaway's own position vis-à-vis the characters'
relation to one another and to the natural world.

BEYOND THE FRAME:
THE GREEN MAN AS THE SPIRIT OF THE PLACE

The presence of the Green Man has received diverse interpretations.
Michael Walsh calls it "the most obviously antinaturalist device in the
film" (266). William Johnson sees it as a "device for making fun of the
aristocrats" (38). For David Pascoe it is "the emblem of the director's
stylistic excesses" (91). Greenaway himself has suggested several possible meanings for the figure, noting that initially it was to play a much

greater role in the film, but that a lot of its significance was lost once the film was cut from its original three and a half hours (Boujut 7). In interviews, Greenaway has proposed several interpretations for this figure. He suggests that it be taken, alternatively, as a prank statue reminiscent of the hollow statues connected to water taps that were designed to squirt water on the unsuspecting passerby; as a Greek or Roman memento of the landed gentry's travel expeditions; as a live person, a servant playing the part of a Greek or Roman statue; and even as a figure analogous to the fool (or trickster), who in the literary tradition serves to comment on the pretensions of power and wisdom (Jaehne 15). Greenaway has also referred to this figure as a Genius Loci, or the Spirit of Place; it is this latter interpretation of the figure that I am favoring here.

In elucidating this figure's presence in the film, Greenaway refers to the tradition of the Green Man in British literature and architecture, and to the fact that the figure also symbolizes nature and gardens (Bouju 8). In fact, the tradition of the Green Man goes back much farther than Greenaway acknowledges. William Anderson, in a comprehensive study of the iconography of the Green Man, traces its recurrences and disappearances from antiquity to the present. This figure generally appears as a head entwined with vegetation and branches sprouting out of its mouth. A composite figure symbolizing the union of humanity and the vegetable world, he also stands for an animistic conception of nature. Anderson describes it as an archetype expressing unity, renewal, and rebirth, who also shares resemblances with the archetypal figure of the fool, joker, or trickster, particularly the qualities of unexpectedness and unconventional wisdom (29–30).

The Green Man's remote origins can be found in the matriarchal religion of the Neolithic period, around the Danube Basin. In Roman art, the Green Man appears in the context of Dionysiac mysteries. In the Christian context, the Green Man is first seen on tombs dating from the fourth or fifth centuries (Anderson 46). His presence continues to be felt throughout the Middle Ages in Europe where he is often seen adorning Gothic cathedrals. Matthew Fox notes in particular the powerful presence of the Green Man in the twelfth century, "the same century that saw the reemergence of the goddess" (23). In studying the various associations between the portrayal of the Green Man in European cathedrals and the goddess, Fox suggests that "the Green Man represents the internalization of the goddess by men. He is a symbol that the goddess, and the revolution she brings in her wake, is as much for men as women" (25).

Anderson also documents the periods during which the presence of the Green Man in representations retreats and almost disappears. Of interest for my purposes here is the fact that while the Green Man was still being represented up to the first half of the eighteenth century, he vanishes from representations in art and architecture in the later part of that century, only to reappear at the end of the nineteenth century with the revival of Renaissance and Palladian styles of architecture. *The Draughtsman's Contract* is set in 1694, so before the Green Man's retreat from iconography.

When the Green Man is understood allegorically, his presence in the film reminds us of the Greek conception of the earth as a single living organism that breathes and pulsates. In the words of Plato, the earth is "a living creature, one and visible, containing within itself all living creatures."[11] The Greeks, however, associated it with the figure of the goddess Gaia, Earth Mother, and not with that of the Green Man, a clearly masculine figure who, in the film, is spotted prancing around naked in the gardens. The Greek notion of the earth as alive and spirited continued to flourish into the Middle Ages and Renaissance, until the seventeenth century, when "the medieval outlook was replaced by the [modern] Cartesian image of the world as a machine."[12] There have been a number of attempts since the seventeenth century to revive this animistic view of nature as a harmonious whole, notably by the Romantic writers and poets, and more recently in the visual arts[13] and the scientific arena. Starting in the early twentieth century with a shift toward a view of nature as a living organism, the increasing importance of a holistic understanding of natural processes is visibly present in contemporary systems thinking, quantum physics, ecology, and in the development of the Gaia hypothesis by the atmospheric chemist James Lovelock.[14]

The images of Gaia and of the Green Man evoke a view of nature, and of humanity's relationship to nature, that constitutes a metaphysics based on a different set of assumptions than those emphasized by the mechanistic worldview: wholeness, process, internal relations, nonlinearity, unpredictability, and plurality.[15] It is not surprising, then, that Greenaway would have chosen a figure he associates with the natural world to "spit out" the pineapple, the product of artifice and the fruit of the labor of those who uphold values that are antithetical to those associated with Gaia.

Within the film's plot, the Green Man goes unnoticed by most of the characters, save in a few instances when he is briefly seen by a child and a servant. He appears as an animated statue, played by a servant roaming about in the gardens; he is thus a mobile statue that changes posture and location at his own will. His actions are neither contained nor controlled. He is clearly not an inanimate object, for he acts on his own volition. Since he is not a "real" statue, he is not a representation. He is playful and sometimes irreverent and unpredictable. He often blends with the natural features of the landscape, such as moss-covered rocks, becoming "invisible" to most of the characters in the film. He might best be thought of as a wandering spirit. He is, above all, a puzzle for the audience of the film since he plays no definable role in furthering the narrative. One commentator suggests that the Green Man "is outside the narrative 'reality' as it is defined by the film's ruling class" (Johnson 39). In other words, he does not belong to the world of this ruling class and therefore does not exist for them. He does, however, exist for the audience of the film, and for a small group of characters in the film who themselves are powerless within the world of this ruling class. This fact has prompted critics to conclude that the Green Man, like those who can see him, is "impotent, even irrelevant" (Johnson 39).

However, when we look at this figure as an allegory, the knowledge he carries is not irrelevant, as one might assume. Through the presence of the Green Man, the film opens up the means for viewers to reflect on the history of humanity's relationship to the rest of nature, on the state of our current perceptions of and relations to nature, and on our place *within* the natural world. Whether he is taken to represent the Green Man of medieval iconography (whose human head, from which sprouts vegetation, suggests a fusion of the human and the nonhuman), or the Genius Loci of pagan animism, the enigmatic figure serves a double function: he stands in for nature as a living organism and character in the film, but also for a different relational model among humans, and between the human and the nonhuman world. This relational model gives primacy to integration, cooperation, and mutuality over alienation, dominion, and antagonism. More than an enigma to be solved, the Green Man is a trickster who beckons the audience to, in the words of Erazim Kohák, "set aside the learned ways of *perceiving* the world as dead matter for your use and *see* if you can recover again your actual *perception* of the world as a community of beings to whom you are meaningfully related."[16] This quotation suggests that the problem and the solution rest in our modes of perception, our ways of seeing and of representing.

The film ends with the death of the draughtsman, framed and betrayed by those who hired him, and literally blinded by fire as a result of his perceptual blindness. The film's final image, however, belongs to the Green Man who spits out the pineapple in an act of rejection of the bitter fruit. As such, his gesture once again invites us to reconsider the values represented and upheld by the characters in the film: greed, power, money, ownership, and knowledge for the purpose of control and dominance. Present-day ecological understanding shows us that these values are ultimately not ecologically sustainable; in other words, they are not hospitable to our and other species' continued survival on the earth. To the extent that the Green Man can be seen as emblematic of Greenaway's own presence in the film,[17] *The Draughtsman's Contract* calls for a new way of seeing the world *before* our eyes, and *before* our representations of it. It calls for a new contract with the natural world, a contract that it does not, however, explicitly draw up for the viewer.

Vernon Gras has noted that two of the three main actions performed by the Green Man are mocking of human power, arrogance, and hubris: He removes a commemorative obelisk from its pedestal in order to take its place, and he dismounts from a statue of a saddled horse (129). Gras also notes that before spitting out the pineapple the figure "looks derisively at the viewer" (130). Is Greenaway proposing this archetypal figure and the values associated with it as an alternative to the ethos of exploitation, displacement, and conquest represented by the estate owners and the draughtsman? Lawrence's analysis supports the notion that "Greenaway persists in this hope for a natural world" (62). The film should not, however, be taken as merely expressive of a naïve or romantic impulse on the part of the filmmaker, as Lawrence implies, but as fundamental to Greenaway's artistic vision.

Vernon Gras writes that in all of Greenaway's films "nature usually renews herself while the artist dies" (126). While Greenaway's self-reflexive style of filmmaking may account for the fact that many of his protagonists are artists, it does not explain why these artists so often die at the end of the films, or abandon their craft as in the case of Prospero in *Prospero's Books*. Do their deaths mean anything, aside from being convenient to the other characters in the film and to the resolution of the narrative? Do they carry a "message" for the audience? Do they bring significant change to the world within the film? Do they invite a reassessment of the world outside the film? Answering these questions naturally entails having an overall theory about Greenaway's artistic aims and methods. My approach to the film has been to draw attention to the ecological implications of two elements: on the one hand, of Greenaway's casting of the Green Man as the embodiment of a living nature and of his giving this character the last word, so to speak; and, on the other hand, of Greenaway's meditation on the motivations behind and the effects of our representational technologies, such as perspectivism, maps, grids, and the frame, on the living world.

Many theorists of technology have stressed the fact that technologies, including representational technologies, are neither morally neutral nor value-free, since their existence cannot be dissociated from their use. Leonardo da Vinci, for example, is said to have destroyed certain of his inventions for fear they would be put to harmful use (Davis 217). Jacques Ellul says there is no essence of technology apart from its use, but that the current degree of investment in modern technology demands that it be used no matter the consequences (Davis 42). Neil Postman contends that every technology—including language, which for him is our most fundamental technology—contains its ideological bias and a "predisposition to construct the world as one thing rather than another, to value one thing over another, to amplify one sense or skill more loudly than another" (13). The study of the effects of a technology, whether artistic or scientific, on our ways of seeing, thinking, acting, and being is crucial to an understanding of the culture that creates and uses that technology.

The rules of perspective elaborated in the mid-fifteenth century by Filippo Brunelleschi and Leon Battista Alberti were a fundamental technological achievement that shaped ways of seeing for centuries to come (Harvey 240–46). Perspectivism, and its extension into more sophisticated optical technologies such as the camera, enabled the creation of a mathematically unified world, a world viewed from an "outside" position. These technologies also imply the possibility of knowing the world in its totality, and of containing and conquering space for human occupation and use. As Greenaway shows in *The Draughtsman's Contract*, the technologies that enable us to represent the world are prescriptive forces that define and regulate how we see, think, and act, and consequently what we value.

Most commentators on Greenaway's cinema have noted that at the end of a Greenaway film there is not much about the culture he portrays that is worth salvaging. However, while Greenaway does not offer a plan, or a map, to lead us into a more ecologically sound era, his films—with few exceptions—end with victory on the side of biological, not technological, reproduction. Cultural productions are shown to be less fundamental than the organic cycles of reproduction that ultimately sustain life. What Greenaway's films do suggest is that it is advisable to reexamine the appropriateness of our chosen systems of knowledge, and of the paradigms guiding our interactions with and representations of the world. The first necessary step is to become fully conscious of what these paradigms are and of their effects. To the extent that our representations of the world can tell us something about how we *perceive* the world and our place within it, and thus what paradigms we construct from these perceptions, they can also perhaps reveal to us the dangers of our misperceptions.

NOTES

An earlier version of this essay was published in *Green Letters* 6 (Winter 2005): 9–23, and is used here with permission from the Association for the Study of Literature and Environment (ASLE-UK).

1. *Prospero's Books* is a partial exception, as Greenaway incorporates most of Shakespeare's *The Tempest* into the script.

2. For other discussions of environmental themes in Greenaway's films, see my "The Exploitation of Human and Nonhuman Nature in Peter Greenaway's *A Zed and Two Noughts*," *Interdisciplinary Studies in Literature and Environment* 10.1 (Winter 2003): 55–74; "*Prospero's Books*, Postmodernism, and the Reenchantment of the World," *Peter Greenaway's Postmodern/Poststructuralist Cinema,* ed. Paula Willoquet-Maricondi and Mary Alemany-Galway (Lanham, MD: Scarecrow Press, 2001), 177–201; and "Fleshing the Text: *The Pillow Book* and the Erasure of the Body," *Postmodern Culture: An Electronic Journal of Interdisciplinary Criticism* 9.2 (February 1999).

3. See Elliott and Purdy, "Artificial Eye/Artificial You: Getting Greenaway or Mything the Point?" *Literature and the Body,* ed. Anthony Purdy (Amsterdam: Rodopi, 1992), 2–11.

4. See part 2 of Jean Jacques Rousseau's *Discourse on the Origins of Inequality* in *Basic Political Writings,* trans. Donald A. Cress (Indianapolis: Hackett Publishing, 1987). Rousseau identifies several developments along the path leading to the establishment of property: language, technology, agriculture, and accumulation of both goods and information.

5. *Drowning by Numbers* (1988) is the only true departure from this pattern among the feature films. It is mostly set outdoors in an environment dominated by the presence of water, primarily the ocean, swimming pools, water towers, and bathtubs. *The Draughtsman's Contract* takes place mostly in the gardens of the Compton Anstey estate, thus technically out of doors. This outdoors environment is thoroughly fashioned by the human hand. As if to dramatize this fact, Greenaway uses filters to exaggerate the greenness of the lawns of the estate.

6. For a discussion of Caliban and of Prospero as representing, respectively, what Morris Berman has called the "participating consciousness" of premodern times, and the "non-participating" consciousness of modernity, see my "*Prospero's Books*, Postmodernism, and the Reenchantment of the World." For Berman's elaboration on these concepts, see *The Reenchantment of the World* (Ithaca, NY: Cornell Univ. Press, 1981). I am also indebted to Max Oelschlaeger's critical analysis of the project of modernity as being one of a

divorce from nature in *The Idea of Wilderness: From Prehistory to the Age of Ecology* (New Haven, CT: Yale Univ. Press, 1991).

7. See Jean-Louis Baudry's discussion of the relationship between the cinematic apparatus and perspectivism in painting in "The Ideological Effects of the Basic Cinematographic Apparatus," *Film Quarterly* 28.2 (1974–75): 39–47. For a phenomenological discussion of linear perspective as a technique and way of knowing that has redefined the world "to suit the eye" and the self as a "spectator behind a window," see Robert Romanyshyn, *Technology as Symptom and Dream* (London: Routledge, 1989), 32, 33, 65.

8. See Peter Greenaway, *Peter Greenaway: Paintings, Drawings, Collages* (Theassaloniki: Mylos Art Gallery, 1996), 29, and Leon Steinmetz and Peter Greenaway, *The World of Peter Greenaway* (Boston: Charles E. Tuttle, 1995), 84.

9. For a discussion of the role of photography in perpetuating this ideology, see Deborah Bright, "The Machine in the Garden Revisited: American Environmentalism and Photographic Aesthetic," *Art Journal* 51.2 (1992): 60–71.

10. See also Lawrence's discussion of this scene (70).

11. Quoted in Kirkpatrick Sale, *Dwellers in the Land: The Bioregional Vision* (Philadelphia: New Society Publishers, 1991), 3.

12. See Fritjof Capra, *The Web of Life: A New Scientific Understanding of Living Systems* (New York: Anchor Books, 1996), 22.

13. See, for example, the 1999 special issue of *Art Journal* (51.2) on art and ecology that explores the relevance and function of art in relation to ecological awareness.

14. Lovelock proposed the notion that the biosphere, Gaia, is a living and self-regulating system in which "the living matter, air, oceans, and land surface form a complex system which can be seen as a single organism and which has the capacity to keep our planet a fit place for life." Quoted in Carolyn Merchant, *Radical Ecology: The Search for a Livable World* (New York: Routledge, 1992), 98.

15. This set of assumptions corresponds to the ecological paradigm advocated by the Deep Ecology movement, whose scientific roots can be found in quantum theory. For a fuller discussion, see Carolyn Merchant, *Radical,* 85–109, and also Fritjof Capra, *Web of Life.*

16. My emphasis. Quoted in Laura Sewall, "The Skill of Ecological Perception," *Ecopsychology: Restoring the Earth, Healing the Mind,* ed. Theodore Roszak, Mary E. Gomes, and Allen D. Kanner (San Francisco: Sierra Club Books, 1995), 201.

17. The drawings are also destroyed by fire at the end of the film.

WORKS CITED

Alemany-Galway, Mary. "Postmodernism and the French New Novel: The Influence of *Last Year at Marienbad* on *The Draughtsman's Contract*." *Peter Greenaway's Postmodern/Poststructuralist Cinema.* Ed. Paula Willoquet-Maricondi and Mary Alemany-Galway. Lanham, MD: Scarecrow Press, 2001. 115–35.

Anderson, William. *Green Man: The Archetype of our Oneness with the Earth.*
    London: Harper Collins, 1990.

Andrews, Nigel. "A Walk through Greenaway," *Sight and Sound* 48.2 (1979): 94–95.

Boujut, Michel. "Peter Greenaway: un inspiré en sa demeure. *L'Avant scène du
    cinéma* 333 (1984): 4–9.

Brown, Robert. "Greenaway's Contract," *Sight and Sound* 51.1 (1981–82): 38–41.

Davis, Gregory H. *Technology—Humanism or Nihilism: A Critical Analysis of the
    Philosophical Basis and Practice of Modern Technology.* Washington, DC: Univ.
    Press of America, 1988.

The Draughtsman's Contract. Dir. Peter Greenaway. British Film Institute and
    Channel Four Films, 1982.

Elliott, Bridget, and Anthony Purdy. *Peter Greenaway: Architecture and Allegory.*
    London: Academy Editions, 1997.

Fox, Matthew. *The Hidden Spirituality of Men: Ten Metaphors to Awaken the Sacred
    Masculine.* Novato, CA: New World Library, 2008.

Garcias, Jean-Claude. "L'été meurtrier de 1694, ou les eaux glacées du canal
    égoiste." *L'Avant scène du cinéma* 333 (1984): 35–37.

Gras, Vernon. "Dramatizing the Failure to Jump the Culture/Nature Gap: The
    Films of Peter Greenaway." *New Literary History* 26 (1995): 123–43.

Harvey, David. *The Condition of Postmodernity.* Cambridge, MA: Blackwell, 1990.

Jaehne, Karen. "The Draughtsman's Contract: An Interview with Peter
    Greenaway." *Cineaste* 13.2 (1984): 13–15.

Johnson, William. "*The Draughtsman's Contract.*" *Film Quarterly* 37.2 (1983): 34–40.

Lawrence, Amy. *The Films of Peter Greenaway.* Cambridge: Cambridge Univ. Press,
    1997.

McKibben, Bill. *The End of Nature.* New York: Random House Trade Paperbacks,
    2006.

Mitchell, W. J. T. *Picture Theory: Essays on Verbal and Visual Representation.* Chicago:
    Univ. of Chicago Press, 1994.

Pascoe, David. *Peter Greenaway: Museums and Moving Images.* London: Reaktion
    Books, 1997.

The Pillow Book. Dir. Peter Greenaway. Kasander/Wigman Production, 1996.

Postman, Neil. *Technopoly: The Surrender of Culture to Technology.* New York: Vintage
    Books, 1992.

Prospero's Books. Dir. Peter Greenaway. Allarts, 1991.

Purdon, Noel. "Immaculate Conceptions." Originally published in *Real Time* 12
    (1996): 19–20. http://web.archive.org/web/19990221080032/www.december
    .org/pg/text/articles/purdon.htm. Retrieved 20 June 2007.

Shepard, Paul. *Man in the Landscape: A Historic View of the Esthetics of Nature.* 1967.
    College Station: Texas A&M Univ. Press, 1991.

Solnit, Rebecca. *Savage Dreams: A Journey into the Hidden Wars of the American West.*
    San Francisco: Sierra Club Books, 1994.

Spieler, Reinhard. "Breaking Through the Frame." *Art and Landscape. Topos:
    European Landscape Magazine* 14 (1996): 113–23.

Walsh, Michael. "Allegories of Thatcherism: The Films of Peter Greenaway." *Fires Were Started: British Cinema and Thatcherism*. Ed. Lester Friedman. Minneapolis: Univ. of Minnesota Press, 1993.

Watney, Simon. "Gardens of Speculation: Landscape in *The Draughtsman's Contract*." *Picture This: Media Representations of Visual Arts and Artists*. Ed. Philip Hayward. London: John Libbey, 1988. 183–92.

CONTRIBUTORS

BETH BERILA is Assistant Professor and Director of the Women's Studies Program at St. Cloud State University. Her research explores representations of gender, race, class, and sexuality in U.S. popular culture. Her published work includes "Toxic Bodies? ACT UP's Disruption of the Heteronormative Landscape of the Nation," in *New Perspectives on Environmental Justice: Gender, Sexuality, and Activism*.

LYNNE DICKSON BRUCKNER is Associate Professor of English at Chatham College, where she teaches courses in literature and the environment, ecofeminist literature, women and science fiction, organic gardening, and ecocritical Shakespeare. Her pedagogical publications focus on study abroad and student writing, the literature of adoption, and ecofeminism and Atwood. She is lead editor for *Ecocritical Shakespeare* and has published on *Macbeth*, Sidney's *Arcadia*, and Chaucer's *Wife of Bath*.

ELIZABETH HENRY is Lecturer in the School of Communication at the University of Denver where she teaches film studies. Her own films are experimental forays into the ecocritical possibilities of the image and have been screened across the country, winning various awards, including at the Humboldt International Film Festival and the Black Maria Film Festival. She has published on experimental cinema in *The Independent*, *Moviemaker*, and *Film Forum*.

JOSEPH K. HEUMANN is Professor of Communication Studies at Eastern Illinois University. He is the author, with Robin Murray, of *Ecology and Popular Film: Cinema and the Edge*. Their essays on ecocritical readings of genre films have appeared in *Film Quarterly*, *Jump Cut*, *Studies in American Culture*, and *Interdisciplinary Studies in Literature and Environment*.

HARRI KILPI is a full-time researcher and freelance critic. He teaches film studies at the University of East Anglia where he is completing his doctorate. His research interests include ecocriticism, cognitive film theory, and contemporary Hollywood cinema. He is the author of "Green Frames: Exploring Cinema Ecocritically," published in *WiderScreen*.

JENNIFER MACHIORLATTI is Assistant Professor in the School of Communication at Western Michigan University where she teaches media and cultural studies, video/media production, and intercultural communication. Her published research and media art include documentary and multimedia installations, Aboriginal/First Nation and Native media, and feminist media. She has published essays on women and film, Aboriginal media, and popular culture.

MARK MINSTER is Assistant Professor of English and Comparative Literature at Rose-Hulman Institute of Technology. His areas of research include romantic poetry, literature and environment, and religion and literature.

ROBIN L. MURRAY is Associate Professor of English at Eastern Illinois University where she teaches courses in film and literature, women's studies, and ecocriticism and nature writing. She is the author, with Joseph Heumann, of *Ecology and Popular Film: Cinema and the Edge*. Their essays on ecocritical readings of genre films have appeared in *Film Quarterly*, *Jump Cut*, *Studies in American Culture*, and *Interdisciplinary Studies in Literature and Environment*.

TIM PALMER is Associate Professor of Film Studies at the University of North Carolina Wilmington. He regularly contributes essays on Japanese cinema to the journal *Film International*. He has published research on French, Asian, and classical Hollywood cinema in *Cinema Journal*, *Studies in French Cinema*, *Journal of Film and Video*, and *Senses of Cinema*. His book in progress, *Brutal Intimacy: Contemporary French Cinema*, is under contract at Wesleyan University Press.

CORY SHAMAN is Assistant Professor at Arkansas Tech University where he teaches environmental literature and American studies courses. His work focuses on environmental literature of the American South and Southwest, with a particular emphasis on environmental justice issues and questions of ecological discourse and risk theory.

RACHEL STEIN is Professor of English and Director of Women's and Multicultural Studies at Siena College. She is the author of *Shifting the Ground: American Women Writers' Revisions of Nature, Gender, and Race*; coeditor of *The Environmental Justice Reader: Politics, Poetics, and Pedagogy*; and editor of *New Perspectives on Environmental Justice: Gender, Sexuality, and Activism*. Her research focuses on intersections of gender, sexuality, race, and nature.

PAULA WILLOQUET-MARICONDI is Associate Professor and Chair of Media Arts, and Coordinator of the Cinema Studies minor at Marist College. Her essays on ecocriticism and film have appeared in *Interdisciplinary Studies in Literature and Environment*, *Green Letters*, and *Postmodern Culture*. She is the editor of *Pedro Almodóvar: Interviews* and coeditor of and contributor to *Peter Greenaway's Postmodern/Poststructuralist Cinema*, revised edition.

UNDER THE SIGN OF NATURE

EXPLORATIONS IN ECOCRITICISM

Rinda West
Out of the Shadow: Ecopsychology, Story, and Encounters with the Land

Bonnie Roos and Alex Hunt, editors
Postcolonial Green: Environmental Politics and World Narratives

Paula Willoquet-Maricondi, editor
Framing the World: Explorations in Ecocriticism and Film